Advanced ECDL

Module 5: Database

Matthew Strawbridge

PAYNE-GALLWAY

Published by Payne-Gallway Publishers Limited
Payne-Gallway is an imprint of Harcourt
Education Ltd, Halley Court, Jordan Hill,
Oxford, OX2 8EJ

Tel: 01865 888070
Fax: 01865 314029

E-mail: orders@payne-gallway.co.uk
Web: www.payne-gallway.co.uk

Text © Matthew Strawbridge, 2006

First published 2006

09 08 07 06
10 9 8 7 6 5 4 3 2 1

British Library Cataloguing in Publication Data
is available from the British Library on request.

10-digit ISBN 1 904 46790 3
13-digit ISBN 978 1 904467 90 8

Microsoft product screen shots reprinted with
permission from Microsoft Corporation.

Designed and typeset by Direction Marketing
& Communications Ltd.

Printed by Printer Trento S.r.l

With thanks to Jim Strawbridge for his help
with testing the exercises.

Ordering Information

You can order from:

Payne-Gallway
FREEPOST (OF1771),
PO Box 381, Oxford OX2 8BR

Tel: 01865 888070
Fax: 01865 314029

E-mail: orders@payne-gallway.co.uk
Web: www.payne-gallway.co.uk

Contents

Introduction

Who is this book for?

This book is suitable for anyone studying for the **ECDL Advanced Module 5: Databases**, whether at school, in an adult class, or at home. Students are expected to have a level of knowledge of **Microsoft Access** equivalent to the basic-level ECDL Databases module.

The approach

The approach is very much one of 'learning by doing'. Students are guided step by step through creating real databases, with numerous screenshots showing exactly what should appear on the screen at each stage.

Chapter 1 (Basic concepts) covers topics that are not explicitly in the ECDL syllabus, but which are either important foundation topics or useful tips.

In subsequent chapters, syllabus topics are introduced whenever they are needed during the development of the database. This helps to demonstrate **why**, as well as **how**, to use these advanced features. Each of these chapters ends with a **Test yourself** section, which contains exercises that consolidate the skills learned in that chapter.

Software used

For this module you will be using **Microsoft Access**, one of many database packages. **Access 2003** has been used in this book, but you should still be able to follow the steps (with a little common sense) if you are using a different version.

Chapter 5 (Importing & exporting) also requires **Microsoft Excel**, but only a very basic level of competence is required.

Extra resources

The exercises have been designed so that you do not need to load documents from a CD-ROM or the Internet – you create them as you go along. The one exception to this is the large database **auction.mdb**, which is used in the **Test yourself** sections throughout the book. It would be impractical to ask you to create this from scratch, so instead you should download it from the publisher's web site: www.payne gallway.co.uk/ecdl. This web site also contains lots of other useful supporting material.

About this book

As well as the main text, you will find useful information in special boxes throughout this book. Two types of information are presented in this way. The first references the ECDL topic that is being covered.

> **Syllabus ref: AM5.X.X.X**
> Boxes like this show which topic from the ECDL syllabus you are covering.

The second, more general, box is home to occasional tips, notes and warnings. These provide extra information, for example, about why Access does something a certain way, and you should make sure that you read them all.

> **TIP**
> Tips, notes and warnings appear in boxes like this one. Make sure that you read these – they are usually important.

You will also find two types of list.

This is an **information list** item.

This is an **action list** item. You should perform the actions given in every action list item you come to. It is a good idea to read the whole action before starting to do it, because long actions often contain hints that clarify what you should be doing.

Make sure that you save any files you create somewhere safe – you will usually need them again in later chapters (you can also download them from the publisher's web site at www.payne-gallway.co.uk/ecdl).

1 Basic concepts

Introduction

This introductory chapter follows a slightly different format to those that follow – there is much more information and there are fewer practical steps for you to perform.

However, the chapter provides a solid foundation for the more advanced topics. I think you will find that it is well worth the effort to carefully read and remember the information presented here. Although you will not be tested directly on most of the tools and techniques, a thorough knowledge of them will make you a more productive user of Access.

In this chapter, you will:

- learn what is meant by some of the **terms** that will be referred to throughout the book

- learn the use of each of the commands on the most common toolbars

- acquire a useful list of **keyboard shortcuts**

- create the blank database – **sandbox.mdb** – that you will be using throughout the rest of the book.

Common terms

Names of keys

This book assumes that you are familiar with the names of the keys on the computer keyboard. Where it is necessary to press a combination of keys to run a particular command, a plus sign is used in the text. For example, you can copy text by highlighting it then pressing **Ctrl+C** (meaning that you must hold down the **Ctrl** key while you tap **C**).

Graphical user interface

Figure 1.1 gives the names of some of the **graphical user interface** (**GUI**) elements that will be referred to throughout the book. It is well worth getting used to calling these things by their correct names, so that you will be better able to communicate with other people when asking for or providing help.

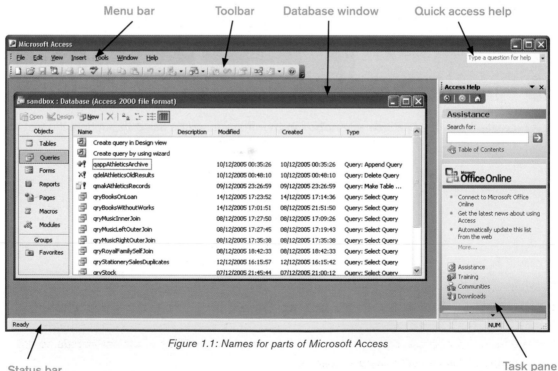

Figure 1.1: Names for parts of Microsoft Access

Toolbars

Menu bar

The **menu bar** is traditionally docked at the top of the window, although you are free to move it if you wish (this is not recommended). You can undock a toolbar by clicking the drag handle (vertical dots) on the left of the toolbar and dragging it into the main window area.

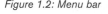

Figure 1.2: Menu bar

By default, Access keeps track of which menu options you use most often and customises the menus to match. Figure 1.3 (a) shows a **Tools** menu with options that have not been used recently hidden from view — to get to these, you must click on the down arrow at the bottom of the menu.

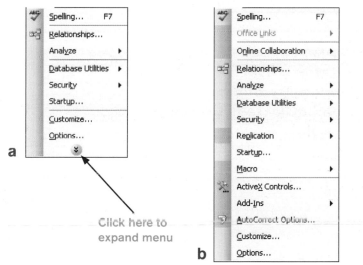

Figure 1.3: Tools menu (a) compressed and (b) expanded

These dynamic menus can be useful for beginners, so they don't have to search through lots of commands to find the ones that they use frequently. However, for more advanced users this feature can be annoying; you will probably find it simpler to have the menus always expanded, so that you never need to waste a click expanding them and the positions of the commands do not keep changing. You can set this up as follows:

 Start Access, if you have not already done so.

Right-click anywhere in the **menu bar**, then select **Customize**. The **Customize** dialogue box appears, as shown in Figure 1.4.

Click on the **Options** tab to display it, then make sure that **Always show full menus** is ticked.

 Press **Close** to confirm the change.

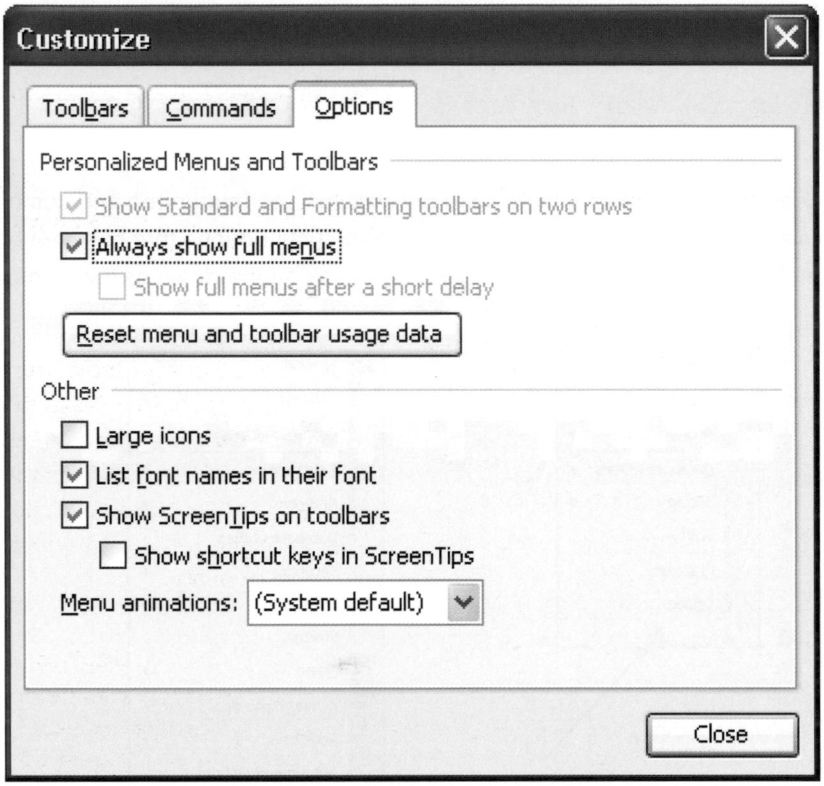

Figure 1.4: Setting options for how menus and toolbars are displayed

Database toolbar

The **Database** toolbar contains buttons that provide quick access to the commands that you need to use when the **Database** window is selected.

Figure 1.5: Database toolbar

The commands provided, reading from left to right, are as follows:

 New quickly creates a new database file.

 Open lets you browse for a database to open.

 Save saves the current object.

 File Search opens the **File Search** task pane.

 Print prints the currently selected object to the default printer.

 Print Preview shows what the currently selected object will look like when it is printed.

 Spelling performs a spell check on the currently selected object.

 Cut, **Copy** and **Paste** move or duplicate one or more objects.

Undo lets you correct mistakes by undoing the last action (such as the pasting of a new database object).

Office Links lets you act upon the current object using another Office application: **Merge It with Microsoft Office Word**, **Publish It with Microsoft Office Word** or **Analyze It with Microsoft Office Excel**.

 The **Analyze** menu provides access to the following tools: **Analyze Table**, **Analyze Performance** and **Documenter**.

 Code lets you edit a Visual Basic module. You are unlikely to need this.

 Microsoft Script Editor is used for editing data access pages. You are unlikely to need this.

Properties displays the **Properties** dialogue box for the currently selected object. You can achieve the same thing by pressing **Alt+Enter**, by selecting **View**, **Properties** from the main menu, or by right-clicking the object and selecting **Properties** from the menu that appears.

 Relationships displays the **Relationships** window. You can also do this by selecting **Tools**, **Relationships** from the main menu.

 The **New Object** menu allows you to quickly create a new object: an AutoForm, an AutoReport, a Table, a Query, a Form, a Report, a Page, a Macro, a Module or a Class Module.

Help displays Access's help task pane.

Design toolbars

Common buttons

The following buttons appear on each of the toolbars used for designing database objects:

 The **View** menu (always the first icon on the design toolbars) allows you to change your view of the currently selected object. You can use the drop-down menu to select a specific view, or click the button to go directly to the view signified by its icon (which is generally the one you want, since it toggles between design and display views).

 Build opens a dialogue box offering you a choice between three builder tools: **Expression Builder**, **Macro Builder** and **Code Builder**.

Database Window provides a quick way of switching from the current object back to the **Database Window**.

> **TIP**
>
> It is important that you understand how the **View** button works. You will be using it time and time again as you work through this book.

Table Design toolbar

The **Table Design** toolbar appears when a table is open in **Design** view.

Figure 1.6: Table Design toolbar

Buttons specific to this toolbar are as follows:

 Primary Key sets the currently selected field as a primary key (or several fields as a joint primary key).

 Indexes shows a list of the indexes that are set up for the current table, and allows you to modify them.

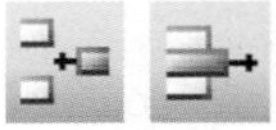

Insert Rows and **Delete Rows** allow you to insert and delete fields from the table design.

Query Design toolbar

The **Query Design** toolbar appears when a query is open in **Design** view.

Figure 1.7: Query Design toolbar

Buttons specific to this toolbar are as follows:

 The **Query Type** menu allows you to change the type of query, enabling you to modify data. This is covered in detail in Chapter 9.

 Run executes the current query and displays the results.

 Show Table opens the **Show Table** dialogue box, allowing you to add another table to the query.

Σ **Totals** allows you to use grouping functions. We cover this in Chapter 9.

 The **Top Values** control allows you to set a maximum number or proportion of results to return from the query. This is particularly useful when querying very large databases.

Form Design and Report Design toolbars

These toolbars are so similar that they can be treated together. The only difference between them is that the **Report Design** toolbar has a **Sorting and Grouping** button (boxed in Figure 1.9), which the **Form Design** toolbar does not have.

Figure 1.8: Form Design toolbar

Figure 1.9: Report Design toolbar

Buttons specific to these toolbars are as follows:

Insert Hyperlink allows you to insert a hyperlink to another file, typically a web page.

Field List displays a floating **Field List** window, which provides a quick way of adding fields from the **Record Source** to the design.

Toolbox shows or hides the **Toolbox** palette of controls.

 Sorting and Grouping shows or hides the **Sorting and Grouping** dialogue box.

AutoFormat displays the **AutoFormat** dialogue box, allowing you to quickly apply different styles to the design.

Formatting toolbar

The **Formatting** toolbar provides quick access to commands that let you change the format of the currently selected control in a form or report.

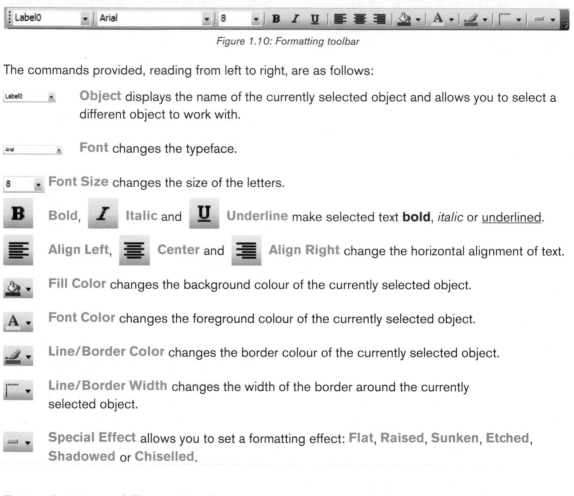

Figure 1.10: Formatting toolbar

The commands provided, reading from left to right, are as follows:

Object displays the name of the currently selected object and allows you to select a different object to work with.

Font changes the typeface.

Font Size changes the size of the letters.

B Bold, *I* Italic and **U** Underline make selected text **bold**, *italic* or underlined.

Align Left, Center and Align Right change the horizontal alignment of text.

Fill Color changes the background colour of the currently selected object.

Font Color changes the foreground colour of the currently selected object.

Line/Border Color changes the border colour of the currently selected object.

Line/Border Width changes the width of the border around the currently selected object.

Special Effect allows you to set a formatting effect: **Flat**, **Raised**, **Sunken**, **Etched**, **Shadowed** or **Chiselled**.

Datasheet and Form toolbars

These toolbars are so similar that they can be treated together. The only difference between them is that the **Form** toolbar has a **Properties** button (boxed in Figure 1.12), which the **Datasheet** toolbar does not have. (For the second icon from the right of each toolbar, a different default object type is selected, although this button opens the **New Object** menu in both cases.)

Figure 1.11: Datasheet toolbar

Figure 1.12: Form toolbar

Buttons specific to these toolbars are as follows:

Filter By Selection filters the data so that only those records whose fields match the current selection are shown.

Filter By Form displays a form into which you can type values to use for the filter.

Apply Filter provides a quick way to turn the last-used filter on and off.

Find displays the **Find and Replace** dialogue box.

New Record takes you to the next blank record so that you can enter new values into the database.

Delete Record deletes the current record from the database.

The Properties dialogue box

The exercises in later chapters often refer to the **Properties** dialogue box. Unlike most other dialogue boxes, the **Properties** dialogue box does not show its name in its title bar; instead, the title changes to reflect the name of the currently selected object, the properties for which are being displayed. An example **Properties** dialogue box for a form is shown in Figure 1.13. You can keep the **Properties** dialogue box open – it stays on top of the main window.

There are four ways to turn the **Properties** dialogue box on and off: Press the **Properties** button on the toolbar; select **View**, **Properties** from the main menu; right-click on an object and select **Properties** from the menu that appears; or press **Alt+Enter**.

Properties

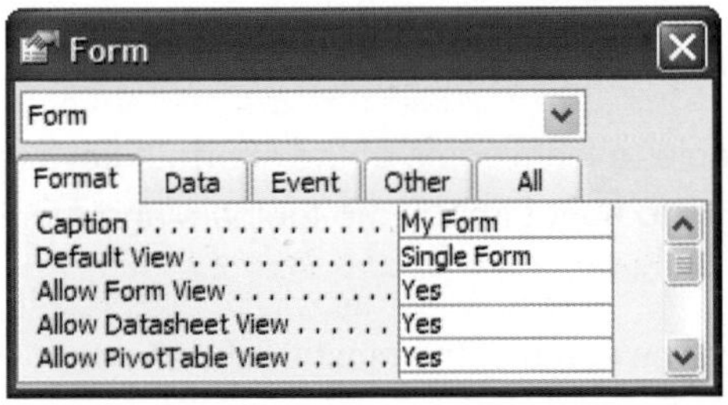

Figure 1.13: The Properties dialogue box for a form

Installed features

Some of the wizards (dialogue boxes that guide you through complex tasks) used in this book are not included in a default installation of Access 2003. Instead, they are installed the first time they are used.

The following wizards are used during the course of this book, but not installed if the **Typical Wizards** option was chosen when Access was installed on your PC. (All of the wizards are installed if **Additional Wizards** was chosen during installation.)

 Find Duplicates Query Wizard.

 Find Unmatched Query Wizard.

 Input Mask Wizard.

 Option Group Wizard.

 Subform/Subreport Wizard.

Because of this, it may be necessary to install further software from your Microsoft Office installation CD-ROM as you work through this book. If this is the case, Access will prompt you for the CD-ROM at the appropriate times.

Regional settings

This book assumes that you are using a Windows PC that has been set up with British regional settings. You can change your regional settings via the **Control Panel** in Windows. Note that if your PC is set up with other regional settings (such as for the US) then Access's treatment of date and currency values will be different.

Commands

Keyboard commands

It is well worth taking the trouble to learn some of the shortcut keys that Access assigns to its commands. Rather than having to hunt through the toolbars and menus, it is often quicker to use the keyboard shortcut.

The following list (Table 1.1) gives some of the most useful shortcut keys; you can find more by searching Access's help.

Command	Shortcut		Command	Shortcut
Undo	Ctrl+Z		Paste	Ctrl+V
Redo	Ctrl+Y		Cancel edit	Esc
Save	Ctrl+S		Find & Replace	Ctrl+F
Select All	Ctrl+A		Bold	Ctrl+B
Copy	Ctrl+C		Italic	Ctrl+I
Cut	Ctrl+X		Underline	Ctrl+U

Table 1.1 Useful shortcut keys

Online help

Do not forget that one of the quickest and easiest ways to find out how to do something in Access is to consult its online help.

 From the menu, select **Help, Microsoft Office Access Help**.

The **Access Help** task pane appears, as shown in Figure 1.14.

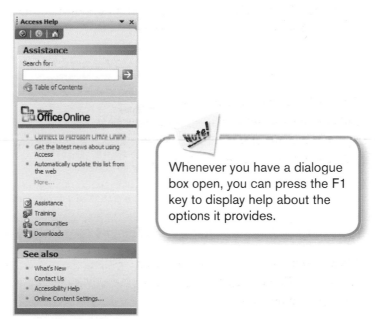

Figure 1.14: The Access Help task pane

Whenever you have a dialogue box open, you can press the F1 key to display help about the options it provides.

 In the **Search for** box, type **about** and press **Enter**.

A list of help topics with the word **about** appears – many of these are introductions to complex topics, so click on any that catch your eye. You may also like to search for **troubleshoot**.

Creating the sandbox

What is the sandbox?

The word **sandbox** (the American term for a **sandpit**) is used in computing to refer to a container from which untrusted programs can be run, and by extension to areas in which users can try out features of software packages without causing harm if anything goes wrong.

This book uses two databases: **auctions.mdb** (an example database with a significant chunk of data, used in the **Test yourself** exercises at the end of each chapter) and **sandbox.mdb** (which you will create for yourself from scratch, and is used for everything else).

Creating the new database

 Open Access if it isn't already running.

 From the menu, select **File**, **New**. The **New File** task pane appears, as shown in Figure 1.15.

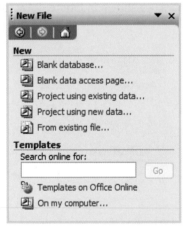

Figure 1.15: New File task pane

Click the **Blank database** link. The **File New Database** window appears.

Navigate to the location where you wish to save your work files (it will be neater if you create all of the files in a dedicated folder). Type **sandbox.mdb** as the **File name** and press **Create**.

You are now ready to work through the exercises presented in the rest of this book.

2 Table design

Introduction

In this chapter we will create a database table containing information about the ten wealthiest countries in the world. We will experiment on this table to understand the benefits and consequences of changing the data types used to store the various fields.

In this chapter, you will:

 learn about the different **data types** supported by Access

 create a table by typing in its data and letting Access automatically determine the data types it uses

 apply and modify data types assigned to fields in your table, and understand the consequences of doing so.

Data types

Introduction to data types

Consider the number **40 000** stored in a database. What might this represent?

 It could be a straightforward number: a staff ID or the number of items a factory has produced in a day.

 It could be a currency amount: an item with a value of €40 000 or a cost of £40 000.

It could even be a date! Access stores dates as the number of days since the 30th December 1899 (since this takes less space than storing the date as a string or a group of numbers for the day, week and month separately). In this scheme, 40 000 equates to 6th July 2009.

> **Note!**
>
> The choice of equating 30th December 1899 with zero is rather strange: there are 31 days in December, so the new century starts on day number 2 (where you might think 1 would make more sense).

Every field in a database must have an associated data type, so that the software knows how to treat th1e data.

Creating a simple table

There are several ways to create a database table in Access. We will start by using the simplest method, in which we can just enter the data into a table and Access will guess what data type to use for each field from the data it contains. After this, we will modify the data types to be exactly what we want. We will repeat this two-step process for most of the tables we create when working through this book.

We are going to create a simple table that records information about the ten wealthiest countries in the world.

> **Note!**
>
> The term **GDP** means *gross domestic product*, which is a measure of the total value of goods and services produced by a nation. The **GDP per capita** is calculated by dividing a nation's GDP by the population size. In simple terms, countries with a high GDP per capita have a wealthier population than those with lower values.

 Open the database **sandbox.mdb** that you created in the previous chapter.

With **Tables** selected on the left-hand side of the **Database** window, double-click on **Create table by entering data**, as shown in Figure 2.1.

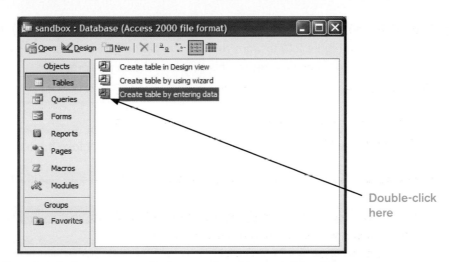

Figure 2.1: Opting to create a table from raw data without specifying data types

An empty grid of cells appears. Adding real data to this grid is a useful way of designing the structure of a table, and has the benefit that the data you enter at this stage will be imported into the new table automatically.

Double-click where it says **Field1**, then type **Country** and press **Enter**. This is how to assign names to the database fields in the table we are creating.

Give the following names to **Field2** through **Field5** respectively: **GDP per capita**, **Date of GDP estimate**, **Population (thousands)** and **Government web site**.

> **TIP**
>
> You can resize the columns by hovering your mouse pointer over the vertical line between two column headings and then clicking and dragging your mouse. If you double-click a dividing line, the column to its left will automatically be resized to fit its contents.

Type in the data for ten countries exactly as it is given in Figure 2.2. Notice that there are commas after the thousands and that the **Government web site** for Switzerland is spelt **parlament**, not **parliament**.

Country	GDP per capita	Date of GDP estimate	Population (thousands)	Government web site
Luxembourg	34,400	2004	469	www.government.lu
United States	23,400	2004	295,734	www.whitehouse.gov
Guernsey	23,300	2003	65	www.gov.gg
Norway	23,300	2004	4,593	www.stortinget.no
Jersey	23,300	2003	91	www.gov.je
British Virgin Islands	22,500	2004	23	
Bermuda	21,000	2003	65	
San Marino	20,200	2001	29	www.esteri.sm
Hong Kong	20,000	2004	6,899	www.info.gov.hk
Switzerland	19,700	2004	7,485	www.parlament.ch

Figure 2.2: Creating a table by entering data. (Data adapted from The World Factbook.)

Save the table as **tblGDP** (see the tip if you are not sure how to do this). A message appears (see Figure 2.3) to warn you that you did not set a primary key on this table. We do not need a primary key for this simple table, so just press **No**.

TIP

There are several ways to save an object in Access: select **File**, **Save** from the menu; click the **Save** icon in the **Table Datasheet** toolbar; or close the object and hope that Access asks you whether you wanted to save it!

Save

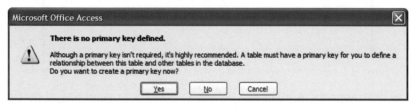

Figure 2.3: The warning message you get when you save a table without defining a primary key

---

TIP

A **primary key** is assigned to large tables to improve their efficiency. It is an index, the values of which must all be unique – this means that Access can find a record very quickly from its primary key, even if there are very many records in the database table.

Design View

 Press the **Design View** button on the **Table Datasheet** toolbar.

The **Design** view appears, as shown in Figure 2.4. The **Data Type** column shows that Access has recognised some of the fields as text and the remainder as numbers.

Field Name	Data Type	Description
Country	Text	
GDP per capita	Number	
Date of GDP estimate	Number	
Population (thousands)	Number	
Government web site	Text	

Field Properties

General | Lookup

Field Size	50
Format	
Input Mask	
Caption	
Default Value	
Validation Rule	
Validation Text	
Required	No
Allow Zero Length	Yes
Indexed	No
Unicode Compression	Yes
IME Mode	No Control
IME Sentence Mode	None
Smart Tags	

Figure 2.4: Design view showing the data types that were automatically assigned to the fields in the new table

Data types and their uses (size in bytes given in parentheses)

Text	A string of letters, numbers and other characters. The default field size is 50 characters and the maximum is 255.
Memo	A text field that can be much larger than Text (up to 64KB) but takes extra storage space.
Number	A numerical value. There are several number subtypes:

Byte (1)	A whole number between 0 to 255.
Integer (2)	A whole number between −32 768 and 32 767.
Long Integer (4)	A whole number between −2 147 483 648 and 2 147 483 647.
Single (4)	A fractional number between approximately $\pm 3.4 \times 10^{38}$.
Double (8)	A fractional number between approximately $\pm 1.79 \times 10^{308}$.
Replication ID (16)	A GUID (globally unique identifier) assigned automatically by Access. This type of field is used for managing databases that will need to be merged later. You are unlikely to need this unless you work on large databases that are updated independently on different sites.
Decimal (12)	A precise number with up to 29 digits and up to 28 decimal places. You will probably not need to use this unless you are dealing with scientific data.

Date/Time (8)	A date, stored as a floating point number in which the integer part represents the date (the number of days after the 30th December 1899) and the fractional part represents the time. Access provides many ways to format dates and times, so you rarely need to understand how it stores the data.
Currency (8)	A fixed-point number designed for accurate financial calculations. This format comprises 15 digits and 4 decimal places.
AutoNumber (4)	A whole number assigned automatically by Access. It is typically incremental (1, 2, 3, …) but can also be set up to be a Replication ID (see above).
Yes/No (1 bit)	A logical field used for representing data that must have exactly one of two states. Such values can be interpreted as Yes/No, True/False or On/Off, depending on what they represent.
OLE Object	An embedded object, such as an image or a document. A typical example would be a human resources database that showed a photo of each member of staff.
Hyperlink	A link to a file, typically a web page on the Internet.

Look at the above list of data types and think about which of them are appropriate for the table you have just created.

Applying and modifying data types

Syllabus ref: AM5.1.1.1
Apply, modify data types such as text, memo, hyperlink, currency, date & time in a field, column.

Syllabus ref: AM5.1.1.2
Understand the consequences of modifying data types such as text, memo, hyperlink, currency formats, date & time in a field, column.

Let's go through the fields one by one.

1 Country

Country has type **Text**. This seems reasonable, so we can leave it as it is.

2 GDP per capita

GDP per capita has type **Number**, **Long Integer**. This might seem excessive, since the largest value it holds is only five digits and the **Long Integer** field can hold numbers of up to ten digits. However, the next smaller field for whole numbers is **Integer**; this has a maximum value of only 32 767, which isn't enough. Because these values are all in British pounds, the best data format to use is **Currency**.

TIP

If we had used a pound sign when we typed in the original data then Access would have correctly detected that we were entering values in pounds and would have set the data type to **Currency** automatically.

 Change the **Data Type** to the right of the **GDP per capita** field to **Currency**.

 Click the **Datasheet View** icon. Press **Yes** when asked whether you wish to save the table.

Datasheet
View

The table looks much like it did before (see Figure 2.2) except that the GDPs are displayed without commas and are right-aligned. You might have expected them to be displayed with pound signs, but they are not. This is easy to change.

Note!

If you are using an earlier version of Access then you might find that the GDPs are displayed with commas, although they are still right-aligned.

 Switch back to **Design** view and change the **Format** of the **GDP per capita** field from **Standard** to **Currency**, as shown in Figure 2.5. Save the design.

In the **Datasheet** view, confirm that the GDP values are now shown with pound signs.

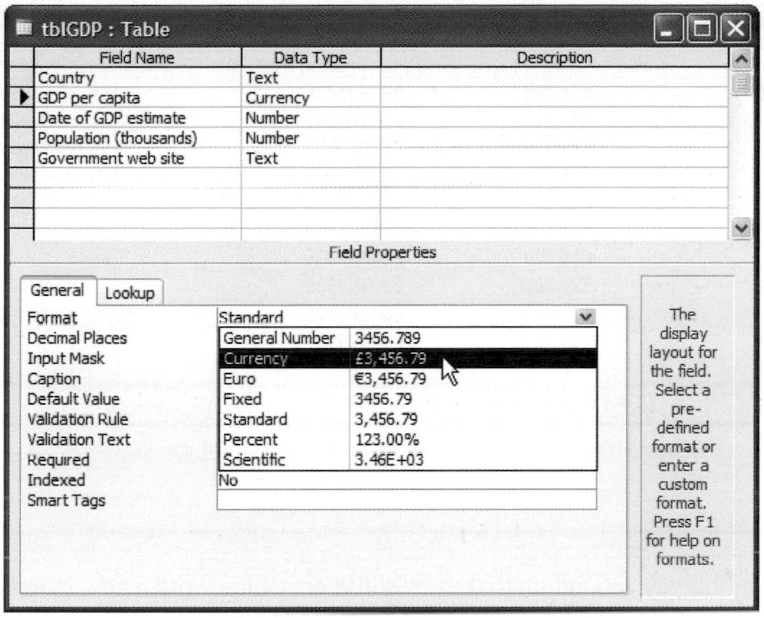

Figure 2.5: Changing the GDP per capita field to Currency format

It is important to understand that this latest change has not altered the way the values are stored in the table, only the way in which they are displayed. You can change the **Format** parameter as often as you like without risking damage to your data. The same is **not** true of the **Data Type** parameter, as we shall see now.

3 Date of GDP estimate

Date of GDP estimate has type **Number**, **Long Integer**. Let's see what happens if we change this to a **Date/Time** field.

Change the **Data Type** of **Date of GDP estimate** to **Date/Time**.

Save the design and view the table.

You should find that the table looks like Figure 2.6. Look at the format of the dates: they are all in 1905, which is not what we wanted at all! The strange dates have appeared because Access stores dates as the number of days since the 30th December 1899, so the year values we are storing are interpreted as meaning approximately 2000 days into the 20th century. This happens to fall in June 1905.

Country	GDP per capita	Date of GDP estimate	Population (thousands)	Government web site
▶ Luxembourg	£34,400	26/06/1905	469	www.government.lu
United States	£23,400	26/06/1905	295,734	www.whitehouse.gov
Guernsey	£23,300	25/06/1905	65	www.gov.gg
Norway	£23,300	26/06/1905	4,593	www.stortinget.no
Jersey	£23,300	25/06/1905	91	www.gov.je
British Virgin Islands	£22,500	26/06/1905	23	
Bermuda	£21,000	25/06/1905	65	
San Marino	£20,200	23/06/1905	29	www.esteri.sm
Hong Kong	£20,000	26/06/1905	6,899	www.info.gov.hk
Switzerland	£19,700	26/06/1905	7,485	www.parlament.ch

tbIGDP : Table

Record: 1 of 10

Figure 2.6: Changing to a date format has not had the desired effect!

> **TIP**
>
> Had we known the day and month that each of the estimates were made, instead of just the year, we could have written the dates in full (for example, **1/11/2004**) when we were designing the table. Access would have recognised these as dates and set the data type appropriately.

Because of this problem, we should change the **Date of GDP estimate** back to being a **Number** field.

 Make the change and confirm that the years are displayed properly again.

4 Population (thousands)

Population (thousands) has type **Number**, **Long Integer**. This seems reasonable. If the United States value were not in the list, we might consider changing the data type to **Integer** (since all of the other values are less than **32 767**, the maximum value that an **Integer** field can hold).

In the spirit of experimentation (this is the **sandbox** database, after all), let's make the change anyway to see what happens.

Change the **Field Size** of **Population (thousands)** from **Long Integer** to **Integer**, as shown in Figure 2.7.

Figure 2.7: Making a foolhardy change from Long Integer to Integer

 Save the table.

The warning message shown in Figure 2.8 appears. It tells us that the proposed change will delete data from exactly one field. If we were to press **No** at this point, the table would not be saved to disk – we could choose to close it and discard the change.

Figure 2.8: A warning that data will be lost if you proceed

Because we were expecting this change to cause problems with our population data for the United States, we will carry on.

 Press **Yes** to instruct Access that we wish to proceed in spite of the lost data.

 Look at the contents of the table. You should find that everything is intact, apart from the **Population (thousands)** value for **United States**; this has been deleted.

So now we know. If a smaller field size is applied to an existing numerical field then any data that no longer fits is simply deleted. Let's change back again and restore the deleted data.

 Change the **Field Size** for **Population (thousands)** back to **Long Integer**.

In **Datasheet** view, type in the population of the United States: **295 734**.

Note!

The comma is optional; it is part of the number's formatting. (Notice that this field's **Format** property is set to **Standard** rather than **General Number**. You can see from Figure 2.9 that this format includes commas.) Before storing a number, Access is clever enough to strip out any commas you typed.

5 Government web site

Government web site has type **Text**.

We can go one better by converting these into working hyperlinks.

TIP

If we had put **http://** in front of these values, Access would have automatically recognised them as hyperlinks.

 In **Design** view, change the **Data Type** of **Government web site** to **Hyperlink**. Save the table and switch it to **Datasheet** view.

The table should now appear with blue underlined values in the **Government web site** column, as shown in Figure 2.9.

Country	GDP per capita	Date of GDP estimate	Population (thousands)	Government web site
Luxembourg	£34,400	2004	469	www.government.lu
United States	£23,400	2004	295,734	www.whitehouse.gov
Guernsey	£23,300	2003	65	www.gov.gg
Norway	£23,300	2004	4,593	www.stortinget.no
Jersey	£23,300	2003	91	www.gov.je
British Virgin Islands	£22,500	2004	23	
Bermuda	£21,000	2003	65	
San Marino	£20,200	2001	29	www.esteri.sm
Hong Kong	£20,000	2004	6,899	www.info.gov.hk
Switzerland	£19,700	2004	7,485	www.parlament.ch
*			0	

Record: 1 of 10

Figure 2.9: Hyperlinks in a table

 If you are connected to the Internet, click on the link for www.whitehouse.gov. Your web browser should load and display the home page for The White House.

 Close your web browser.

Back in Access, if you hover your mouse pointer over one of the hyperlinks, the pointer changes to a hand. A tooltip displays the web address of the hyperlink. This is important because a hyperlink field can have a display value that is different from the hyperlink itself.

 Right-click on www.whitehouse.gov and hover over the **Hyperlink** submenu to expand it, as shown in Figure 2.10. Change the value of **Display Text** to **The White House** and press **Enter**.

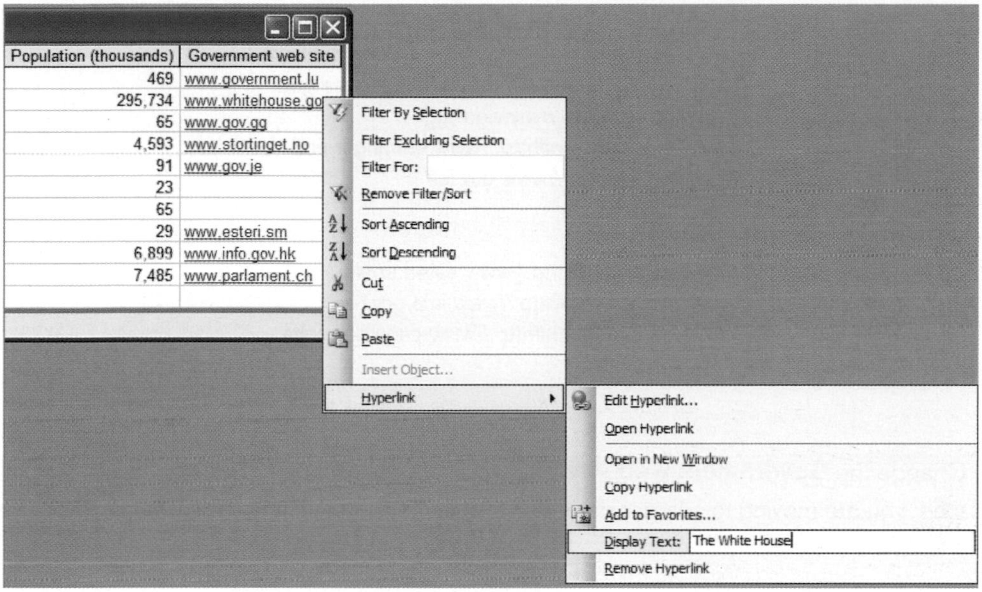

Figure 2.10: Changing the display text for a hyperlink

The value now appears to be **The White House**. However, notice that the tooltip still displays http://www.whitehouse.gov and the link still works. We have only changed the display value. To see how Access stores this information, we will temporarily switch the field type back to plain text.

Change the **Data Type** for **Government web site** back to **Text** and save the table. The warning shown in Figure 2.11 appears.

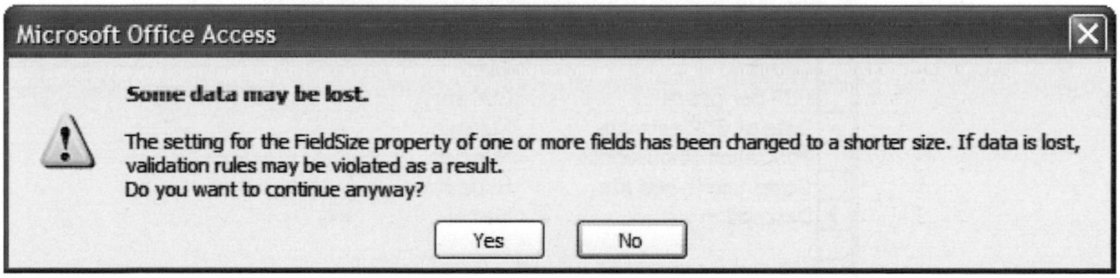

Microsoft Office Access

⚠ **Some data may be lost.**

The setting for the FieldSize property of one or more fields has been changed to a shorter size. If data is lost, validation rules may be violated as a result.
Do you want to continue anyway?

[Yes]   [No]

Figure 2.11: A warning that data may be lost by truncating a text field

This warning is less useful than its numerical equivalent (Figure 2.8) because it only tells us that some data might possibly be lost – the other warning told us exactly how many records were affected. We will carry on regardless.

Press **Yes** to confirm that you wish to proceed.

Your text should look like Figure 2.12. The value for The White House shows how each hyperlink is stored as a string with three parts: the display name, the web address, and an optional location in the document (which we have not used – this would go on the end). Each pair of values is separated by a **#**.

Government web site
www.government.lu#http://www.government.lu#
The White House#http://www.whitehouse.gov#
www.gov.gg#http://www.gov.gg#
www.stortinget.no#http://www.stortinget.no#
www.gov.je#http://www.gov.je#
www.esteri.sm#http://www.esteri.sm#
www.info.gov.hk#http://www.info.gov.hk#
www.parlament.ch#http://www.parlament.ch#

Figure 2.12: Hyperlinks displayed as text

Change the **Government web site** back to a **Hyperlink** again. There is no warning this time: you are moving to a larger data type and so cannot lose any information in this direction.

Adding a memo field

Because you cannot create a **Memo** field using **Create table by entering data**, we have not used one of these so far. For the sake of completeness, let's add a **Memo** field to hold the description of each country.

In **Design** view, type a new **Field Name** of **Description** and set its **Data Type** to **Memo**, as shown in Figure 2.13.

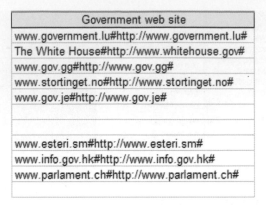

Field Name	Data Type	
Country	Text	
GDP per capita	Currency	
Date of GDP estimate	Number	
Population (thousands)	Number	
Government web site	Hyperlink	
Description	Memo	

Figure 2.13: Adding a Memo field

In **Datasheet** view, type the following text into the new **Description** field for **Luxembourg**. (If you prefer you may type something else, even complete gibberish, so long as it is longer than 255 characters and you make a note of how it ends.)

Founded in 963, Luxembourg became a grand duchy in 1815 and an independent state under the Netherlands. It lost more than half of its territory to Belgium in 1839, but gained a larger measure of autonomy. Full independence was attained in 1867. Overrun by Germany in both World Wars, it ended its neutrality in 1948 when it entered into the Benelux Customs Union and when it joined NATO the following year. In 1957, Luxembourg became one of the six founding countries of the European Economic Community (later the European Union), and in 1999 it joined the euro currency area.

Source: *The World Factbook*

What do you think will happen if we change this back to a **Text** field?

 Change the **Description** field back to **Text** and give it a **Field Size** of **255** (the maximum that **Text** will support).

Confirm that this results in the description being truncated. Was this what you expected to happen?

Conclusions

This exercise has demonstrated the following points.

A table field must have a **Data Type**. Changing the **Data Type** may cause data to be lost if the new type is more restrictive (uses less storage space) than the old type.

If a smaller field size is applied to an existing field, any data that no longer fits is deleted (set to null).

If a smaller field size is applied to an existing textual field, any data that no longer fits is truncated.

Access warns you if you change the design of a table in such a way that some data might get lost. If this happens, you can choose to close the table without saving its changes.

A table field may have a **Format**. This affects only the way the data is displayed, not the underlying data. Therefore, the **Format** may be changed freely without any risk of losing data.

Test yourself

Auction database

Throughout this book, most of the 'Test yourself' exercises will apply to an example database used by an auctioneer. This will let you see how the syllabus topics fit into a larger, more realistic database than the ones you will create when working through the chapters. The initial database – **auction.mdb** – is available from the publisher's web site: www.payne-gallway.co.uk/ecdl.

Because the act of changing data types is straightforward, there are no exercises here on that subject. You should, however, make sure that you have a thorough understanding of the conclusions listed on the previous page.

3 Form design I

Introduction

In this chapter we will create a form that could be used for noting down telephone messages (an electronic equivalent to the telephone message pads found in most offices). This form will be unusual in that it will not be attached to a table; users can enter details about a telephone message and then print the form, but the data will not be stored in the database – in other words, the controls will be **unbound**. (It would be easy to extend the form to store the information in a table, but this is not necessary for this exercise.)

In this chapter, you will:

- learn about the different **types of control** that can be added to a form

- **add unbound controls** to a form

- change the **sequential order** of the controls (for tabbing between the fields)

- **record a macro** to print and close the form

- learn how to **run a macro**

- **attach a macro** to a button on the form.

Message

For_____

From_____of_____

Time_____Date_____

Phone_____

❑ Urgent ❑ Call them ❑ They'll call back

_____

_____

_____

_____

_____

_____

_____

_____

Message taken by_____

Telephone message pad

Creating a form

In this chapter we will develop a simple form that people within a business could use to record telephone messages. Each of the fields on a database form is usually **bound** to data from a table or query and the form displays the data from a single record in the database. For this form, all of the controls will be **unbound**. You can still enter data into an unbound control, but it will not be saved in the database. These controls are still useful – you will see that we can print the form once it has been filled in.

Open **sandbox.mdb** if it is not already open.

Click **Forms** from the **Objects** list on the left-hand side of the **Database** window, and double-click **Create form in Design view**, as shown in Figure 3.1.

Figure 3.1: Creating a new form

A new form appears. Resize the form by clicking and dragging its edges until it is 8 cm wide and 6 cm tall, as shown in Figure 3.2. (Select **View**, **Ruler** if you don't already have the horizontal and vertical guides.)

> **TIP**
>
> You can turn the gridlines on and off by selecting **View**, **Grid** from the main menu. They can help you to align the components, but tend to obscure any text on the form.

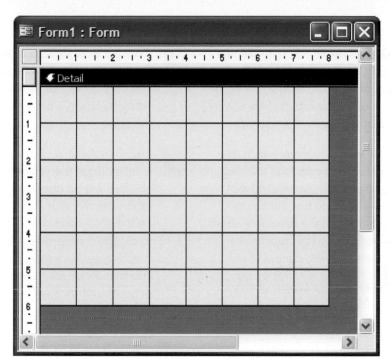

Figure 3.2: A blank form that has been resized

Adding components

Syllabus ref: AM5.3.1.1
Create bound and unbound controls.

Syllabus ref: AM5.3.1.2
Create, edit a combo box, list box, check box, option groups.

Now we need to add some controls to the blank form. Let's look at what is on offer. Figure 3.3 shows the **Toolbox**; your one will probably be a different shape (as with other toolbars, you can resize it by dragging one of its edges) but should have the same buttons available.

Figure 3.3: Toolbox for adding controls to a form

Tools

 Select Objects With this tool selected you can click on an object on the form to select it, or click and drag a rectangle to select all of the objects that are (even partly) in the rectangle.

 Control Wizard If this is selected then Access will automatically load a wizard when you add certain types of control (option group, combo box, list box or command button) to the form. The wizard will guide you through the process of applying settings to the control.

Label This is used for fixed text, such as a title or the name of one of the other controls.

 Text Box This is a box for displaying and/or inputting text (typically bound to a field in the database).

Option Group This is a bounding rectangle that modifies the behaviour of any on/off controls within it so that only one control can be 'on' at a time (that is, the previously 'on' control is turned off whenever a new selection is made). This is typically used for option buttons, but also works with toggle buttons and check boxes.

Toggle Button This control can be clicked once to press in the button and once more to return it to its original state.

Option Button This type of button is most frequently used in an option group.

 Check Box This is the more traditional way of representing a toggle button (i.e. for values that are either true or false).

Combo Box This is a combination (hence the name) of a list box and a text edit control. You can select a new value either by typing it or by selecting it from the list.

List Box A list of choices. If the control is tall enough then all of the possible choices will be displayed at once, otherwise the user must click the arrow on the right-hand side of the control to display a drop-down list. A list box can display more than one column of information for each choice, although only one of these will be bound to its value. If a list box is not bound then users can be allowed to select more than one value at once.

Command Button This control doesn't represent a value. Instead it is usually connected to a macro to allow the user to perform some action.

 Image This is used to add a fixed image, such as a logo, to a form.

Unbound Object Frame This control allows you to add any object from an application that supports OLE (Object Linking and Embedding). You are unlikely to need to do this.

 Bound Object Frame This control can be bound to an OLE data field in a table or query. For example, in a human resources database it could be used to display a staff member's picture.

 Page Break This tool allows you to add a page break to a multi-page form.

Tab Control This tool allows you to create, on a single form, a set of pages that the user can switch between by clicking on the named tab at the top of each.

 Subform/Subreport This tool allows you to embed one form inside another. See Chapter 11.

 Line This tool allows you to draw a line on a form, for example to separate two groups of controls.

 Rectangle This tool allows you to draw a rectangle on a form. Unlike an option group, a rectangle does not alter the behaviour of any controls that you put inside it.

 More Controls This button allows you to insert any ActiveX control on to your form. You are unlikely to want to do this.

TIP

If you want your form to be easy to understand, you should use check boxes in preference to option buttons for yes/no values, and option buttons inside option groups for fields that have only a small number of possible values.

Note!

The difference between combo boxes and list boxes is purely that you can type a value in a combo box but not in a list box. This does not necessarily mean that every value typed will be accepted as valid. A combo box may have its **Limit To List** property set to **Yes**, in which case users may still type values, but only those values that are also in the drop-down list will be accepted by the control.

 Click **Format** on the main menu and make sure that **Snap to Grid** is turned on (has a tick next to it).

Select the **Text Box** tool and click and drag a rectangle on the form in the location shown in Figure 3.4(a). When you release your mouse button, the form should look like Figure 3.4(b).

Text Box

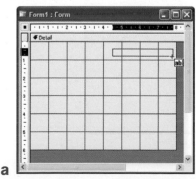

a

b

Figure 3.4: Adding a text field to the form – (a) during the drag and (b) on releasing the mouse button

A label that is created automatically to accompany another control is attached to that control. If you drag the control or its label then your mouse pointer will change to a hand symbol (🖑) and both the control and its label will move together. If you wish to move one of these components without the other then click and drag the black square in the top left of the component that you wish to move – your mouse pointer will change to a finger shape (👆) to show that you are moving only one component. You can resize controls and labels by dragging their respective resize handles.

Notice that a label (**Text0:**) has been added automatically. This is often a useful feature, since most text boxes have accompanying labels to tell the user what type of information the box contains. However, in this case we don't need a label, so we can delete it.

Click the label and then press the **Delete** key on your keyboard.

TIP

Clicking a control that is not already selected will select it (it will get selection handles around it – see Figure 3.5(a)). Clicking a selected control will allow you to change the **Control Source** without having to display the **Properties** dialogue – see Figure 3.5(b).

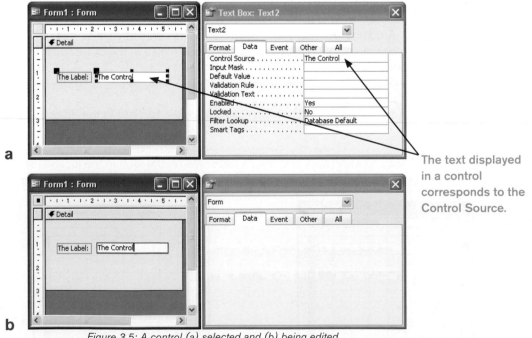

a

b

Figure 3.5: A control (a) selected and (b) being edited

The text displayed in a control corresponds to the Control Source.

Now add the other text fields shown in Figure 3.6. Notice that the labels have been retained for most of the text fields.

TIP

If you double-click on a tool, it will remain selected so that you can create several controls of the same type one after the other (if you just single-click on a tool, as soon as you add a new control Access will automatically change to the **Select Objects** tool). Having double-clicked on a tool, you can deselect it again by clicking on it once or by clicking the **Select Objects** tool.

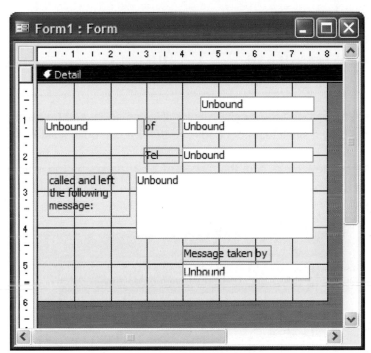

Figure 3.6: Text fields on the message form

Save the form as **frmTelephoneMessage** (do not close it).

It is easy to test a form as you are designing it. Let's try this.

Click the **Form View** button on the **Form Design** toolbar.

Try typing an example telephone message, as shown in Figure 3.7.

Figure 3.7: Typing data into the telephone message form

There is nowhere to record who the message is for. We can add a combo box for this (supposing the form is to be used by a small team of people, so that we can build a list of names into it).

Control Wizards

Combo Box

Back in **Design** view, make sure that the **Control Wizards** button is not pressed in and then use the **Combo Box** tool to add a new control in the top left of the form, as shown in Figure 3.8.

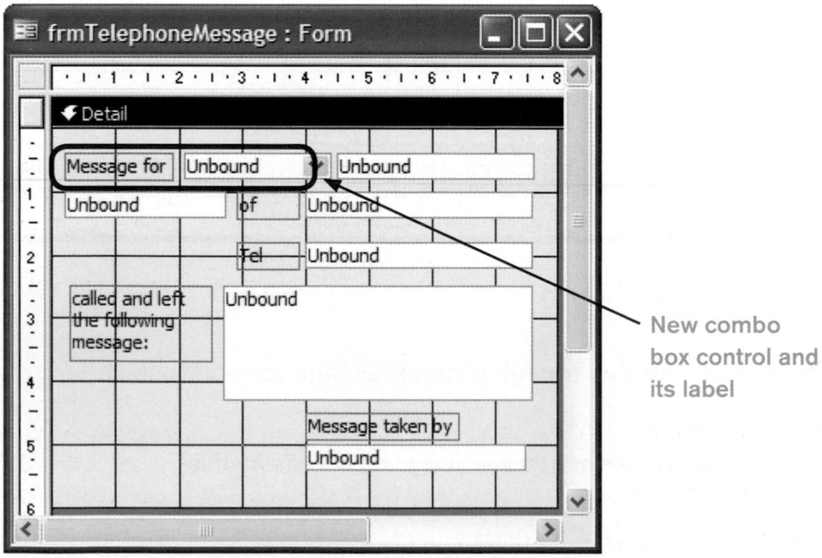

New combo box control and its label

Figure 3.8: Adding a combo box to hold the name of person whom the message is for

If the **Properties** window is not already open, right-click the new control (not its label) and select **Properties** from the menu that appears.

Switch to the **Data** tab and change the **Row Source Type** to **Value List**. For the **Row Source**, type **Matthew;David;James;Chee**.

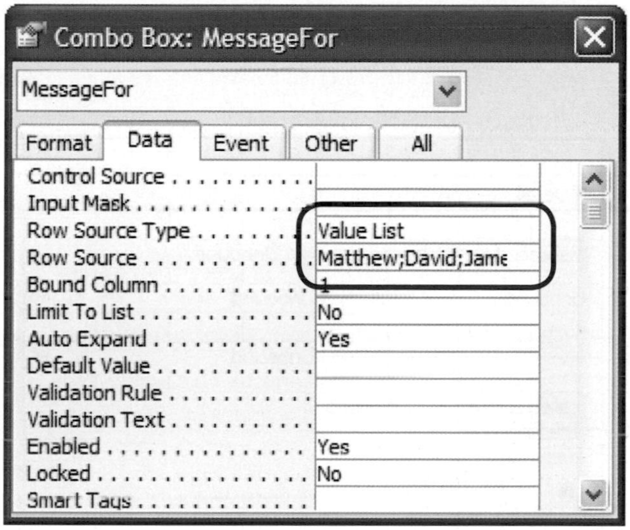

Figure 3.9: Setting values for the drop-down list of names

This tells Access that we will be using a hard-coded list of values (rather than looking them up in a table). We supply four names for the list: Matthew, David, James and Chee.

 Go back to **Form** view and try out the new control. Notice that you can type a name even if it isn't in the list.

The **Option Group Wizard** may not be available if your copy of Access was installed with the **Typical Wizards** option (see page 10). If this is the case, Access will ask you to insert the Microsoft Office CD to install the wizard when you try to do the next step.

The next control we will be adding – an option group – is unusual because it is a **container control**. The user doesn't interact directly with an option group; instead the option group modifies the behaviour of other controls placed within it. Refer back to the description on page 30 for more details.

**Control
Wizards**

**Option
Group**

Back in **Design** view, make sure that the **Control Wizards** button is pressed in and then use the **Option Group** tool to draw a control in the bottom left of the form as shown in Figure 3.10. The **Option Group Wizard** appears.

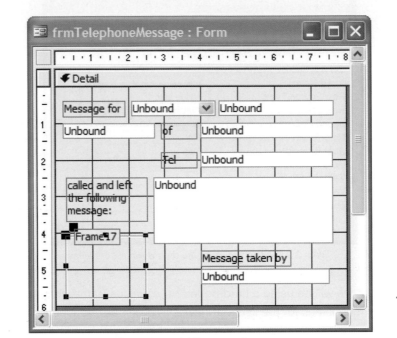

Figure 3.10: Adding an option group

Type two **Label Names**: **Call them** and **They'll call back**. Press **Next**.

This step of the wizard asks if we want a default value. Select the **No, I don't want a default** option and then press **Next**.

This step of the wizard allows us to assign values to the various options in the group. This would be important if this control was going to be bound to a data field, but the values do not matter in this example. Press **Next**.

This step of the wizard (Figure 3.11) allows us to change how the option group is drawn. Try the different options to see how they affect the preview, but switch back to the values shown in Figure 3.11 before continuing. When you are ready, press **Next** to go to the final screen.

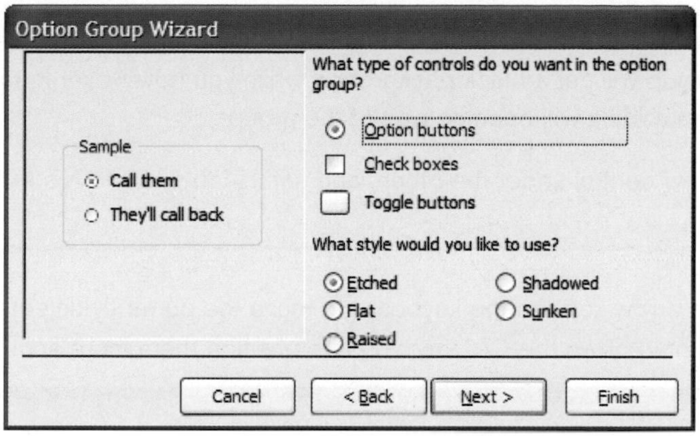

Figure 3.11: Styles that could be assigned to an option group

Type a caption of **What next?** and then press **Finish**.

The option group appears on the form, as shown in Figure 3.12. You may want to move the controls about slightly so that none of them overlap.

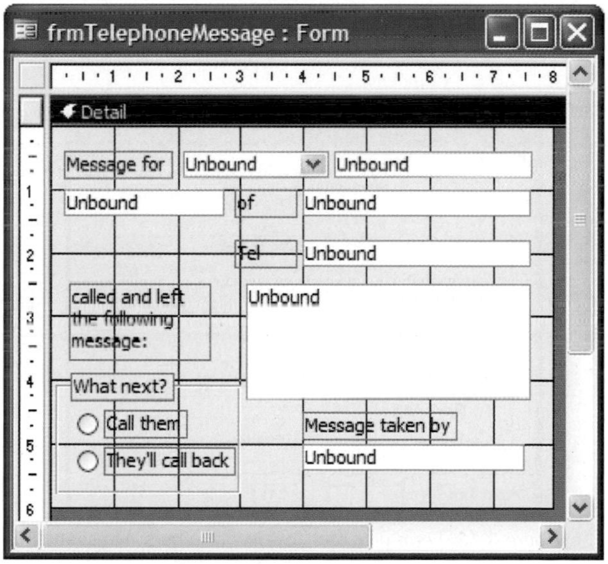

Figure 3.12: The option group added to the form

Save your form and try out the option group in **Form** view.

Notice that when you first use the form there is no **What next?** value selected, but as soon as you have selected one there will always be a value selected. Let us add a third option – **No action** – to the group.

In **Design** view, resize the form and the option group if necessary to make space for a third option below the existing two.

Option Button

Select the **Option Button** tool and click on the bottom of the **What next?** option group (the option group will get a black background while you hover over it, to show that the control you are adding will become part of the group).

Line up the new control under the others and set its label text to **No action**.

TIP

You can use the arrow keys on the keyboard to move the currently selected controls. Note that if you hold down the **Ctrl** key, you can position them more accurately

Save the form and test that the new control works with the others in its group.

It would be useful if the person filling in the form could easily flag the message as urgent. We will add a check box to allow this.

Check Box

Use the **Check Box** tool to add a check box in the bottom right of the form (you can just click once where you want it to appear – you don't have to draw a rectangle). Change the label text to **Urgent?**

Save and test your form. It should look something like Figure 3.13.

Figure 3.13: Form with a check box for urgent messages

Setting the sequence of the controls

In **Form** view you can use the **Tab** key to move from one control to the next and **Shift+Tab** to move back in the other direction. The order of the controls is determined by the order in which they were added to the form.

Use **Tab** and **Shift+Tab** to move between the controls on your form. Notice that the order would not be very helpful to someone filling in the form.

It is straightforward to change this tabbing order, as you will see.

Switch to **Design** view and select **View**, **Tab Order** from the menu.

The **Tab Order** dialogue appears. The **Custom Order** list shows the order of the controls; because we have just left them with the default names that Access assigned, the list is difficult to understand. We should go back and give the controls meaningful names.

 Press **Cancel** to close the **Tab Order** dialogue box.

 Go through each control in turn, setting its **Name** via the **Other** tab of the **Properties** dialogue box. We only need to name the controls, not the labels (see the following tip). Use the following names: **MessageFor**, **DateTime**, **WhoCalled**, **Company**, **Telephone**, **Message**, **WhatNext** (make sure you select the whole option set), **TakenBy** and **Urgent**.

> **TIP**
>
> We only need to rename the controls (generally white rectangles), not their labels (grey rectangles). For **WhatNext**, make sure that you select the bounding rectangle rather than the text label in the top left of the rectangle. If the current name of the thing you are renaming starts with **Label** then you have selected the wrong thing!

 From the menu, select **View**, **Tab Order**. The **Tab Order** dialogue box appears. All the controls in the **Custom Order** list should now have sensible names – if you have missed any then press **Cancel** and change them.

> **TIP**
>
> If you have accidentally renamed a label instead of its control then you will have to change the label's name because all of the names must be unique.

 Press the **Auto Order** button. The order should change to that shown in Figure 3.14. (If the order is different then you might need to move the controls slightly on the form – Access goes through the controls from top to bottom, left to right when assigning its automatic order. If a control on the right of the form is higher than a control on the left then it will come first: move the high control down slightly.)

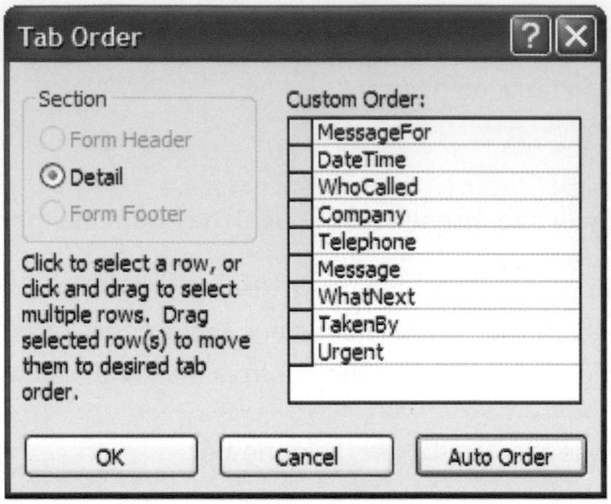

Figure 3.14: The tab order after pressing the Auto Order button

The order suggested by Access is pretty good. The fields are ordered according to their position, reading left-to-right and top-to-bottom. Suppose that we want the **DateTime** field to be last – it's easy to fill this in at the end of the call, whereas the others might need to be filled in while the call is still in progress.

 Click the grey box to the left of **DateTime** in the list. The **DateTime** line gets a black background to show that it is selected.

 Click the (now black) box to the left of **DateTime** and drag it to the bottom of the list, as shown in Figure 3.15. Press **OK** to confirm the change.

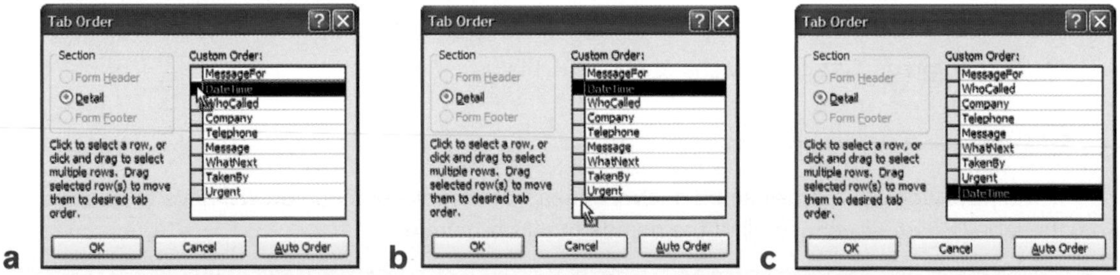

a   b   c

Figure 3.15: Dragging a field name to change its order – (a) before, (b) during and (c) after

 Save the form and test its new tab order in **Form** view.

Macros

Introduction to macros

You may be familiar with macros in Word and Excel, where you can record a sequence of commands and key presses then play them back later. Macros in Access have the same purpose but a different technique: you can play back only certain commands, and you must select them from a list.

Let's see how this works by adding a command button that will print and close our form.

In the **Database** window, click **Macros** in the **Objects** list and then press **New**, as shown in Figure 3.16.

Syllabus ref: AM5.5.1.1
Record a simple macro (e.g. close a form).

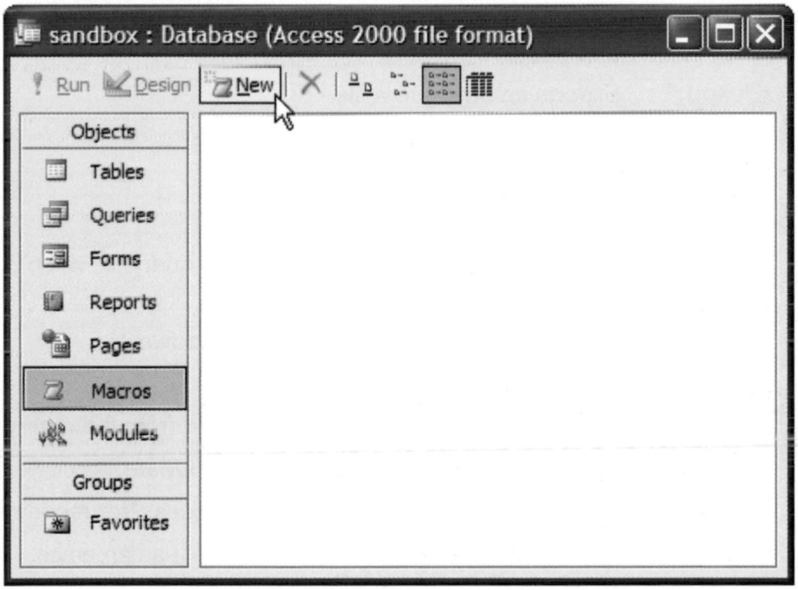

Figure 3.16: Creating a new macro

The **Macro** window appears, from which you can select a sequence of actions to perform and optionally add comments. If you click in the **Action** column of the first blank row of the grid, and then on the drop-down arrow that appears, you will see a list of the actions that can be part of a macro.

There are lots of possible actions, and there is only space for a brief overview here. You can search Access's help files for more detailed information. I have split the actions up into three groups – those actions that do exactly what you would expect from the name, actions that need some explanation, and actions that you are unlikely to need to use (for example, those that only apply to projects, not to desktop databases).

The following actions are self-explanatory: **ApplyFilter**, **Beep**, **CopyObject**, **DeleteObject**, **FindNext**, **FindRecord**, **GoToControl**, **GoToPage**, **GoToRecord**, **Hourglass**, **Maximize**, **Minimize**, **OpenForm**, **OpenQuery**, **OpenReport**, **OpenTable**, **Rename**, **Restore**, **RunMacro**, **Save**, **SelectObject**, **ShowToolbar**, **StopAllMacros** and **StopMacro**.

The box below lists actions that need some explanation.

CancelEvent	Cancels whichever event caused the current macro to run (for example, preventing the user from printing if certain validation checks have failed).
Close	Closes either a specific named object, or the active object if no specific name is given.
Echo	Controls whether Access should show the results of the macro while it runs or only when it has finished.
MoveSize	Moves and resizes the current window.
MsgBox	Displays a dialogue box with a message and waits for the user to press OK.
OutputTo	Exports an object to a file.
PrintOut	Prints the active object.
Quit	Exits Access.
RepaintObject	Redraws an object's window.
Requery	Refreshes a control by re-running the query to which it is bound.
RunApp	Runs the specified executable in Windows.
RunCode	Executes a Visual Basic function.
RunCommand	Runs a command as if it were selected from the menu.
RunSQL	Executes the supplied SQL query or update.
SendKeys	Sends the specified string of key presses. Not recommended.
SendObject	Outputs a database object and sends it as an email.
SetValue	Changes the value of a control or property.
SetWarnings	Controls whether warning dialogue boxes should be closed automatically.
ShowAllRecords	Removes any filters.
TransferDatabase	Exports/imports objects.
TransferSpreadsheet	Exports/imports spreadsheet objects.
TransferText	Exports/imports text files.

For the sake of completeness, here is a list of the other action types (you are unlikely to need these): **AddMenu**, **CopyDatabaseFile**, **OpenDataAccessPage**, **OpenDiagram**, **OpenFunction**, **OpenModule**, **OpenStoredProcedure**, **OpenView**, **SetMenuItem**, **TransferSQLDatabase**.

We want to create a simple macro that prints the telephone message form and then closes it.

Set the first action to **PrintOut**. Notice that **Action Arguments** appear at the bottom of the window, allowing you to fine-tune the action. We do not need to change these in this case.

> **TIP**
>
> If you don't have a printer connected, or if you just want to save paper, feel free to select **Beep** as the first action instead of **PrintOut**. You will just have to imagine that the form is printing when you press the **Print & Close** button later on!

Set the second action to **Close**. Add some comments if you like (this macro is easy to understand, but adding comments is a good habit to get into).

Your window should look something like Figure 3.17.

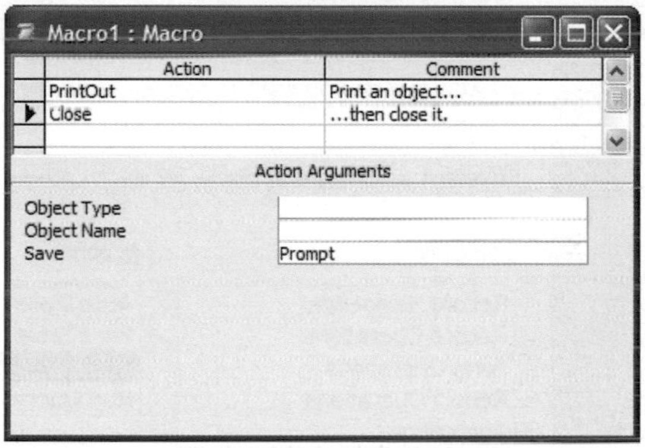

Figure 3.17: Setting up a macro

Save your macro as **mcrPrintAndClose** and close the window.

> **Syllabus ref: AM5.5.1.2**
> Run a macro.

Make sure that **frmTelephoneMessage** is open and in **Form** view. Save it and ensure that it is the current active window.

From the menu, select **Tools**, **Macro**, **Run Macro**. The **Run Macro** dialogue box appears, as shown in Figure 3.18.

Figure 3.18: Running a macro

Press **OK**. The macro runs, and your form should print (or beep!) and close.

Syllabus ref: AM5.5.1.3
Assign/attach a macro to a form, report, control.

Open **frmTelephoneMessage** in **Design** view and use the **Command Button** tool to add a new button to the bottom right of the form. The **Command Button Wizard** appears.

Select **Miscellaneous** from the **Categories** list and **Run Macro** from the **Actions** list, as shown in Figure 3.19. Press **Next**.

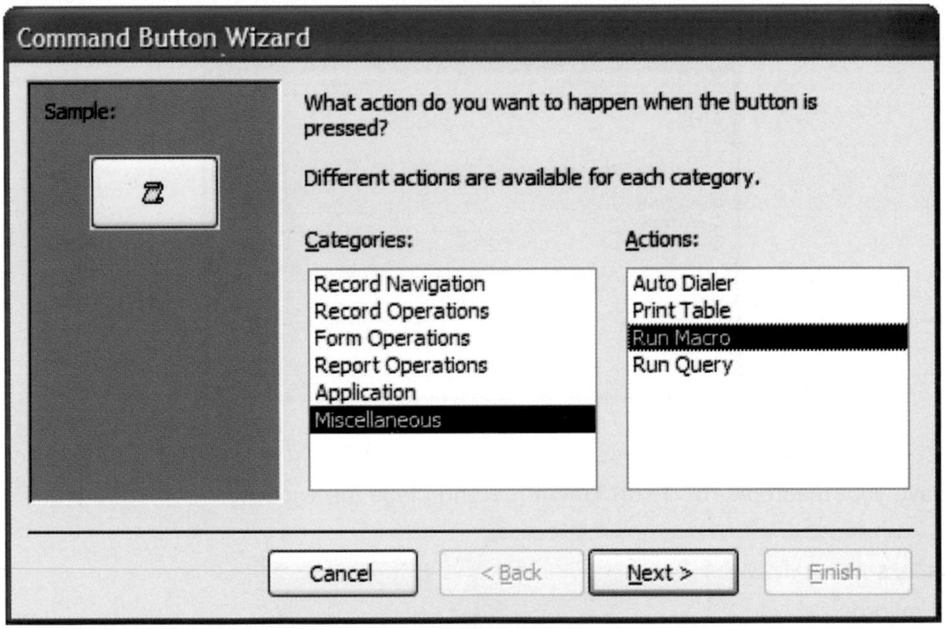

Figure 3.19: Adding a button to run a query

Because **mcrPrintAndClose** is the only macro we have created, it is automatically selected. Press **Next**.

Select the **Text** option and set its value to **&Print && Close**, as shown in Figure 3.20.

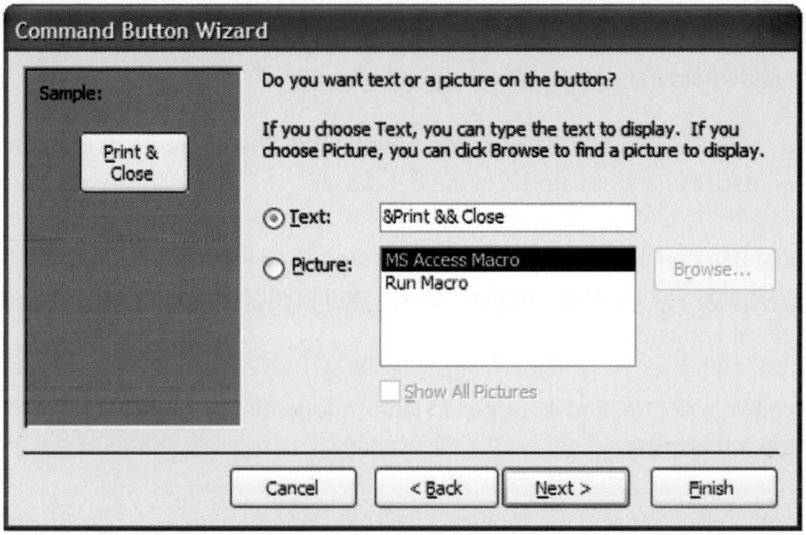

Figure 3.20: Adding text to the command button

Note!

In a button name, the **&** symbol is used before the letter that will act as a shortcut key. In Figure 3.20 you can see that using **&P** at the beginning of the text has caused the **P** in the preview to become underlined. This shows that **Alt+P** is a shortcut key that will activate this button. Because **&** has a special meaning, we have to type **&&** to get a single ampersand.

Press **Next** and name the button **PrintAndClose**. Press **Finish**.

Save the form and then test your new button.

The final form should look like Figure 3.21.

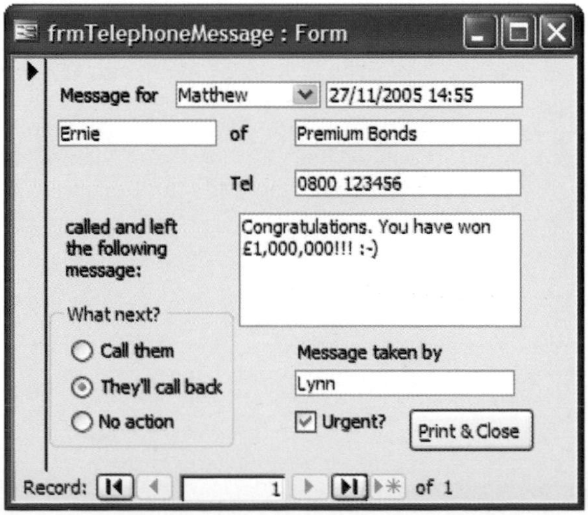

Figure 3.21: Finished telephone message form

Conclusions

This exercise has demonstrated the following points.

 Controls can be bound to a data source or unbound. The contents of unbound controls can be printed, but are not stored in the database.

 You should use check boxes for fields with yes/no values, option buttons inside option groups for fields with a small range of values, and combo boxes or list boxes for fields with larger sets of known values.

 You can move a control and its attached label independently by dragging the black squares in their top-left corners.

If you double-click a tool in the toolbox, it will stay selected until you deselect it by clicking on it again. This is useful when you want to add several controls of the same type to a form.

Use **View**, **Tab Order** to change the sequential order (the tab order used when moving between fields using **Tab** or **Shift+Tab**) of the controls in a form.

You cannot record macros (as you can in Word), but you can construct them for yourself from a sequence of named commands.

Test yourself

Auction database

The auctioneer would like a form that can be filled in and printed out twice whenever a new item is brought in for sale: one copy of the form can be filed at the auctioneer's office and the other copy can be given to the seller as a receipt.

1   Create the form shown in Figure 3.22. An example of the completed form is shown in Figure 3.23.

Figure 3.22: Design of the Auction Item Receipt form

Figure 3.23: An example completed receipt

2   Make sure that you have named all of the controls. Test the form and adjust the sequential order of the controls if necessary.

It will be a common task, after receiving an item, to want to open the **Items** table in order to add the new item.

3   Create a macro, as shown in Figure 3.24, which will close the form and open the **Items** table. Make sure that the form you created in exercises 1 and 2 is open and try running your new macro. The form should close and the **Items** table should open.

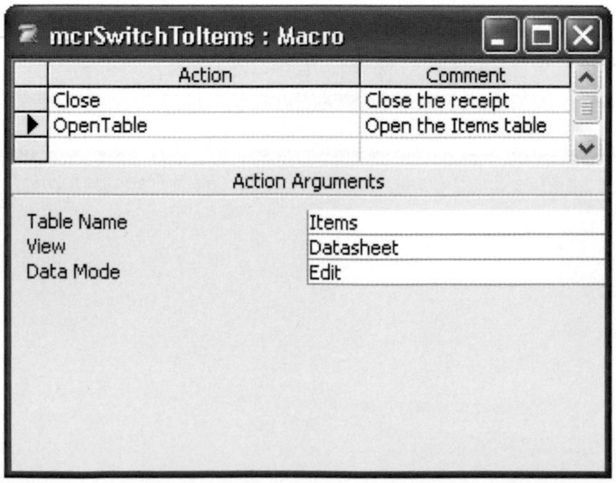

Figure 3.24: Creating a macro to close a form and open a table

4   Add a button to the form so that you can press it to run your new macro.

4 Form design II

Introduction

In this chapter we will create a form that can be used to display or modify the contents of the **tblGDP** table of wealthy nations that you created in Chapter 2.

In this chapter, you will:

 create a form with bound controls

 learn how to **create controls that perform calculations** (both **arithmetic** and **logical**) on other fields on a form

 see how to finc tune the **format** used to display data in a field on a form

 use the different **headers** that a form can have.

Creating a form by using the wizard

In Chapter 2, we created a table called **tblGDP**, which contains information about the ten wealthiest nations. In this chapter, we will create a form with controls bound to the fields in **tblGDP**.

 Open **sandbox.mdb** if it isn't already open.

Open **tblGDP** to re-familiarise yourself with it (Figure 4.1). Close it again when you are done.

Country	GDP per capita	Date of GDP estimate	Population (thousands)	Government web site	
Luxembourg	£34,400	2004	469	www.government.lu	Founded in 962, Luxembourg became
United States	£23,400	2004	295,734	The White House	
Guernsey	£23,300	2003	65	www.gov.gg	
Norway	£23,300	2004	4,593	www.stortinget.no	
Jersey	£23,300	2003	91	www.gov.je	
British Virgin Islands	£22,500	2004	23		
Bermuda	£21,000	2003	65		
San Marino	£20,200	2001	29	www.esteri.sm	
Hong Kong	£20,000	2004	6,899	www.info.gov.hk	
Switzerland	£19,700	2004	7,485	www.parlament.ch	
*			0		

Record: 1 of 10

Figure 4.1: The table we are going to create a form for

In the **Database** window, select **Forms** from the **Objects** list. Double-click **Create form by using wizard**, as shown in Figure 4.2.

sandbox : Database (Access 2000 file format)

Open | Design | New | × |

Objects	
	Create form in Design view
Tables	Create form by using wizard
Queries	frmTelephoneMessage
Forms	
Reports	
Pages	
Macros	
Modules	
Groups	
Favorites	

Figure 4.2: Adding a new form using the wizard

The **Form Wizard** appears. Press **>>** to select all of the fields. With **Description** highlighted in the **Selected Fields** list, press **<** to return it to the list of **Available Fields** – remember that our description was truncated, so let's not display it on the form. The wizard should look like Figure 4.3.

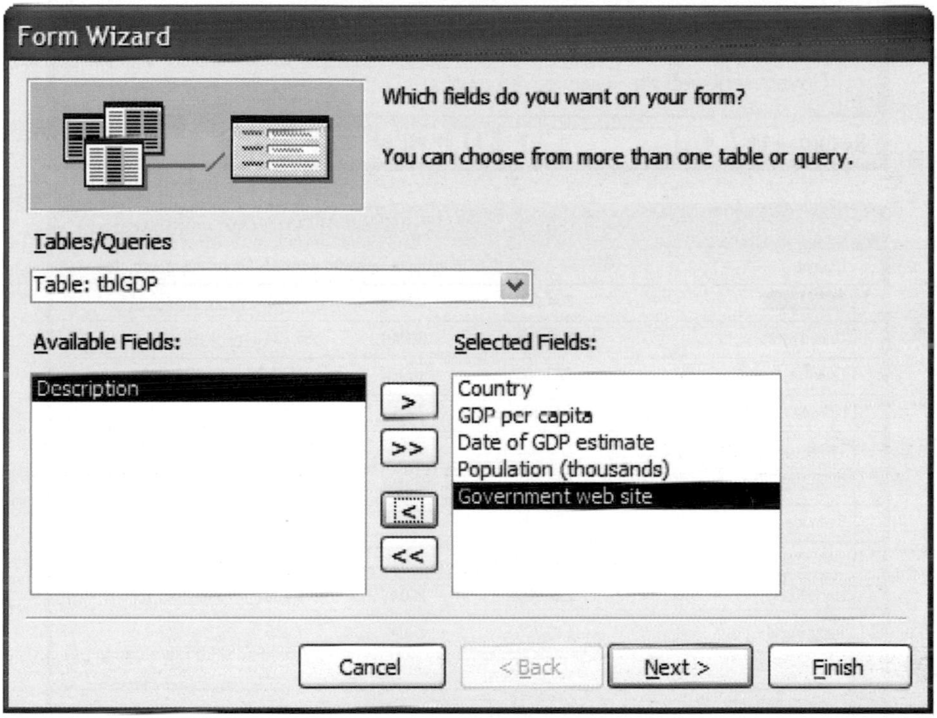

Figure 4.3: Selecting which fields to add to the form

Press **Next** to go on to the next step of the wizard.

This step allows you to choose a format for the form. Pages 52–53 show a gallery of the possibilities. We will use the **Columnar** format for our form.

Columnar form for tblGDP

Country	Luxembourg
GDP per capita	£34,400
Date of GDP estimate	2004
Population (thousand	469
Government web site	www.government.lu

Record: 1 of 10

a

Tabular form for tblGDP

Country	GDP per capita	of GDP estimate	ation (thousands)	Government web site
Luxembourg	£34,400	2004	469	www.government.lu
United States	£23,400	2004	295,734	The White House
Guernsey	£23,300	2003	65	www.gov.gg
Norway	£23,300	2004	4,593	www.stortinget.no
Jersey	£23,300	2003	91	www.gov.je
British Virgin Islands	£22,500	2004	23	
Bermuda	£21,000	2003	65	
San Marino	£20,200	2001	29	www.esteri.sm
Hong Kong	£20,000	2004	6,899	www.info.gov.hk
Switzerland	£19,700	2004	7,485	www.parlament.ch
*		0		

Record: 1 of 10

b

Datasheet form for tblGDP

Country	GDP per capita	Date of GDP estimate	Population (thousands)	Government web site
Luxembourg	£34,400	2004	469	www.government.lu
United States	£23,400	2004	295,734	The White House
Guernsey	£23,300	2003	65	www.gov.gg
Norway	£23,300	2004	4,593	www.stortinget.no
Jersey	£23,300	2003	91	www.gov.je
British Virgin Islands	£22,500	2004	23	
Bermuda	£21,000	2003	65	
San Marino	£20,200	2001	29	www.esteri.sm
Hong Kong	£20,000	2004	6,899	www.info.gov.hk
Switzerland	£19,700	2004	7,485	www.parlament.ch
*		0		

Record: 1 of 10

c

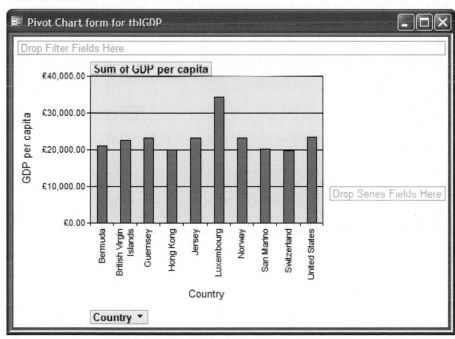

d

e

f

Figure 4.4: Different ways that the Form Wizard could be used to present our data (the title bar of each screenshot explains which option was chosen)

Make sure that the **Columnar** option is selected. Press **Next**.

 The next step lets you choose a style for the background, label text, and other formatting. Select some different styles to see what they look like in the preview. Select **Standard** again and click **Next**.

 Give the form the title **frmGDP** and press **Finish**.

The new form appears, looking like Figure 4.4(a).

Notice the controls at the bottom of the form. These let you move between the different records.

 First Record

 Previous Record

1 **Record Number** – this control shows the number of the currently displayed record, and can also be used to jump directly to a specific record if you know its number.

 Next Record – if you are already on the last record then this is equivalent to **New Record**.

 Last Record

 New Record

 Try using the controls to move through the records.

> **Syllabus ref: AM5.3.1.1**
> Create bound and unbound controls.

Design
View

 Switch the form into **Design** view and select the **Country** field (the white box, not its label). If the **Properties** window isn't on display, press **Alt+Enter** to display it.

> **TIP**
> There are several ways to display the **Properties** window: selecting **View**, **Properties** from the main menu; selecting **Properties** from the right-click context menu; and pressing the keyboard shortcut **Alt+Enter**. You may use whichever method you prefer.

Change to the **Data** tab and click on the down arrow to the right of the **Control Source**, as shown in Figure 4.5. This is how you bind a control to a field in a table or query. For now, just close the **Properties** window without changing the value.

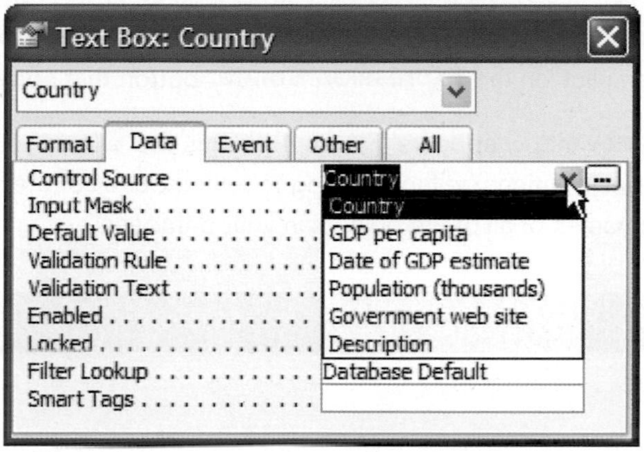

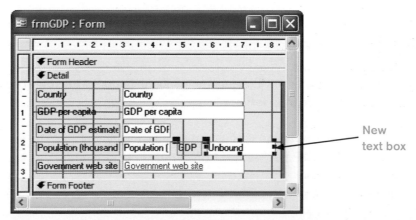

Figure 4.5: The Control Source binds a control to a data field

Calculation controls

You have already covered unbound and bound controls. A calculation field is halfway between the two: its value is generated as a result of a calculation on one or more of the data fields, but it cannot be used to change the values held in the database.

Arithmetic expressions

The easiest way to understand this is to add a calculation control. We can work out a country's total **GDP** by multiplying its **GDP per capita** value by its **Population**.

> **Syllabus ref: AM5.3.1.3**
> Create arithmetic, logical expressions, controls on a form.

Use the **Text Box** tool to add a new control, which will hold the calculated GDP, to the form. Position it as shown in Figure 4.6 and change the label to **GDP**.

ab|
Text Box

Figure 4.6: Adding another control to the form

New text box

55

Expression
Builder

Bring up the **Properties** window for the new control. Click in the **Control Source** property and then click on the **Expression Builder** button that appears next to it.

The **Expression Builder** window appears (Figure 4.7). This tool allows you to construct expressions (queries or calculations) without having to remember all of the syntax of Access's built-in functions or the names of all of the objects in your database.

Common operators

Current object

Other objects in the database

Functions

Components in the current object

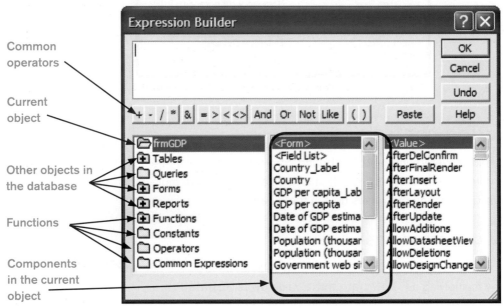

Figure 4.7: The Expression Builder

Double-click **GDP per capita** (not **GDP per capita_Label**) in the middle column. **[GDP per capita]** appears in the main text box.

TIP

If the field names are truncated, make the **Expression Builder** wider (it is resizable).

Click the multiplication (*) operator – the fourth button in the row above the three lists. A * appears in the main text box.

Double-click **Population (thousands)** in the middle column. The full formula is now displayed as **[GDP per capita]** * **[Population (thousands)]**, as shown in Figure 4.8.

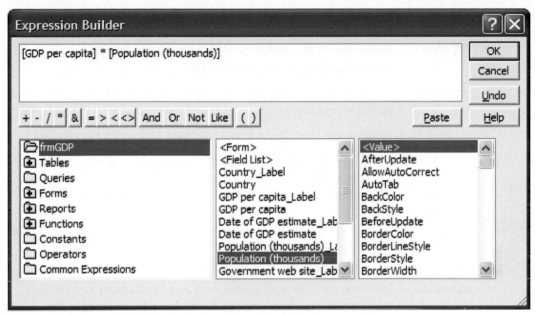

Figure 4.8: The finished calculation

 Press **OK** to close the **Expression Builder**.

 Test the form. For example, you should get a **GDP** of **16133600** for Luxembourg.

Have you spotted the mistake? The population figures are given in thousands – for example, the population data field for Luxembourg holds a value of **469** to record that the population size is actually **469 000**! Therefore our reported GDP values are **1000** times smaller than they should be.

To correct things, we could **multiply by 1000** in our formula to give the correct value. However, the GDP value is already unwieldy; we don't really want to make it any longer. A better strategy is to **divide by 1000** instead, which will give the value in millions. This will be OK as long as we make it clear to the users what this number represents.

 Edit the **Control Source** value for the **GDP** field by adding **/1000** to the end. You can either use the **Expression Builder** or just type the extra text into the **Control Source** text box.

 On the **Format** tab of the **Properties** window, set the **Format** to **£#,###m** by typing it in. (Access will automatically add a **** before the **m** when you leave the field – this is OK.)

This tells Access to display the number from this field as a currency with commas separating the thousands, and to add the character **m** (for million) to the end.

You can use the following characters to control the format of your fields.

full stop (.)	Shows where to position the decimal point (for example, **0.00** will display two decimal places).
comma (,)	Use this when you want a comma between each group of three digits, as in our example.
zero (0)	A mandatory digit. For example, the value **123** with a format of **0000** will be displayed as **0123**.
hash (#)	An optional digit. For example, the value **123** with a format of **####** will be displayed as **123**.
exclamation mark (!)	Force left-alignment.
backslash (\)	Treat the next character literally (for example, \# really displays a # instead of an optional digit).
asterisk (*)	Use whatever character comes next as a fill character and use it to pad out the value to completely fill the control. For example, the value **123** displayed with a format of *=# would be displayed as ========123 (where the number of equals signs would depend on the width of the control).
percent (%)	Display the value as a percentage. For example, **0.5** with a format of **0%** would be displayed as **50%**.
E+/e+/E-/e-	Display the value using scientific notation. For example, **1234** with a format of **0.00E+00** would be displayed as **1.23E+03**. Don't worry – if you do not understand this then you will never need to use it!
[*colour*]	Specify a colour: **[Black]**, **[Blue]**, **[Cyan]**, **[Green]**, **[Magenta]**, **[Red]**, **[Yellow]** or **[White]**. This is useful in combination with semicolons (see below).
semicolon (;)	Use to specify different formats depending on whether the value is positive, negative, zero or null. For example, a format of **0[Green];(0)[Red];-;"Empty"[Yellow]** would display **1** as **1**, **-2** as **(2)**, **0** as **-** and **null** as Empty respectively.
at (@)	Right-align string. For example, **qwerty** with a format of @@@@@@ would have a space as the first character.
ampersand (&)	Left-align string. For example, **qwerty** with a format of @@@@@@ would have a space as the sixth character.
less than (<)	Convert all characters to lower case.
greater than (>)	Convert all characters to upper case.

There are, in addition, many formatting strings to control the way that Access displays dates. Detailed information is available in Access's online help.

Test the form. You should find that the GDP values range from **£518m** in the British Virgin Islands to **£6,920,176m** in the United States.

Logical expressions

The GDP was calculated using an **arithmetic expression** (multiplication using *). You also need to know about **logical expressions**; that is, expressions that evaluate to either true or false.

Some of the estimates in our database are quite old. Let's add a check box control that warns the user about old data becoming ticked if the estimate was made before 2004.

Use the **Check Box** tool to add a check box to the form, labelling it **Old data?** as shown in Figure 4.9.

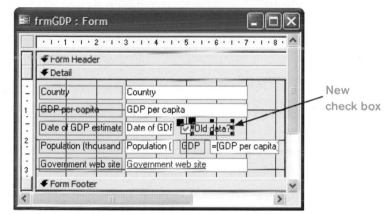

New check box

Figure 4.9: Adding a check box to highlight old data

Either using the **Expression Builder** or simply by typing it in, set the **Control Source** for the new control to the following expression: **=[Date of GDP estimate] < 2004**.

This expression will evaluate to true if the date of the estimate is less than 2004, otherwise it will evaluate to false.

Test your form. Confirm that the check box is ticked for those records with estimate dates before 2004, otherwise it is not ticked.

Note!

If you misspell the field name, Access will ask you to supply it when you run the query (in effect, it is treated as an **input parameter** – see page 188). Correct the spelling and run the query again

TIP

If we had decided to store the estimates as full dates (such as 21/11/2004) instead of just the year, we would have needed to use a more complicated expression:

=[Date of GDP estimate] < DateSerial(2004, 1, 1)

If you need to create an expression that depends on the values of two or more other fields then you can use the functions **And** and **Or** to distil them down to a single true/false value.

For example, **=[Date of GDP estimate] < 2004 And [Population (thousands)] > 50** is only true if both the estimate is old and the population is high. If either one of those conditions is itself false then the whole expression is false.

Similarly, **=[Date of GDP estimate] < 2004 Or [Population (thousands)] > 50** is true if either the estimate is old or the population is large (or both). The expression evaluates to false only if both of its terms evaluate to false.

> **TIP**
>
> You can chain together as many **And** and **Or** operators as you need, grouping expressions together with round brackets if necessary. For example, **([This] Or [That]) And [The other]** is different from **[This] Or ([That] And [The other])**.

Form headers and footers

You may have noticed areas labelled **Form Header** and **Form Footer** when you were editing the form. We can use these areas to hold information about the form, just as you might use a header or footer in a word-processed document to hold the title, date or page number.

> **Syllabus ref: AM5.3.1.5**
> Insert data field to appear within form header, footers on the first page or all pages.

There are actually five distinct areas on a form where you can enter information. First, let's make sure that they are all being displayed.

 Make sure **frmGDP** is in **Design** view, then click on **View** in the main menu. Make sure that both **Page Header/Footer** and **Form Header/Footer** are turned on (have ticks next to them).

You should now be able to see five distinct areas of the form, labelled **Form Header**, **Page Header**, **Detail**, **Page Footer** and **Form Footer**.

Resize the headers and footers by clicking and dragging their borders. Make them all the same size, as shown in Figure 4.10.

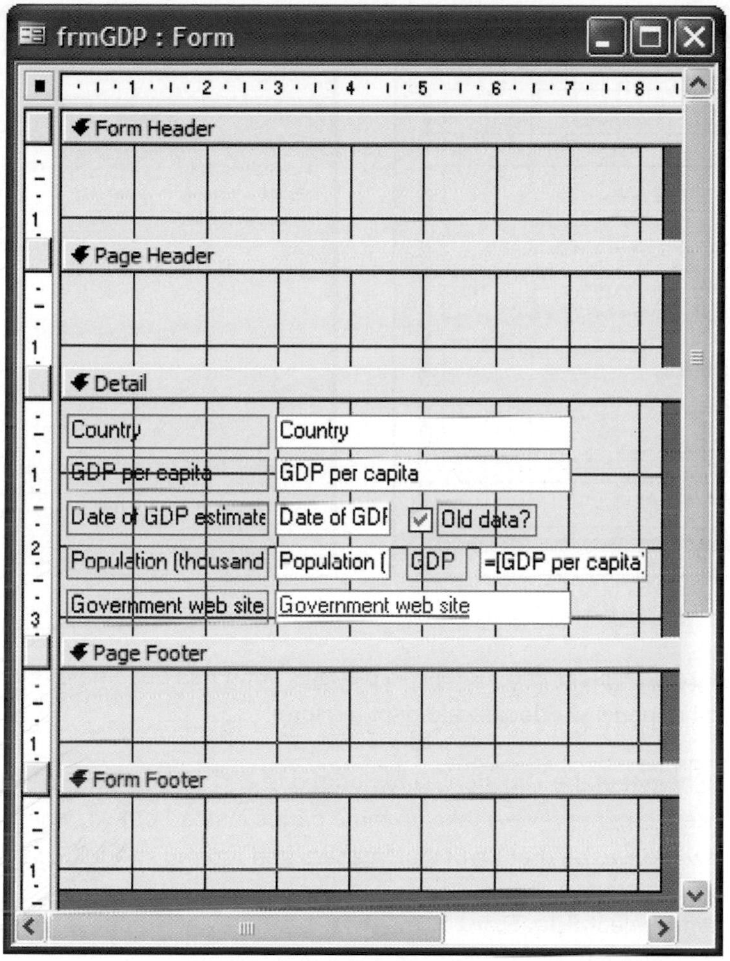

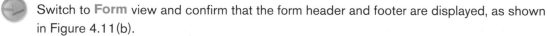

Figure 4.10: Displaying all of the headers and footers on a form

The easiest way to see how these headers and footers work is to label each of them and see where these labels are displayed in the form.

Use the **Label** tool to add labels to the two headers and footers, as shown in Figure 4.11(a). You do not need to be particularly neat, because you will be deleting these labels again soon.

Label

Switch to **Form** view and confirm that the form header and footer are displayed, as shown in Figure 4.11(b).

61

Figure 4.11: The form with its headers and footers labelled – (a) in Design view and (b) in Form view

So, what about the page header and footer? To discover what has become of them, we need to look at what would happen if we decided to print the form.

Increase the height of the **Detail** area to about one and a half times its current height. This will make the print preview take up three pages instead of two, which should make it clearer how the two different types of headers and footers interact.

Maximize

From the menu, select **File**, **Print Preview**. A print preview appears within the form's window – maximize this so that you can see it more clearly.

You should have three pages of print preview. You can display them all at once by clicking the **Multiple Pages** icon on the **Print Preview** toolbar and then selecting **1x3 Pages**, as shown in Figure 4.12.

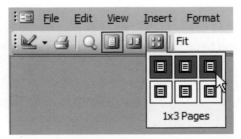

Figure 4.12: Displaying three pages of print preview side-by-side

The actual previews should look like Figure 4.13. Notice that each page starts with a **Page Header** apart from the first, which starts with the only **Form Header**. Every page ends with a **Page Footer**, even the last one, and the **Form Footer** is attached to the bottom of the last form.

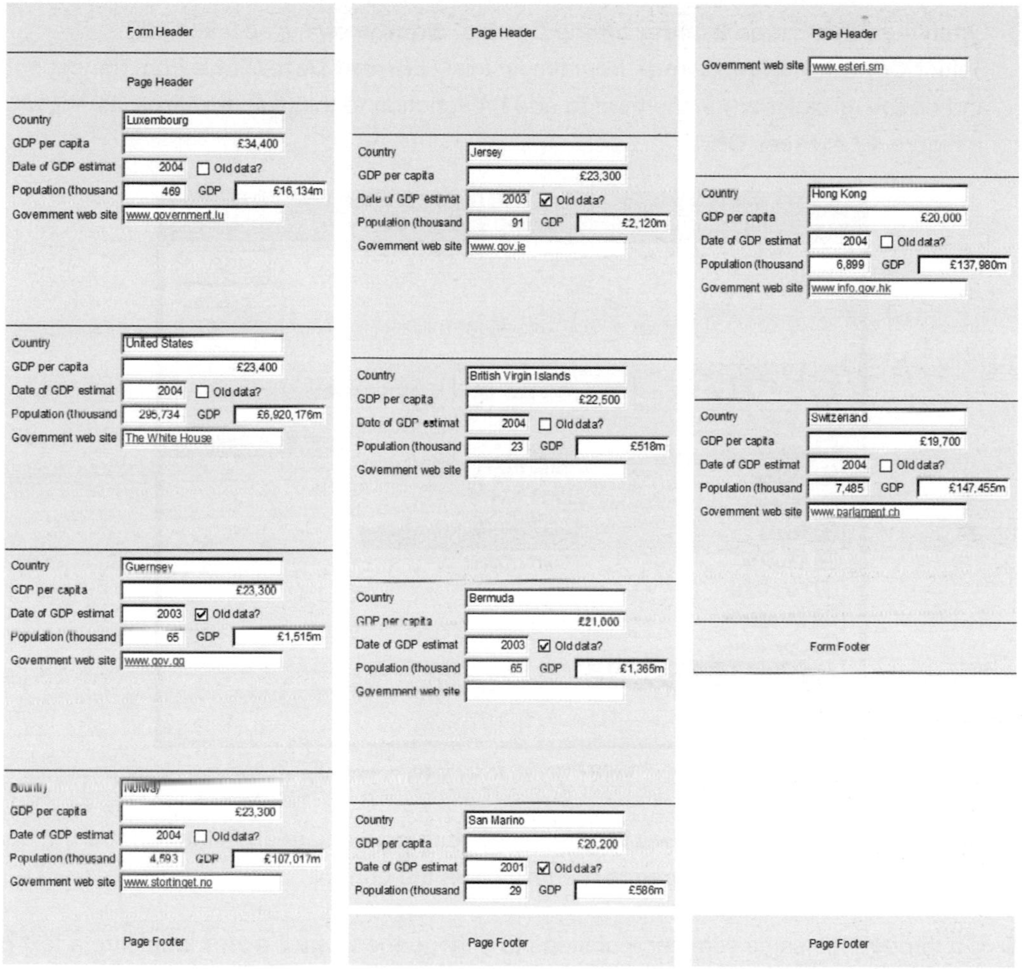

Figure 4.13: Print Preview showing how headers and footers will appear on the printed form

Click on the **Close** button to close the **Print Preview** and return to **Design** view.

Change the label in the **Form Header** to **International Statistics**. Change the font size to **18** and make it bold and centred using the buttons on the **Formatting (Form/Report)** toolbar. (Alternatively, you could change the formatting using the **Properties** window.)

We will add a timestamp at the top of each printed page and the page number at the bottom.

Right-click on the **Page Header** label and select **Change To**, **Text Box**. This saves us the job of deleting the label and creating a new text box.

Open the **Expression Builder** for the **Control Source** of this new text box. Select **Common Expressions** from the first list, **Current Date/Time** from the second, and double-click **Now()** in the third to add the function to the main text area, as shown in Figure 4.14. Press **OK**.

Figure 4.14: Adding the current time and date to the form

Center

Resize the control so that it will be wide enough to hold a date and time. Centre the control and use the **Center** tool to centre the text within the control.

Go through the same sequence of steps to change the **Page Footer** label into a text box, assigning it the **Page N of M** expression (see Figure 4.14) and again centring it.

Note!

Notice how the **Page N of M** expression uses **&** characters to concatenate values, such as **[Page]**, and strings.

Line

Use the **Line** tool to draw a horizontal line above the page number.

Change the **Border Width** of the line to **2 pt** using either the line's **Properties** window or the **Line/Border Width** control on the **Formatting (Form/Report)** toolbar.

Delete the **Form Footer** label and add two thin horizontal lines in its place.

Resize the **Detail** section back to its original height.

Your form should now look like Figure 4.15.

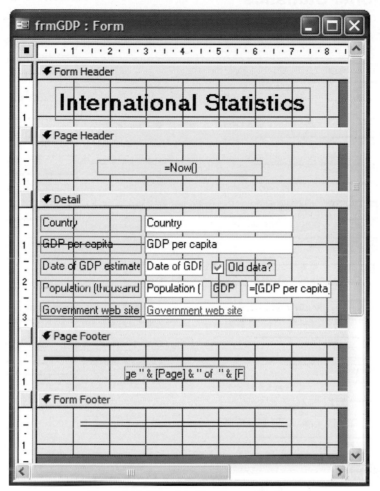

Figure 4.15: Completed headers and footers

Look at your form in **Print Preview**. It should look like Figure 4.16.

International Statistics

29/11/2005 13:17:33

Country	Luxembourg
GDP per capita	£34,400
Date of GDP estimat	2004	☐ Old data?
Population (thousand	469	GDP	£16,134m
Government web site	www.government.lu

Country	United States
GDP per capita	£23,400
Date of GDP estimat	2004	☐ Old data?
Population (thousand	295,734	GDP	£6,920,176m
Government web site	The White House

Country	Guernsey
GDP per capita	£23,300
Date of GDP estimat	2003	✔ Old data?
Population (thousand	65	GDP	£1,515m
Government web site	www.gov.gg

Country	Norway
GDP per capita	£23,300
Date of GDP estimat	2004	☐ Old data?
Population (thousand	4,593	GDP	£107,017m
Government web site	www.stortinget.no

Country	Jersey
GDP per capita	£23,300
Date of GDP estimat	2003	✔ Old data?
Population (thousand	91	GDP	£2,120m
Government web site	www.gov.je

Country	British Virgin Islands
GDP per capita	£22,500
Date of GDP estimat	2004	☐ Old data?
Population (thousand	23	GDP	£518m
Government web site	

| Country | Bermuda |

29/11/2005 13:17:33

GDP per capita	£21,000
Date of GDP estimat	2003	✔ Old data?
Population (thousand	65	GDP	£1,365m
Government web site	

Country	San Marino
GDP per capita	£20,200
Date of GDP estimat	2001	✔ Old data?
Population (thousand	29	GDP	£586m
Government web site	www.esteri.sm

Country	Hong Kong
GDP per capita	£20,000
Date of GDP estimat	2004	☐ Old data?
Population (thousand	6,899	GDP	£137,980m
Government web site	www.info.gov.hk

Country	Switzerland
GDP per capita	£19,700
Date of GDP estimat	2004	☐ Old data?
Population (thousand	7,485	GDP	£147,455m
Government web site	www.parlament.ch

Figure 4.16: A printout of the completed form (two pages side-by-side)

Conclusions

This exercise has demonstrated the following points.

 The **Form Wizard** can be used to create several different types of form: **Columnar**, **Tabular**, **Datasheet**, **Justified**, **Pivot Table** and **Pivot Chart**.

 You can create controls that perform **arithmetic** on other values, for example adding together the values in two other controls on the form.

 You can create controls that evaluate **logical expressions** (true/false). These are often represented by check boxes.

 A set of special characters is available to let you fine-tune the **format** used to display the data in a control.

 If a form has a **Page Header** and **Page Footer** then they come at the top and bottom of each page in general. The exception is that the **Form Header**, if present, will come above the **Page Header** on the first page. If the form has a **Form Footer** then it will come immediately after the last of the data.

Test yourself

Auction database

1   Use the **Create form by using wizard** option to automatically create a form called **frmLots** (see Figure 4.17) based on the **Lots** table.

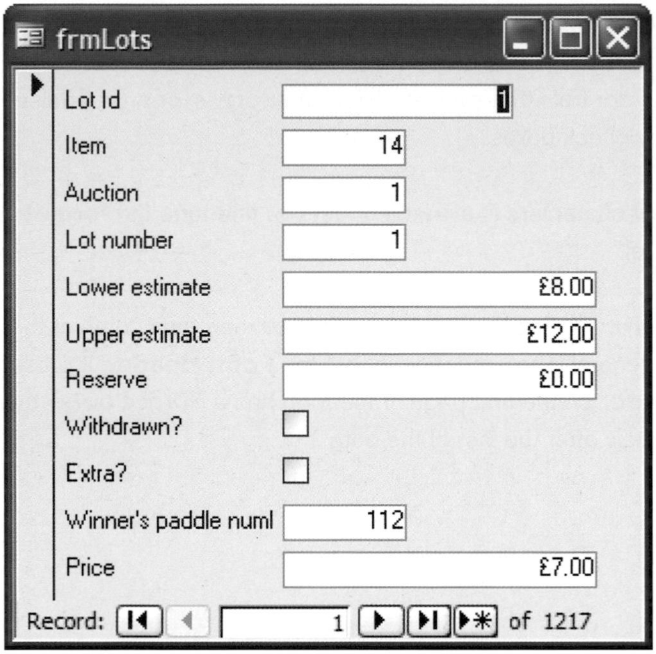

Figure 4.17: frmLots generated by the wizard

2   Delete the fields **Reserve**, **Withdrawn?**, **Extra?** and **Winner's paddle number**. Create the **Sold** check box shown in Figure 4.18. Set its **Control Source** to =[Price]>0. Test the form in **Form** view, and confirm that the check box is ticked for those records where the price is not zero, and is not ticked when the price is zero.

3   Make sure that the **Control Wizards** option is selected in the toolbox and then add the **Price Range** option group shown in Figure 4.18. Set the **Control Source** for the option group to =IIf([Price]<[Lower estimate],1,IIf([Price]>[Upper estimate],3,2)). Test the form in **Form** view, and confirm that the new control correctly shows whether each record is below, within or above its estimate.

The **IIf** (if) function takes three parameters: a comparison to perform, a value to return if the comparison is true, and a value to return if the comparison is false.

The formula **=IIf([Price]<[Lower estimate],1,IIf([Price]>[Upper estimate],3,2))** checks whether **[Price]** is less than **[Lower estimate]**. If it is, the value **1** is returned (which happens to be the value assigned to the first option in the option group). If the first comparison is false (so that **[Price]** is greater than or equal to **[Lower estimate]**) then the value of **IIf([Price]>[Upper estimate],3,2)** is returned. This evaluates to **3** if **[Price]** is greater than **[Upper estimate]**, or **2** otherwise.

4   Create a text box control, labelled **Difference**, as shown in Figure 4.18. Set its **Control Source** to **=[Price]-([Upper estimate]+[Lower estimate])/2**, which is the difference between the actual price that the item sold for and the middle of the two estimates. Set the control's **Format** property to **Currency**. Test the form in **Form** view, and confirm that the correct difference is calculated. (For example, in the first record the lower estimate is £8 and the upper estimate is £12, so the average estimate is £10. The lot sold for only £7, so the calculated difference should be −£3.)

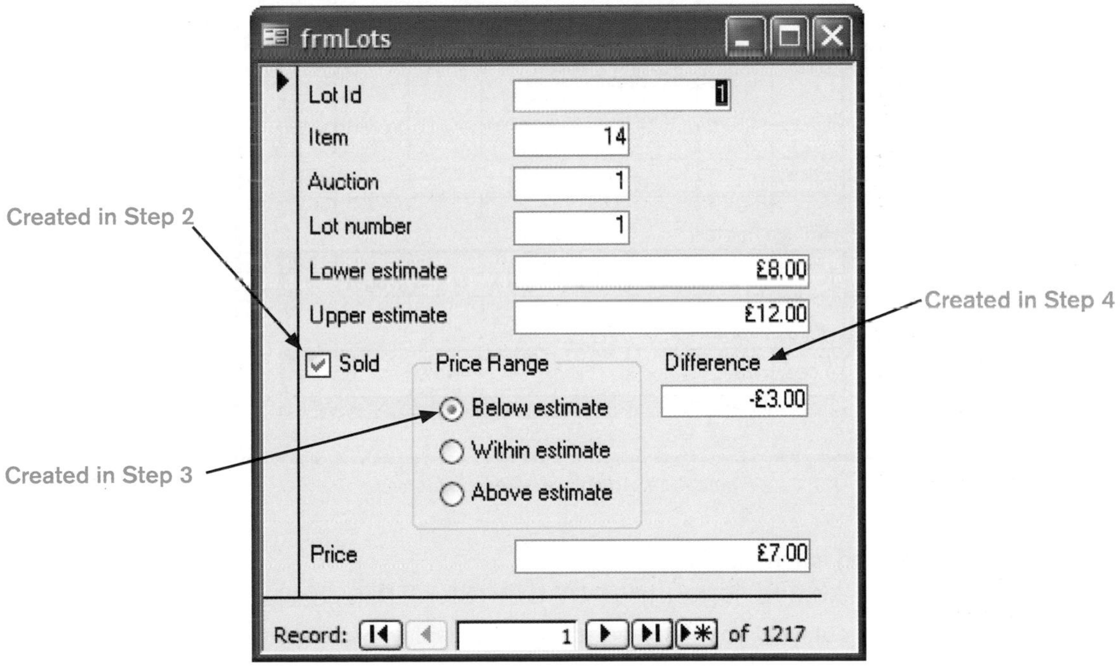

Figure 4.18: Calculated fields on a form

5   Add headers and footers to the form as shown in Figure 4.19. Format the **Form Footer** as a **Short Date**.

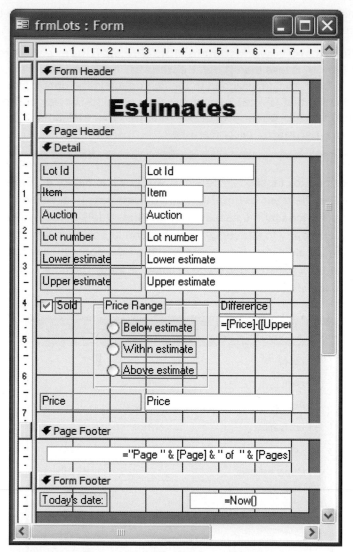

Figure 4.19: Adding headers and footers

6   Look at the following format string:
    £#,##0.00[Blue];-£#,##0.00[Red];"SPOT ON!"[Blue]. Refer back to the table on page 58 and work out what you think this format will display. Set this as the **Format** for the **Difference** control and test the form – does it do what you expected?
    (Tip: Record 86 should be spot on!)

5 Importing & exporting

Introduction

In this chapter we will export a series of tables from **auctions.mdb** (that is, save them to a different format understood by other types of software). This simulates the process for moving data from Access to another application.

After this, we will import them again, this time into **sandbox.mdb**. This simulates the process of bringing new data into Access from another application.

In this chapter, you will:

 export data in several different formats

 import the exported data

 import a linked table so that changes made to the data by another application are automatically detected by Access.

Exporting data

Syllabus ref: AM5.6.1.2

Export data in spreadsheet, txt, dBASE, and Paradox formats.

Open the database **auction.mdb**.

We are going to export some of the tables from this database and then import them into **sandbox.mdb**.

Table to be exported	format to be used
People	comma-delimited text
Auction Types	fixed-width text
Auctions	dBASE
Lots	Paradox
Items	Excel

Exporting to a comma-delimited text file

Highlight the table **People** in the **Database** window, and from the menu select **File**, **Export**. A dialogue box entitled **Export Table 'People' To...** appears.

Create New
Folder

Navigate to the folder where your databases are stored and use the **Create New Folder** button to create a new folder. Name it **exports**.

Change the **Save as type** drop-down list to **Text Files (*.txt; *.csv; *.tab; *.asc)**, as shown in Figure 5.1.

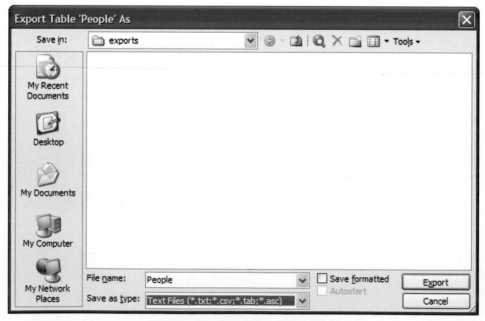

Figure 5.1: Choosing an export type

Note!

Access lists four different file extensions in connection with text files: **txt** (text), **csv** (comma-separated values), **tab** (tab-separated text) and **asc** (ASCII text – equivalent to txt).

Make sure that the **Save formatted** box is not ticked, then press **Export**. The **Export Text Wizard** (Figure 5.2) appears.

Note!

If you are using an earlier version of Access, the **Export** button may be called **Save**, but it does the same thing.

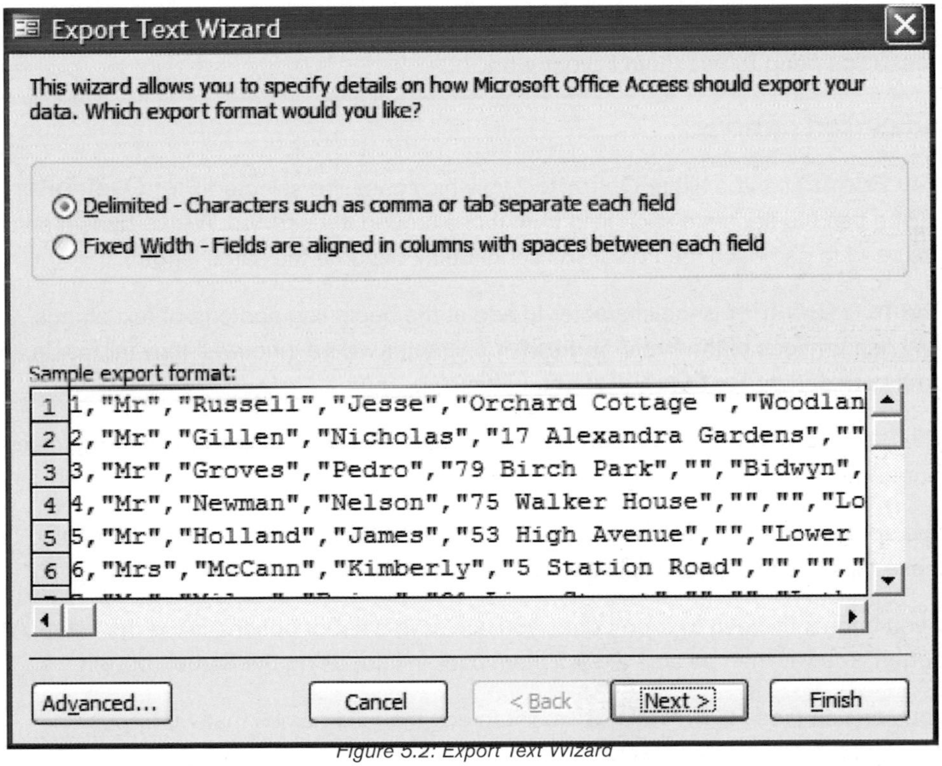

Export Text Wizard
This wizard allows you to specify details on how Microsoft Office Access should export your data. Which export format would you like?
Delimited - Characters such as comma or tab separate each field
Fixed Width - Fields are aligned in columns with spaces between each field
Sample export format:
1 1,"Mr","Russell","Jesse","Orchard Cottage ","Woodlan
2 2,"Mr","Gillen","Nicholas","17 Alexandra Gardens",""
3 3,"Mr","Groves","Pedro","79 Birch Park","","Bidwyn",
4 4,"Mr","Newman","Nelson","75 Walker House","","","Lo
5 5,"Mr","Holland","James","53 High Avenue","","Lower
6 6,"Mrs","McCann","Kimberly","5 Station Road","","","
Advanced...
Cancel
< Back
Next >
Finish

Figure 5.2: Export Text Wizard

Press the **Advanced** button. The **People Export Specification** window (Figure 5.3) appears.

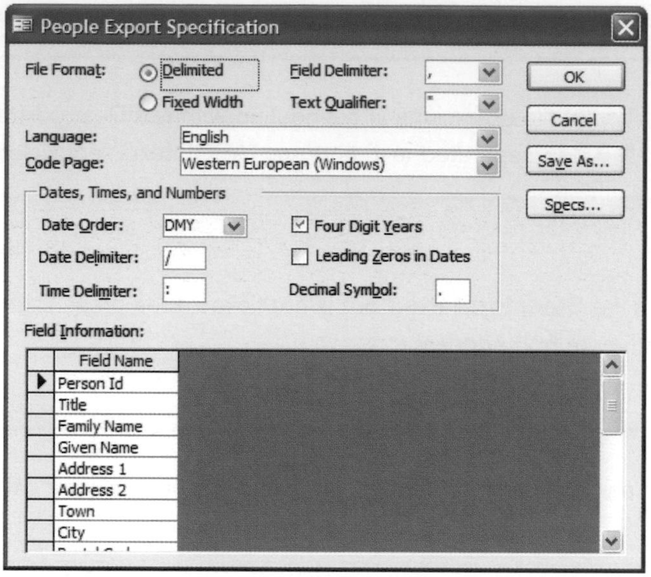

Figure 5.3: Advanced export options

We do not want to change any of these advanced options, but you should familiarise yourself with them in case you need to use them in your work.

Advanced options

File Format can be either **Delimited** (in which case the selected **Field Delimiter** will be used to separate each field from those around it) or **Fixed Width** (where spaces are used to pad each record's fields so that they become the same length).

The **Text Qualifier** is the character to add at the beginning and end of text strings. Any occurrences of the **Field Delimiter** character will be ignored if they fall inside an area bounded by **Text Qualifier** characters.

The **Language** and **Code Page** drop-down lists provide options for exporting foreign languages that might contain special characters.

The options in the **Dates, Times, and Numbers** box let you control the formatting of these things, and are self-explanatory.

If you frequently need to export data, you can save a set of options using the **Save As** button. You will then be able to load them back in later using the **Specs** button.

You can use the **Field Information** list to edit the field names that will appear in the exported file.

Press **Cancel** to dismiss the **People Export Specification** window without making any changes.

Press **Next** to go to the next step of the **Export Text Wizard**.

Leave **Comma** selected as the delimiter and " as the **Text Qualifier**. Click on **Include Field Names on First Row** to tick it, as shown in Figure 5.4. Press **Next**.

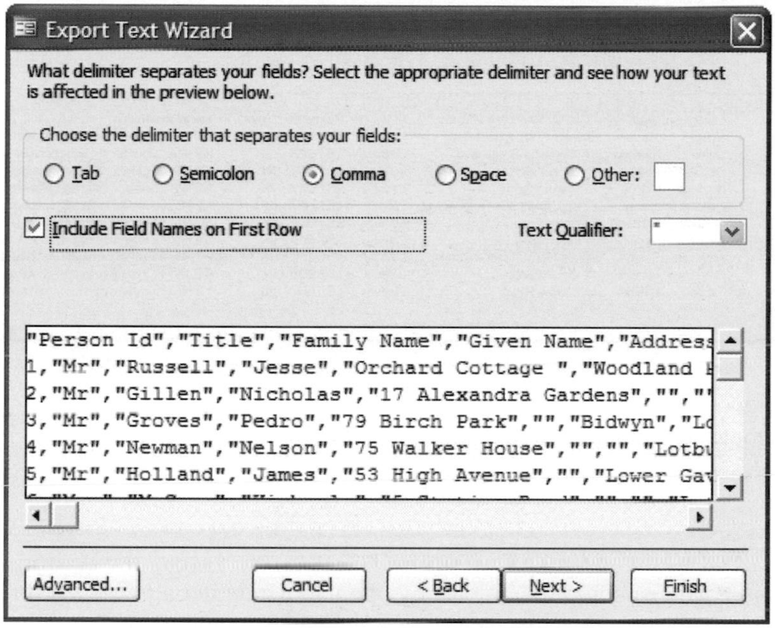

Figure 5.4: Selecting a delimiter and text qualifier

The final step should automatically set the **Export to File** box to be **People.txt** in your new **exports** folder. Change **People.txt** to **People.csv** and then press the **Finish** button.

TIP

Click in the **Export to File** field and press the **End** key to scroll to the end of the path if it is long.

Note!

It would be perfectly acceptable to leave the file extension as **txt** – however, changing it to **csv** is more descriptive, since this is to be a data file containing comma-separated values.

After a short time an alert box appears, as shown in Figure 5.5. Press **OK**. The alert and the wizard both close.

Figure 5.5: Alert box – the export was successful

People.csv

The file **People.csv** should appear in your **exports** folder on disk. Because we saved it as a **csv** file, it should have an icon showing that it can be opened in Excel. Double-click the file to open it in Excel. It should look like Figure 5.6.

	A	B	C	D	E	F	G	H	I	J	K	L
1	Person Id	Title	Family Nai	Given Nam	Address 1	Address 2	Town	City	Postal Coc	Country	Telephone	Email
2	1	Mr	Russell	Jesse	Orchard C	Woodland Road		Lotbury	LB2 5AX	UK	(02345) 55	jrussell@lotburyinternet.com
3	2	Mr	Gillen	Nicholas	17 Alexandra Gardens			Lotbury	LB3 9QB	UK	(02345) 15	nicholas.gillen@lotburyweb.net
4	3	Mr	Groves	Pedro	79 Birch Park		Bidwyn	Lotbury	LB15 7RE	UK	(02345) 47	groves_p@lotburyonline.com
5	4	Mr	Newman	Nelson	75 Walker House			Lotbury	LB2 9NY	UK	(02345) 25	nelson.newman@lotburyontheweb.com
6	5	Mr	Holland	James	53 High Avenue		Lower Gav	Lotbury	LB13 8UH	UK	(02345) 68	james.holland@lotburyemail.com
7	6	Mrs	McCann	Kimberly	5 Station Road			Lotbury	LB2 9LG	UK	(02345) 25	kimberly.mccann@ilovelotbury.com
8	7	Mr	Milne	Brian	31 Lime Street			Lotbury	LB2 6LS	UK	(02345) 42	brian.milne@mylotbury.net
9	8	Ms	Nicholson	Sarah	Wright Hou	St. Mark's Road		Lotbury	LB6 3SL	UK	(02345) 41	sarah.nicholson@lotburyontheweb.com
10	9	Mrs	Surtees	Kimberly	11 Victoria Close			Lotbury	LB2 6DY	UK	(02345) 41	k.surtees@lotburyinternet.com
11	10	Mrs	Jarvis	Donna	11 Charles Road			Lotbury	LB5 5FQ	UK	(02345) 83	d.jarvis@lotburyontheweb.com

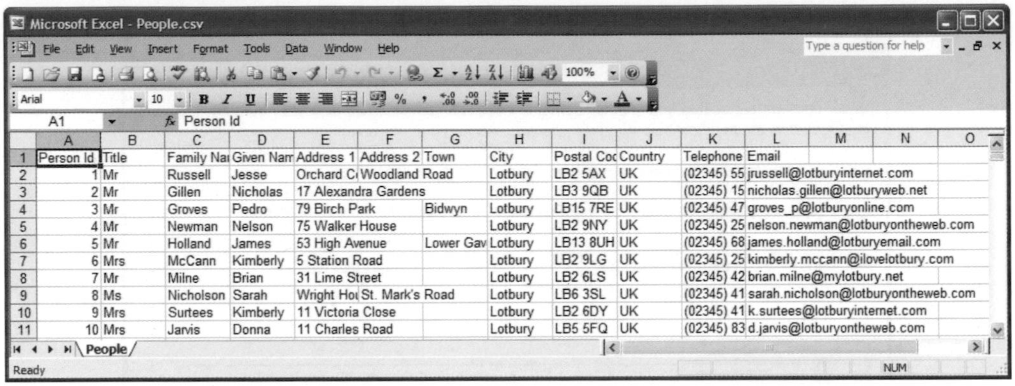

Figure 5.6: Comma-delimited text file produced by exporting from Access

Confirm that the data appears to be correct, then close Excel.

TIP

We could also have inspected the **csv** file by opening it in Notepad. We will do this for the next file, since this will be a fixed-width text file, which is not automatically associated with Excel.

Exporting to a fixed-width text file

Now we will export the **Auction Types** table. We will use a text format again, but this time we will used fixed-width columns instead of delimiters between each column.

Back in Access, click the **Auction Types** table to select it and again choose **File**, **Export** from the menu.

Change the **Save as type** drop-down list to **Text Files (*.txt; *.csv; *.tab; *.asc)**, as before, and press **Export**.

This time, choose **Fixed Width** (see Figure 5.7) and then press **Next**.

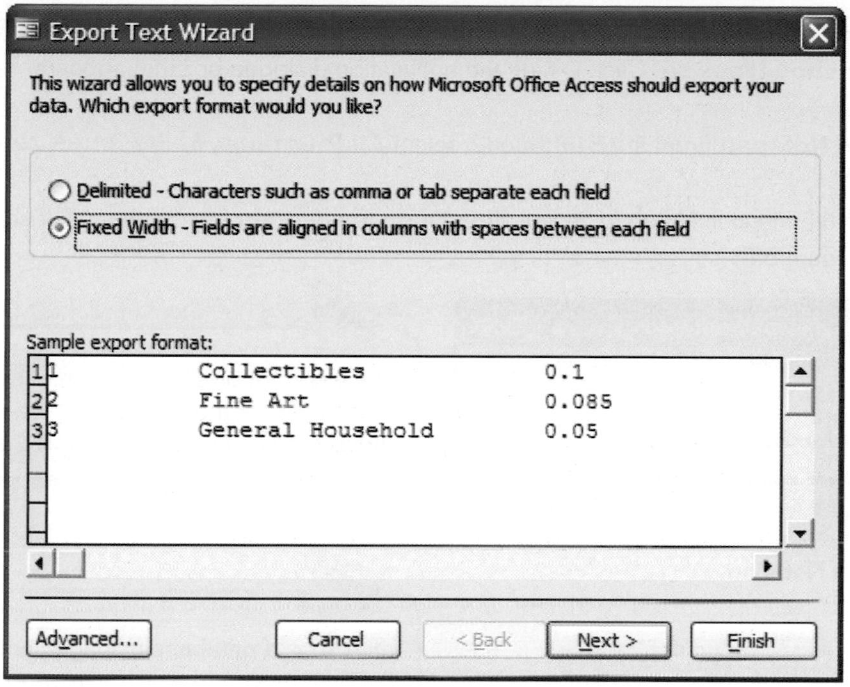

Figure 5.7: Exporting to a fixed-width text file

The next step of the wizard lets you adjust the column widths. Click on the vertical lines and drag them until the columns are wider then their contents, as shown in Figure 5.8.

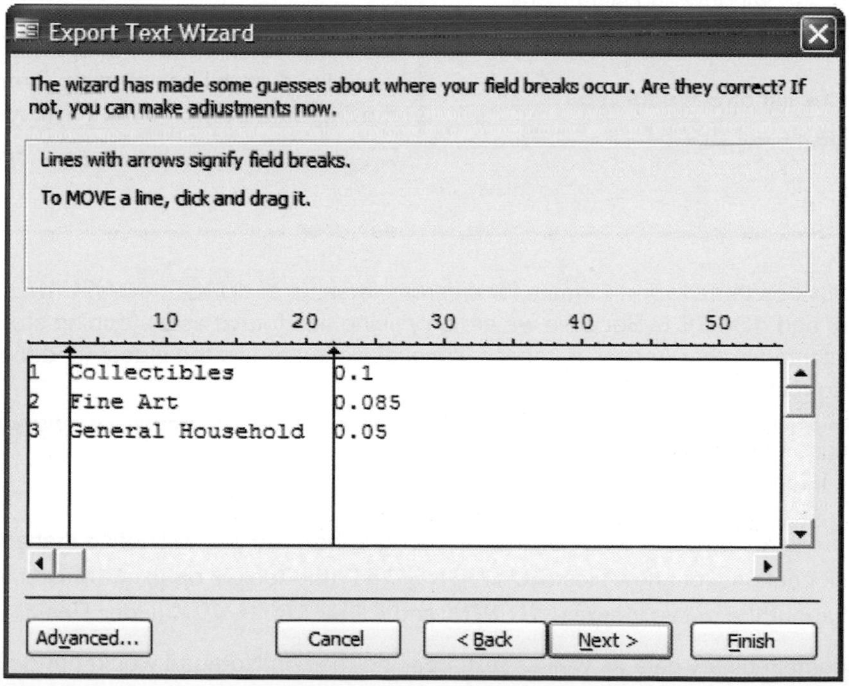

Figure 5.8: Adjusting fixed-width column sizes

Click **Next** to go the final step of the wizard, then click **Finish** to accept the default name of **Auction types.txt**. Click **OK** on the notification dialogue box that appears.

 Open **Notepad** (from the **Start** menu, select **All Programs**, **Accessories**, **Notepad**).

 From the menu in Notepad, select **File**, **Open** to open **Auction types.txt**. It should look like Figure 5.9.

Auction types.txt - Notepad
File Edit Format View Help
1 Collectibles   0.10
2 Fine Art   0.08
3 General Household 0.05

Note! We were not given the option of saving the field names in the first row, so we will have to type them in when we import the table.

Figure 5.9: Fixed-width exported file

 Close Notepad.

Exporting to dBASE files

Next, we will export the **Auctions** table in **dBASE** format.

 Select the **Auctions** table in the **Database** window and select **File**, **Export** from the menu.

 From the list of **Save as type** formats, select **dBASE III** (*.dbf).

Note! dBASE is a database management system, the first version of which was produced around 1980. This software quickly became the most widely-used database software for microcomputers. Because of this success, other database software needed to be able to import and export the **dbf** files created by dBASE. Even today, the **dbf** format is widely supported and so provides a useful intermediary format for moving data between database systems.

Note! Access provides three export formats for different versions of dBASE: **dBASE III**, **dBASE IV** and **dBASE 5**. Because we are only using this format as a stepping stone before importing it into another Access database, it makes sense to use the oldest (and therefore simplest) format – **dBASE III**.

 Press the **Export** button.

This time there is no wizard and no notification dialogue box, but you will notice that your **exports** folder on disk contains four new files: **AUCTIONS.DBF** (the table's data), **Auctions.INF** (information about the data's indexes), **ID.NDX** and **PRIMARYK.NDX** (index files).

These files contain binary data as well as text; opening them in Notepad would not do any harm, but the data will not be well formatted.

TIP

Access truncates long field names when exporting to dBASE or Paradox. If this results in duplicated field names then the export will fail.

Exporting to a Paradox file

Next, we will export the **Lots** table in **Paradox** format.

Note! Paradox is another database management system dating from the late 1980s. Again, its file format is widely supported by other database programs.

 Export the **Lots** table, as you have done for the others, this time choosing **Paradox 3 (*.db)** as the **Save as** type.

Again, you will get no wizard or confirmation dialogue box. A single file – **Lots.DB** – will appear in your **exports** folder. As with the dBASE files, this file is a combination of binary and text data, and so is not suitable for viewing in Notepad.

Exporting to an Excel file

Finally, we will export the **Items** table as an Excel spreadsheet.

Export the **Items** table, as you have done for the others, this time choosing **Microsoft Excel 97–2003 (*.xls)** as the **Save as** type. This time, also tick the **Save formatted** box and then the **Autostart** box before pressing **Export** (see Figure 5.10).

TIP

Save formatted will save the formatting of the **Items** table. **Autostart** will open the exported spreadsheet in Excel once we have finished exporting it.

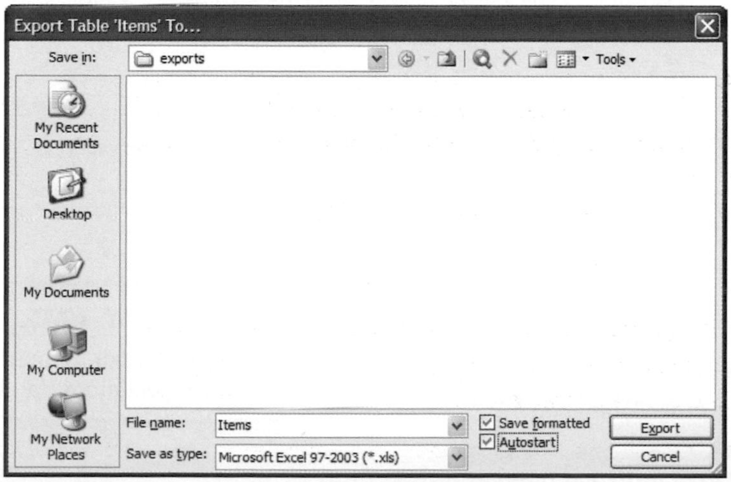

Figure 5.10: Exporting a table as a spreadsheet

After a pause, Excel loads with the new **Items.xls** spreadsheet, as shown in Figure 5.11. Notice how the heading row has been coloured and the columns have been sized sensibly. Also, the dates and insurance values are formatted in the same way as the original table.

	A	B	C	D	E	F	G
1	Item Id	Type	Description	Seller	Date received	Date taken	Insurance value
2	1	SILVER & GOLD	Silver lady's compact	396	03-Jan-06	03-Feb-06	£50.00
3	2	COLLECTIBLES	Mahogany box containing various copper and brass coinage	43	03-Jan-06	03-Feb-06	£50.00
4	3	POTTERY & PORCELAIN	18th century Worcester blue and white transfer Plantation pattern mug	88	03-Jan-06	06-Feb-06	£300.00
5	4	WATCHES & CLOCKS	Gent's rotary 9ct gold wristwatch	30	03-Jan-06	31-Jan-06	£100.00
6	5	POTTERY & PORCELAIN	Continental majolica jardiniere on stand	12	03-Jan-06	31-Jan-06	£600.00
7	6	JEWELLERY	Assorted costume jewellery	24	03-Jan-06	02-Feb-06	£100.00
8	7	WATCHES & CLOCKS	Three silver pocket watches	148	03-Jan-06	02-Feb-06	£100.00
9	8	JEWELLERY	18ct gold, sapphire and diamond ring	55	03-Jan-06	02-Feb-06	£300.00
10	9	FURNITURE	Late Victorian walnut swivel desk chair	93	03-Jan-06	03-Feb-06	£100.00
11	10	FURNITURE	Pine low chest of two short over one long drawer	6	03-Jan-06	06-Feb-06	£50.00
12	11	POTTERY & PORCELAIN	Pair of Royal Worcester porcelain plates	12	03-Jan-06	31-Jan-06	£100.00
13	12	WATCHES & CLOCKS	Gold-plated full hunter pocket watch together with chain	64	03-Jan-06	06-Feb-06	£100.00
14	13	POTTERY & PORCELAIN	Royal Crown Derby porcelain dessert service	27	03-Jan-06	01-Feb-06	£100.00
15	14	GLASS	Brandy glasses, wine glasses etc.	23	03-Jan-06	10-Feb-06	£50.00
16	15	JEWELLERY	Gold and platinum set diamond and peridot three stone crossover ring	16	03-Jan-06	02-Feb-06	£300.00
17	16	SILVER & GOLD	Four piece Georgian-style electroplated tea and coffee set	286	03-Jan-06	02-Feb-06	£100.00
18	17	TOYS	Small collection of die cast model cars	41	03-Jan-06	31-Jan-06	£100.00
19	18	SILVER & GOLD	George V silver sugar caster	5	03-Jan-06	31-Jan-06	£50.00
20	19	POTTERY & PORCELAIN	Poole pottery floral painted vase	31	03-Jan-06	02-Feb-06	£100.00
21	20	MISCELLANY	Art deco bronzed table lamp	31	03-Jan-06	31-Jan-06	£500.00
22	21	FURNITURE	Georgian mahogany dining table	7	03-Jan-06	31-Jan-06	£900.00
23	22	POTTERY & PORCELAIN	Copeland Spode Chelsea pattern dinner service	5	03-Jan-06	31-Jan-06	£200.00
24	23	WATCHES & CLOCKS	9ct gold full hunter pocket watch	150	03-Jan-06	31-Jan-06	£300.00
25	24	COLLECTIBLES	Quantity of assorted military cap badges	15	03-Jan-06	07-Feb-06	£100.00
26	25	FURNITURE	Oak three-tier folding cakestand	97	03-Jan-06	09-Feb-06	£50.00
27	26	WATCHES & CLOCKS	Mid-19th-century oak longcase clock	212	03-Jan-06	31-Jan-06	£1,400.00
28	27	MISCELLANY	Oak cased part canteen of cutlery	134	03-Jan-06	31-Jan-06	£100.00
29	28	COLLECTIBLES	Postcard album containing a large quantity of early 20th century postcards	18	03-Jan-06	02-Feb-06	£200.00
30	29	COLLECTIBLES	Large collection of LP records	30	04-Jan-06	31-Jan-06	£50.00
31	30	FURNITURE	Victorian wall mirror	87	04-Jan-06	07-Feb-06	£100.00
32	31	TOYS	Large quantity of Matchbox and Corgi boxed die cast toys	74	04-Jan-06	31-Jan-06	£200.00
33	32	WATCHES & CLOCKS	Early 20th century oak mantel clock	18	04-Jan-06	31-Jan-06	£100.00

Figure 5.11: Spreadsheet created by exporting a table with formatting from Access

At this stage, the contents of your **exports** folder should look something like Figure 5.12.

Name ▲	Size	Type
Auction types.txt	1 KB	Text Document
AUCTIONS.DBF	1 KB	DBF File
Auctions.INF	1 KB	Setup Information
ID.NDX	1 KB	NDX File
Items.xls	288 KB	Microsoft Excel Worksheet
Lots.DB	96 KB	Data Base File
People.csv	61 KB	Microsoft Office Excel Comma Separated Values File
PRIMARYK.NDX	1 KB	NDX File

Figure 5.12: Contents of the exports folder

Importing data

Having exported five tables in a variety of formats, let's go through the process of importing them into the **sandbox.mdb** database.

> **Syllabus ref: AM5.6.1.1**
>
> Import text, spreadsheet, csv, dBASE, Paradox files into a database.

Close **auction.mdb** and open **sandbox.mdb**.

Importing a comma-delimited text file

From the menu, select **File**, **Get External Data**, **Import**. The **Import** dialogue box appears.

Navigate to the **exports** folder you created (you will not be able to see any of the files it contains at this stage).

Change the **Files of type** drop-down list to **Text files (*.txt; *.csv; *.tab; *.asc)**. The two text-based files (**Auction types.txt** and **People.csv**) are shown.

Select **People.csv** and press the **Import** button. The **Import Text Wizard** appears, as shown in Figure 5.13.

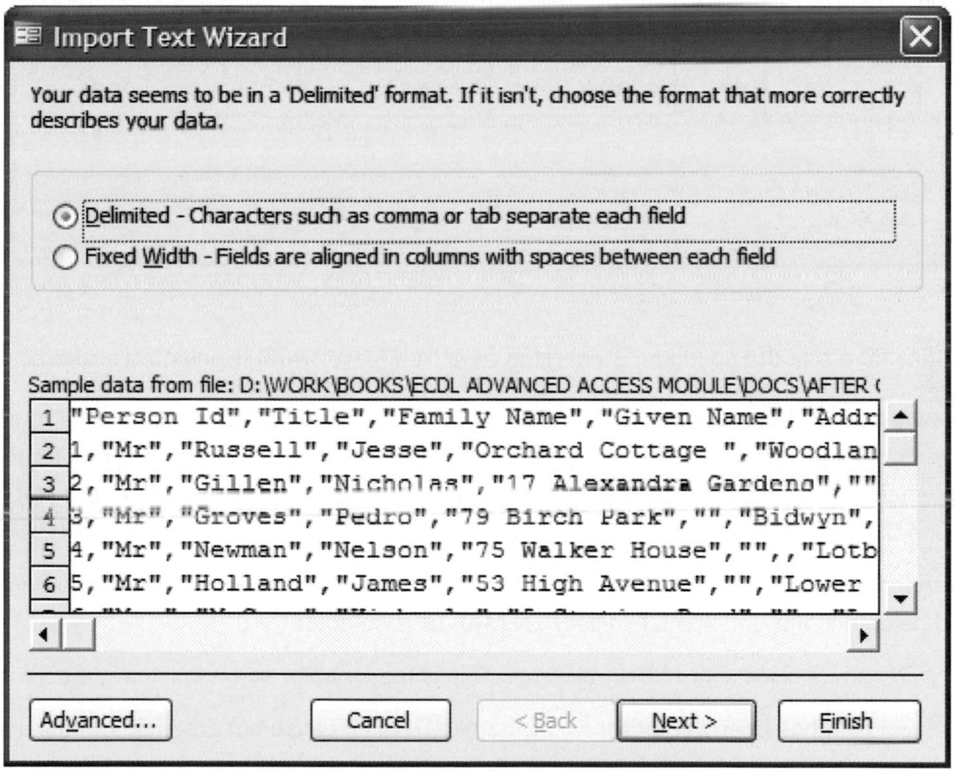

Figure 5.13: Importing a comma-delimited text file

Access has determined that the data file is **Delimited**, which it is, so press **Next**.

In the next step, make sure that **Comma** is selected and that **Text Qualifier** is set to ". Tick **First Row Contains Field Names**, as shown in Figure 5.14. Press **Next**.

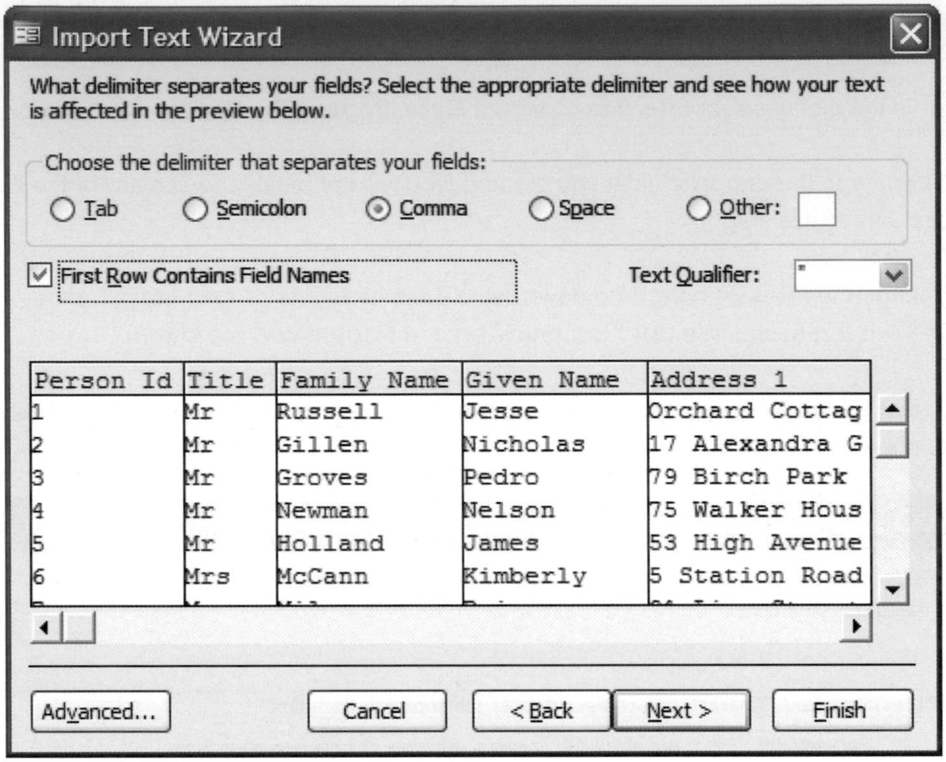

Figure 5.14: Setting the data structure in the Import Text Wizard

 Make sure that the option for storing the data **In a New Table** is selected and press **Next**.

Because we saved the field names as the first row of the exported data, these have all been correctly recognised. However, we did not store any information about the data types for the fields or whether they were indexed. Access tries to work these out from the data, but you should always check them.

The controls in the top half of the **Import Text Wizard** show the values relating to the currently selected column in the bottom half. Initially, **Person Id** is selected.

The **Data Type** has been set to **Long Integer**. This is reasonable, so we will leave it as it is.

The **Indexed** field has been set to **Yes (Duplicates OK)**. Because our first field contains numbers, Access has worked out that we might need to find records from these values and so recommends that we create an index to speed up the search. We can go one step further, since we know that there are no duplicate **Person Ids**.

 Change **Indexed** from **Yes (Duplicates OK)** to **Yes (No Duplicates)** as shown in Figure 5.15.

Import Text Wizard

You can specify information about each of the fields you are importing. Select fields in the area below. You can then modify field information in the 'Field Options' area.

Field Options

Field Name: `Person Id`   Data Type: `Long Integer`

Indexed: `Yes (No Duplicates)`   ☐ Do not import field (Skip)

Person Id	Title	Family Name	Given Name	Address 1
1	Mr	Russell	Jesse	Orchard Cottag
2	Mr	Gillen	Nicholas	17 Alexandra G
3	Mr	Groves	Pedro	79 Birch Park
4	Mr	Newman	Nelson	75 Walker Hous
5	Mr	Holland	James	53 High Avenue
6	Mrs	McCann	Kimberly	5 Station Road

Advanced...   Cancel   < Back   Next >   Finish

Figure 5.15: Changing how an imported field is to be indexed

Note!

We could tick the **Do not import field (Skip)** box if we did not want this field to form part of the imported table.

Click on the other columns in the lower half of the **Import Text Wizard** to see how the controls in the upper half are updated.

Press the **Advanced** button. A dialogue box entitled **People Import Specification** appears, as shown in Figure 5.16.

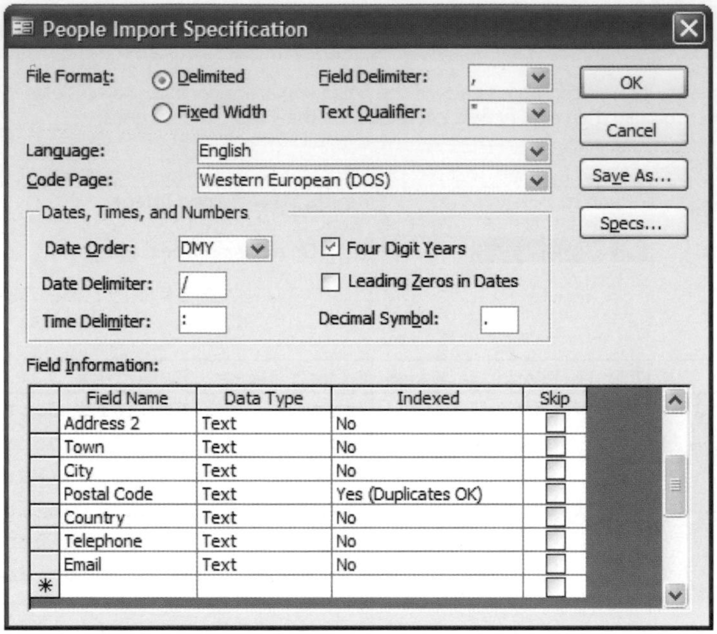

Figure 5.16: Using advanced settings to set the field names

Notice how all of the other fields have been recognised as **Text** with no indexing, apart from **Postal Code**. Access has recognised this as a special case, and is recommending that we add a non-unique index to this field. We are not planning to look up records by **Postal Code**, so we can remove this index.

> **TIP**
>
> To control how Access assigns these automatic indexes, change the **AutoIndex on Import/Create** setting in the **Tables/Queries** tab of the **Options** dialogue box (**Tools, Options**). By default it is **ID;key;code;num** – if any of these four words appear in a field's name it will be assigned an index by default.

Set the **Indexed** property for **Postal Code** to **No** by clicking in the field and then using the drop-down list that appears, as shown in Figure 5.17.

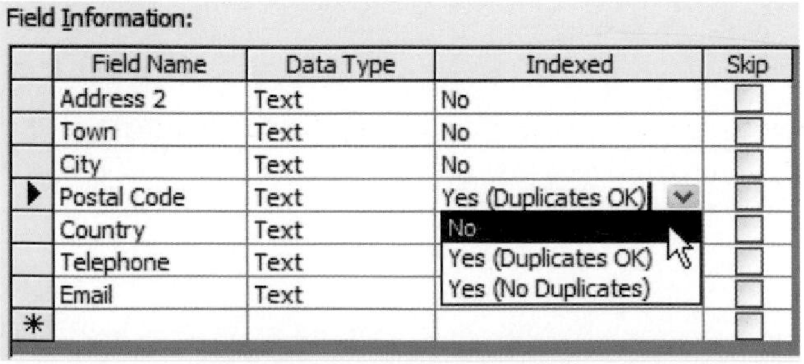

Figure 5.17: Turning off an index

Press **OK** to close the **People Import Specification** window and to apply the changes.

Press **Next** in the **Import Text Wizard**. We already have a field with a unique index that we can use as the primary key, so select the **Choose my own primary key** option and make sure that it is set to **Person Id**. Press **Next**.

The final step of the wizard asks for a table name. We will just accept the default – **People** – so press **Finish**.

A dialogue box should appear to tell you that the import has been successful. Press **OK** to dismiss it.

Open the new **People** table and check its contents. It should look like Figure 5.18. Close the table when you have finished inspecting it.

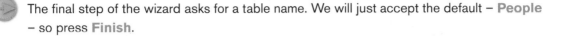

Person Id	Title	Family Name	Given Name	Address 1	Address 2	Town	City	Postal Code	Country	Telephone	Email
1	Mr	Russell	Jesse	Orchard Cottag	Woodland Road		Lotbury	LB2 5AX	UK	(02345) 558607	jrussell@lotbur
2	Mr	Gillen	Nicholas	17 Alexandra G			Lotbury	LD3 9QD	UK	(02345) 152173	nicholas.gillen@
3	Mr	Groves	Pedro	79 Birch Park		Bidwyn	Lotbury	LB15 7RE	UK	(02345) 473448	groves_p@lotbu
4	Mr	Newman	Nelson	75 Walker Hous			Lotbury	LB2 9NY	UK	(02345) 259912	nelson.newman
5	Mr	Holland	James	53 High Avenue		Lower Gavel	Lotbury	LB13 8UH	UK	(02345) 686064	james.holland@
6	Mrs	McCann	Kimberly	5 Station Road			Lotbury	LB2 9LG	UK	(02345) 256167	kimberly.mccar
7	Mr	Milne	Brian	31 Lime Street			Lotbury	LB2 6LS	UK	(02345) 423711	brian.milne@m
8	Ms	Nicholson	Sarah	Wright House	St. Mark's Road		Lotbury	LB6 3SL	UK	(02345) 411307	sarah.nicholson
9	Mrs	Surtees	Kimberly	11 Victoria Clos			Lotbury	LB2 6DY	UK	(02345) 412410	k.surtees@lotb
10	Mrs	Jarvis	Donna	11 Charles Roa			Lotbury	LB5 5FQ	UK	(02345) 838068	d.jarvis@lotbun
11	Mr	Jolly	Gregory	The Cottage	New Road		Lotbury	LB3 7DE	UK	(02345) 607965	jolly_g@ilovelot
12	Mrs	Norman	Grace	9 Chesterton R		Smedley	Lotbury	LB7 9TF	UK	(02345) 448289	gnorman@lotbu
13	Mr	Porter	Christopher	47 Claremont R		Smedley	Lotbury	LB7 8JR	UK	(02345) 537074	christopher.port
14	Mr	Holden	John	6 Manor Avenue			Lotbury	LB4 4PS	UK	(02345) 609012	jholden@ilovele
15	Mrs	Warren	Rachel	58 Salisbury Pl			Lotbury	LB4 9JS	UK	(02345) 890391	r.warren@lotbul
16	Mr	Turner	Jesse	28 Blenheim Ro			Lotbury	LB1 3WP	UK	(02345) 365341	jturner@lotbury
17	Mrs	Bailey	Stephanie	12 Hill Road		Smattering	Lotbury	LB12 1AU	UK	(02345) 548965	s.bailey@mylot
18	Mr	Fahey	Philip	Green House	Green Terrace	Greater Nodd	Lotbury	LB17 5PB	UK	(02345) 284392	philip.fahey@lo
19	Mr	Taylor	Travis	Church House	Winston Hill		Lotbury	LB5 5HZ	UK	(02345) 673782	t.taylor@lotbun
20	Mr	Brock	Travis	20 Claremont V			Lotbury	LB1 5UN	UK	(02345) 660665	brock_t@lotbur

Record: I◄ ◄ [1] ► ►I ►* of 500

Figure 5.18: The People table immediately after it has been imported

Importing a fixed-width text file

From the menu, select **File**, **Get External Data**, **Import**. Access should open the folder you used last time: **exports**. Click on **Auction types.txt** and then press **Import**.

Access should automatically determine the file type and select the **Fixed Width** option. Press **Next**.

Because this is a simple file, Access successfully works out where the field breaks occur (Figure 5.19). Press **Next**.

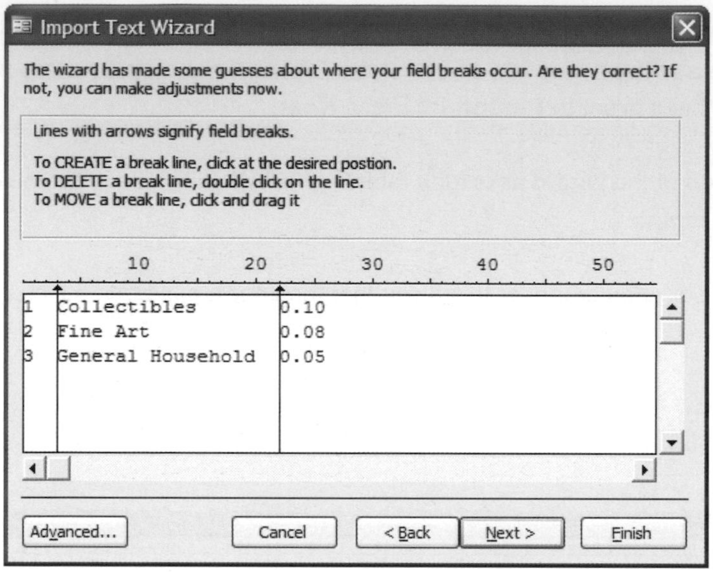

Figure 5.19: Access works out where the field breaks occur in the fixed-width text file

 Select **In a New Table** and press **Next**.

Because we did not save the field names when we exported the data, we will have to type this information in now.

TIP

The boxed text in the wizard explains how to correct the field breaks if Access has got it wrong.

 Change the **Field Name** from **Field1** to **id** and press the **Tab** key to move to the next control on the form.

Note!

Note that Access has automatically changed the **Indexed** control from **No** to **Yes (Duplicates OK)**. It does this because fields called **id** are often used in queries and relationships, so it assumes that we want to index the field to make searches faster. We will go one stage further and change this to **Yes (No Duplicates)**, since we know that all the **id** values are unique.

 Set the **Indexed** field to **Yes (No Duplicates)**.

 Click in each of the other two columns in turn, renaming **Field 2** to **type** and **Field 3** to **commission**. Note that **type** is a text field and **commission** is a double-precision floating point number – we will leave these as they are. Press **Next**.

 As before, click **Choose my own primary key**. The drop-down list will change to **id**, which is the field we want. Press **Next**.

Leave the table name as **Auction types** and press **Finish**. Press **OK** on the confirmation dialogue box that appears.

Check that the new **Auction types** table looks like Figure 5.20. Close it when you have finished.

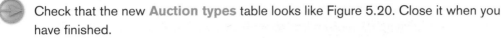

	id	type	commission
▶	1	Collectibles	0.1
	2	Fine Art	0.08
	3	General Housel	0.05
*			

Figure 5.20: The imported Auction types table

Importing dBASE files

From the menu, select **File**, **Get External Data**, **Import**.

From the **Files of type** drop-down list, select **dBASE III (*.dbf)**. The file **AUCTIONS.DBF** is displayed. Select it and press **Import**.

A confirmation dialogue box appears. Press **OK** to dismiss it.

Press **Close** to dismiss the **Import** window.

Open the **AUCTIONS** table. It should look like Figure 5.21. Close it when you have finished.

	AUCTION_ID	DATE	TYPE
▶	1	31/01/2006	1
	2	28/02/2006	1
	3	28/03/2006	1
*			

Figure 5.21: The imported AUCTIONS table

The dBase **dbf** format supports only capital letters for table and field names, so **Auctions**, **Auction Id**, **Date** and **Type** have all been capitalised.

Importing a Paradox file

 From the menu, select **File**, **Get External Data**, **Import**.

 From the **Files of type** drop-down list, select **Paradox (*.db)**. The file **Lots.DB** is displayed. Select it and press **Import**.

 A confirmation dialogue box appears. Press **OK** to dismiss it.

Press **Close** to dismiss the **Import** window.

Open the **Lots** table. It should look like Figure 5.22. Close it when you have finished.

Lot Id	Item	Auction	Lot number	Lower estimate	Upper estimate	Reserve	Withdrawn?	Extra?	Winner's paddle	Price
1	14	1	1	8	12	0	0	0	112	7
2	201	1	2	30	40	0	0	0	111	45
3	218	1	3	30	40	0	0	0	69	8
4	336	1	4	20	30	0	0	0	182	45
5	384	1	5	20	30	0	0	0	11	50
6	3	1	6	100	150	0	0	0	26	160
7	5	1	7	250	350	140	0	0	196	480
8	11	1	8	50	80	40	0	0	175	95
9	13	1	9	30	40	0	0	0	193	30
10	19	1	10	40	60	0	0	0	100	65
11	22	1	11	60	90	32	0	0	54	160
12	35	1	12	20	30	0	0	0	3	35
13	36	1	13	50	80	0	0	0	184	35
14	46	1	14	20	30	0	0	0	34	48
15	47	1	15	30	40	0	0	0	69	65
16	60	1	16	100	150	0	0	0	88	240
17	71	1	17	10	15	0	0	0	29	4
18	78	1	18	40	60	30	0	0	0	0
19	86	1	19	10	15	0	0	0	152	16
20	93	1	20	20	30	0	0	0	183	40
21	107	1	21	70	100	60	0	0	176	90
22	109	1	22	100	150	90	0	0	71	160
23	115	1	23	20	30	0	0	0	156	35
24	116	1	24	30	40	0	0	0	101	10
25	118	1	25	20	30	0	0	0	152	30
26	121	1	26	70	100	55	0	0	113	180
27	129	1	27	20	30	0	0	0	54	22
28	137	1	28	100	150	90	0	0	163	140
29	141	1	29	20	30	0	0	0	80	45
30	151	1	30	40	60	0	0	0	28	55
31	165	1	31	200	300	130	0	0	0	0
32	167	1	32	40	60	0	0	0	174	48
33	168	1	33	30	40	0	0	0	191	42
34	176	1	34	100	150	80	0	0	0	0
35	177	1	35	50	80	0	0	0	78	55

Record: I◄ ◄ 1 ► ►I ►* of 1219

Figure 5.22: Lots table

Importing an Excel file

From the menu, select **File**, **Get External Data**, **Import**.

From the **Files of type** drop-down list, select **Microsoft Excel (*.xls)**. The file **Items.xls** is displayed. Select it and press **Import**. The **Import Spreadsheet Wizard** appears, as shown in Figure 5.23.

Import Spreadsheet Wizard			✕

Microsoft Access can use your column headings as field names for your table. Does the first row specified contain column headings?

☑ First Row Contains Column Headings

	Item Id	Type	Description
1	1	SILVER & GOLD	Silver lady's compact
2	2	COLLECTIBLES	Mahogany box containing
3	3	POTTERY & PORCELAIN	18th century Worcester l
4	4	WATCHES & CLOCKS	Gent's rotary 9ct gold w
5	5	POTTERY & PORCELAIN	Continental majolica jar
6	6	JEWELLERY	Assorted costume jewelle

Cancel	< Back	Next >	Finish

Figure 5.23: The Import Spreadsheet Wizard

The **Import Spreadsheet Wizard** has correctly determined that the first row of the spreadsheet contains column headings, so press **Next** to continue.

Make sure that **In a New Table** is selected and press **Next**.

Note!

Unlike the **Import Text Wizard**, the **Import Spreadsheet Wizard** does not allow you to change the **Data Type** parameter for any of the columns.

As we have done for the other imported files, change the **Indexed** control for the first column to **Yes (No Duplicates)**, as shown in Figure 5.24. Press **Next**.

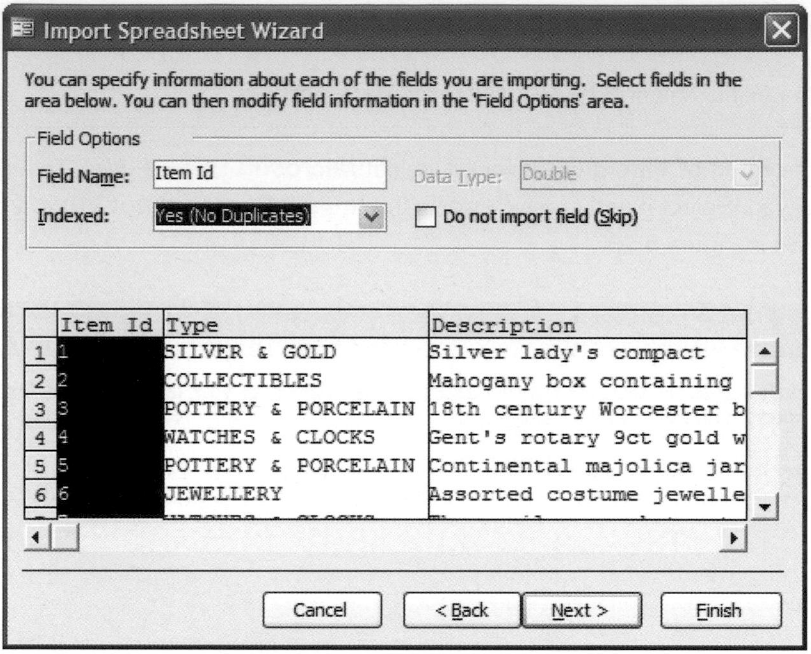

Figure 5.24: Importing a spreadsheet

- Select **Choose my own primary key**, which should become set to **Item Id**. Press **Next**.
- We will keep the table name **Items**, so press **Finish**. Press **OK** on the confirmation dialogue box that appears.
- Open the **Items** table. It should look like Figure 5.25. Close it when you have finished.

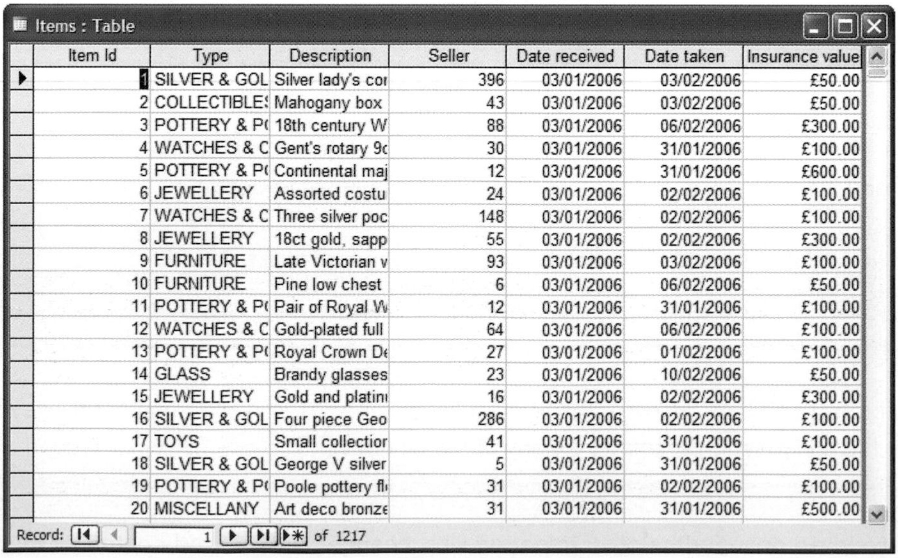

Item Id	Type	Description	Seller	Date received	Date taken	Insurance value
1	SILVER & GOL	Silver lady's co	396	03/01/2006	03/02/2006	£50.00
2	COLLECTIBLE	Mahogany box	43	03/01/2006	03/02/2006	£50.00
3	POTTERY & P	18th century W	88	03/01/2006	06/02/2006	£300.00
4	WATCHES & C	Gent's rotary 9c	30	03/01/2006	31/01/2006	£100.00
5	POTTERY & P	Continental maj	12	03/01/2006	31/01/2006	£600.00
6	JEWELLERY	Assorted costu	24	03/01/2006	02/02/2006	£100.00
7	WATCHES & C	Three silver poc	148	03/01/2006	02/02/2006	£100.00
8	JEWELLERY	18ct gold, sapp	55	03/01/2006	02/02/2006	£300.00
9	FURNITURE	Late Victorian v	93	03/01/2006	03/02/2006	£100.00
10	FURNITURE	Pine low chest	6	03/01/2006	06/02/2006	£50.00
11	POTTERY & P	Pair of Royal W	12	03/01/2006	31/01/2006	£100.00
12	WATCHES & C	Gold-plated full	64	03/01/2006	06/02/2006	£100.00
13	POTTERY & P	Royal Crown D	27	03/01/2006	01/02/2006	£100.00
14	GLASS	Brandy glasses	23	03/01/2006	10/02/2006	£50.00
15	JEWELLERY	Gold and platin	16	03/01/2006	02/02/2006	£300.00
16	SILVER & GOL	Four piece Geo	286	03/01/2006	02/02/2006	£100.00
17	TOYS	Small collectior	41	03/01/2006	31/01/2006	£100.00
18	SILVER & GOL	George V silver	5	03/01/2006	31/01/2006	£50.00
19	POTTERY & P	Poole pottery fl	31	03/01/2006	02/02/2006	£100.00
20	MISCELLANY	Art deco bronze	31	03/01/2006	31/01/2006	£500.00

Figure 5.25: The imported Items table

Linking external data

Once you have imported data in the way that we have just described, there is no link with the original data file. If you need to import updated data you must first delete whatever data you have and then repeat the import procedure.

An alternative way of using external data in Access is to link to the data. By doing this, any changes made to the data will be automatically picked up in Access. We will demonstrate this by linking to the Excel spreadsheet file that we have just imported.

> **Syllabus ref: AM5.6.1.3**
> Link external data to a database.

 From the menu, select **File**, **Get External Data**, **Link Tables**. The **Link** dialogue box appears.

 From the **Files of type** drop-down list, select **Microsoft Excel (*.xls)**. The file **Items.xls** is displayed. Select it and press **Link**. The **Link Spreadsheet Wizard** appears. Apart from the title it looks just like the **Import Spreadsheet Wizard** shown previously in Figure 5.23.

 Click **Next** and change the **Linked Table Name** to **LinkedItems**. Press **Finish**. Click **OK** on the confirmation dialogue box that appears.

Notice that the **LinkedItems** entry that has appeared in the list of tables has a different icon to the tables.

 Load Excel and use it to open the spreadsheet **Items.xls** that is stored in your **exports** folder.

 In Excel, change the **Description** for the first item from **Silver lady's compact** to **Gold lady's compact**. Put the **Insurance value** up to **£200**.

 Save and close the spreadsheet.

 Open the **LinkedItems** table. Notice how it has picked up the updated **Description** and **Insurance value** fields, as shown in Figure 5.26.

Item Id	Type	Description	Seller	Date received	Date taken	Insurance value
1	SILVER & GOL	Gold lady's con	396	03-Jan-06	03-Feb-06	£200.00
2	COLLECTIBLE!	Mahogany box	43	03-Jan-06	03-Feb-06	£50.00
3	POTTERY & P(	18th century W	88	03-Jan-06	06-Feb-06	£300.00
4	WATCHES & C	Gent's rotary 9c	30	03-Jan-06	31-Jan-06	£100.00
5	POTTERY & P(	Continental maj	12	03-Jan-06	31-Jan-06	£600.00

Record: I◀ ◀ 1 ▶ ▶I ▶* of 1217

Figure 5.26: Linked table has updated automatically

 Close this table and open the original imported **Items** table. Confirm that it has not been updated (the first item is still listed as silver and insured for £50).

Conclusions

This exercise has demonstrated the following points.

 You can export data from Access in a variety of formats.

 You can import data into Access from a variety of formats, typically the same ones that Access can export to.

 It is a good idea to use the **.csv** file extension (which stands for **comma-separated values**) if you are exporting data in a comma-delimited format. This extension is usually associated with Excel, which can make it more convenient to edit the data if necessary.

 Access truncates long field names when exporting to dBASE or Paradox. If this results in duplicated field names then the export will fail.

 By default, Access adds indexes to imported fields if their names contain **ID**, **key**, **code** or **num**. You can easily remove these indexes if you do not need them.

 You can link to external data so that the table in Access is always up-to-date even if another program modifies the underlying data.

Test yourself

Auction database

1   Export the **Items** table in each of the following formats in turn: (1) **comma-delimited text** (save the file as **Items.csv**), (2) **fixed-width text** (save the file as **Items.txt**), (3) **dBASE** and (4) **Excel**. Compare the sizes of the exported files on disk (when I did this, the file sizes were as follows: **Items.csv** 129 K, **Items.xls** 175 K, **Items.txt** 462 K and the dBASE files 544 K in total, but yours might differ slightly).

> Importing from and exporting to **Paradox** format is simple (much like **dBASE** format), but has stricter requirements for the format of the data, so we have skipped it here.

2   Import into your **sandbox.mdb** database each of the four tables you exported in Exercise 1 as **Items from csv**, **Items from txt**, **Items from dBASE** and **Items from xls** respectively. In each case, use **Item Id** as the primary key and check that all of the records have been imported successfully.

3   Use **File**, **Get External Data**, **Link Tables** to import a linked version of the comma-delimited text table created in Exercise 1 (**items.csv**). Name the linked table **Items from csv linked**. Use Notepad to change some of the data, and check that it is automatically updated in Access.

Importing files from the Internet

Here is a nifty trick that you might enjoy. If you are connected to the Internet, you can import all sorts of structured information as a database. As an example, let's import the latest BBC News headlines.

4   Import a table as you normally would. Choose **XML (*.xml; *.xsd)** as the **Files of type** and use a URL (http://newsrss.bbc.co.uk/rss/newsonline_uk_edition/front_page/rss.xml) as the **File name**. Just press **OK** when you get the dialogue box shown in Figure 5.27. Three new tables will be created: **image**, **item** and **channel**. The interesting information is in **item**.

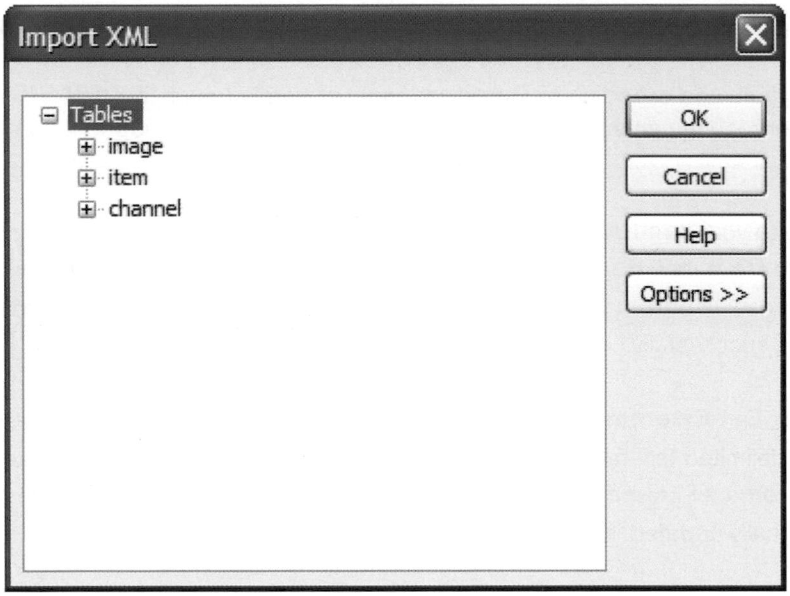

Figure 5.27: Importing news headlines from the Internet

Note!

The address of the BBC's RSS (Really Simple Syndication) news feed is, of course, subject to change. If it moves, you should be able to find the new URL by visiting the BBC's web site.

6 Data integrity

Introduction

In this chapter we will use the example of an art gallery to look at the various ways in which constraints can be put in place to protect against users entering invalid data into a database.

In this chapter, you will:

- specify that certain fields in a table are **mandatory** and cannot be left empty

- assign **default values** to the fields in a table and a form

- use **input masks** (both pre-defined and custom) to control what the user is allowed to type in a field in a table or a form

- set **validation rules** to control what Access will accept as a valid value for a field in a table or a form

- learn how to use the **Like** keyword to support **wildcards** in a query.

Mandatory fields

A database may acquire invalid data if important fields are left blank, either by someone entering information and choosing not to put in a value, or because data is missing in an imported file. To protect against this you can specify any important fields in a table as mandatory.

> **Syllabus ref: AM5.1.1.7**
> Set a mandatory data field, column.

⊙ Open **sandbox.mdb** if it is not already open.

⊙ With **Tables** selected in the **Objects** list, double-click **Create table in Design view** icon. A window opens to allow you to specify the structure of the new table.

⊙ Type four field names – **Title**, **Artist**, **Century** and **Style** – as shown in Figure 6.1. Leave all of their **Data Types** as **Text**. You can type in the **Descriptions** shown in Figure 6.1 if you like.

Table1 : Table

Field Name	Data Type	Description
Title	Text	The name of the exhibit
Artist	Text	The name of the painter
Century	Text	The century in which the work was created
Style	Text	The school/style of the work

Field Properties

General | Lookup

Field Size	50
Format	
Input Mask	
Caption	
Default Value	
Validation Rule	
Validation Text	
Required	No
Allow Zero Length	Yes
Indexed	No
Unicode Compression	Yes
IME Mode	No Control
IME Sentence Mode	None
Smart Tags	

The field description is optional. It helps you describe the field and is also displayed in the status bar when you select this field on a form. Press F1 for help on descriptions.

Figure 6.1: Simple table for a gallery

⊙ Press **Ctrl+S** to save the table. Use the name **tblGallery**.

⊙ You will get a warning that there is no primary key. Although it is good form to have one, it would only complicate things in this example. Press **No**.

Press the **Datasheet View** button to change the new **tblGallery** table into **Datasheet** view. Type **The Hay Wain** as the **Title** for the first record, but do not type anything else. Move your cursor to the second row, as shown in Figure 6.2. By leaving the first record, we have saved it to the database; Access is perfectly happy that three of the fields in this record have been left blank.

Datasheet View

Figure 6.2: A record with fields deliberately left blank

Press the **Design View** button. With the cursor in each of the four data fields in turn, change the **Required** setting in the bottom half of the window from **No** to **Yes**, as shown in Figure 6.3.

Design View

Figure 6.3: Marking a data field as Required (mandatory)

Press the **Datasheet View** button.

A warning appears saying that you must save the table. Press **Yes**.

Another dialogue box appears, as shown in Figure 6.4, warning us that the data must be checked against the changed rules. It says that the process may take a long time, but as we have only a single record in the database, it will not! Press **Yes**.

Datasheet View

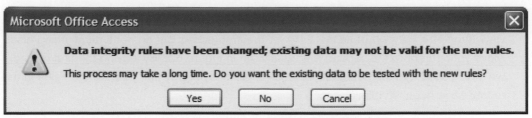

Figure 6.4: Warning that Access must check the data against the new integrity rules

 Another warning appears (Figure 6.5) stating that the **Artist** field violates the mandatory setting we just applied. We know that this is true, so press **Yes** to continue.

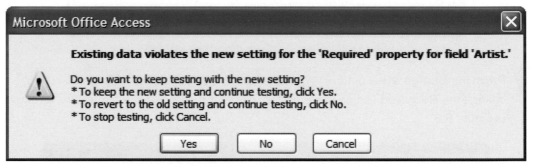

Figure 6.5: A data violation has occurred

 Two more warning dialogue boxes appear, one each for the **Century** and **Style** fields. Press **Yes** for each.

 In the second row (as a new record) type a **Title** of **The Scream**. Press the **down arrow** key to leave the record. The warning dialogue box shown in Figure 6.6 appears because we are trying to submit a record without filling in all of the mandatory fields. Press **OK** to dismiss the warning dialogue.

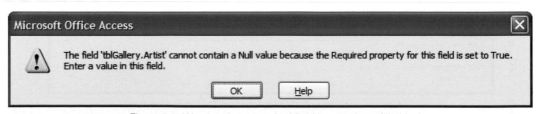

Figure 6.6: Warning that a required field has not been filled in

 Fill in the three remaining fields with **Edvard Munch**, **19** and **Expressionist**. Now you should be able to move freely to a different record.

 Right-click in the grey box to the left of the first record and select **Delete Record** from the menu that appears. Press **Yes** in the warning dialogue box. The table should now look like Figure 6.7.

Figure 6.7: Gallery table with a single record having no empty fields

Default values

Suppose that the gallery specialises in 20th Century Cubist paintings. We can use defaults to reduce the amount of typing that will be required for the average record.

> **Syllabus ref: AM5.1.1.6**
> Apply, modify default values in a field, column.

Default values in tables

In **Design** view, select the **Century** field and set its **Default Value** to **20**, as shown in Figure 6.8.

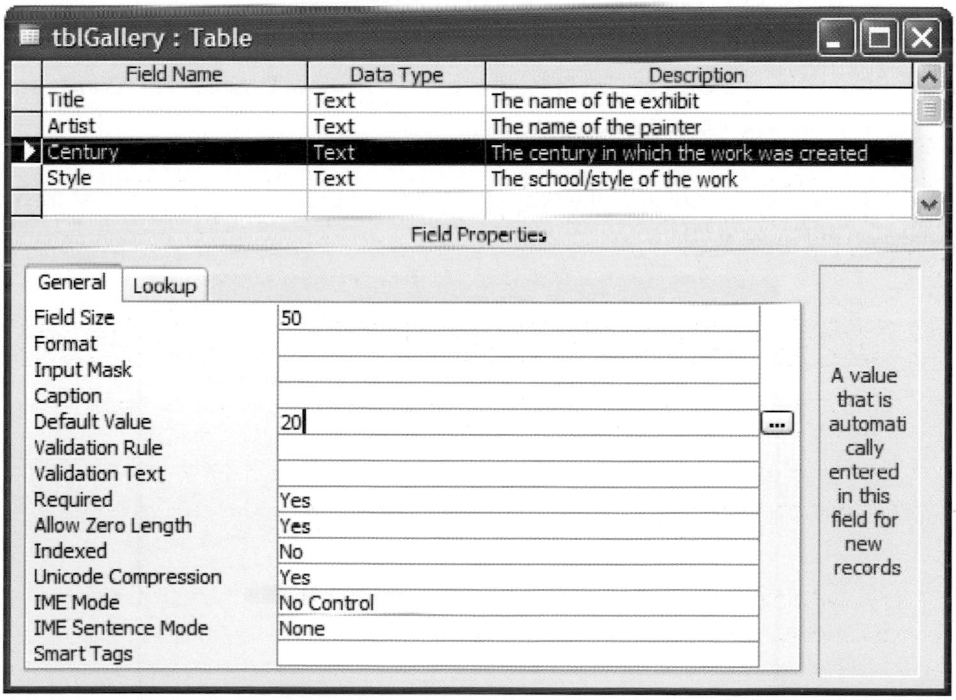

Figure 6.8: Setting a default value for a field

Use the same method to change the **Default Value** of the **Style** field to **Cubist**.

Save the table and switch back to **Datasheet** view.

Notice how the row that you would use to enter a new record already has the values **20** and **Cubist** filled in.

	Title	Artist	Century	Style
▶	The Scream	Edvard Munch	19	Expressionist
∗			20	Cubist

tblGallery : Table

Record: ◀◀ ◀ 1 ▶ ▶▶ ▶∗ of 1

Figure 6.9: Default values are now supplied for Century and Style

Default values in forms

Suppose that the gallery is planning to hold a special exhibition of Monet paintings, all of which will need to be entered into the database. It would be useful if the **Artist**, **Century** and **Style** were set to default values so that the person entering the details would only need to type the **Title** for each painting.

We could change the table defaults to achieve this. However, it might be better to create a temporary form that overrides the table's defaults. Let us see how this works.

 Close **tblGallery**.

Select **Forms** in the **Objects** list in the **Database** window. Double-click **Create form by using wizard**. The **Form Wizard** appears.

Select **Table: tblGallery** from the drop-down list and press **>>** to select all of the fields, as shown in Figure 6.10.

Form Wizard

Which fields do you want on your form?

You can choose from more than one table or query.

Tables/Queries

Table: tblGallery

Available Fields:

Selected Fields:

Title
Artist
Century
Style

Cancel   < Back   Next >   Finish

Figure 6.10: Creating a simple form

Work through the wizard: select **Columnar** layout and **Standard** style, and name the form **frmGallery** (it defaults to the table name, **tblGallery**). Press **Finish**.

The new form appears, looking like Figure 6.11(a). Press the **New Record** button and the form should look like Figure 6.11(b), showing the same defaults as the underlying table.

New Record

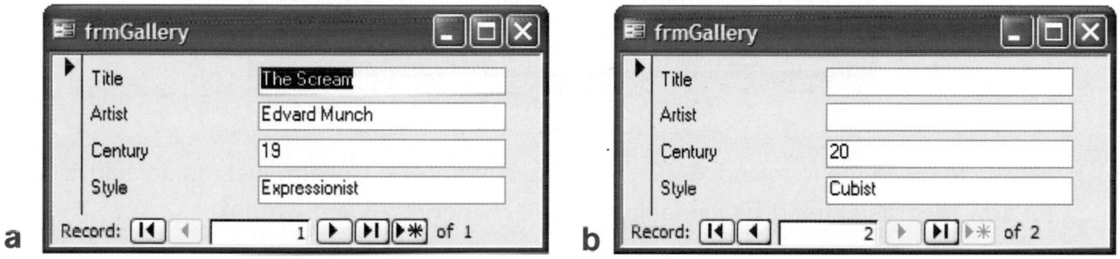

a

b

Figure 6.11: The form uses the table's defaults unless they are overridden

Switch into **Design** view. Right-click the **Artist** field and select **Properties** from the menu that appears. A **Properties** window entitled **Text Box: Artist** appears.

Click on the **Data** tab. Notice that **Default Value** is blank. Change this to **Claude Monet** as shown in Figure 6.12 (Access will add the quotation marks automatically if you omit them).

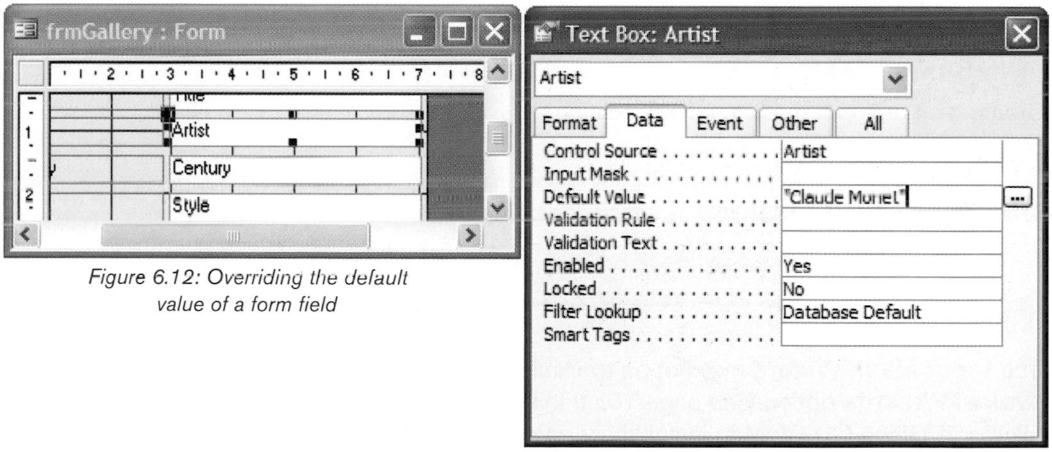

Figure 6.12: Overriding the default value of a form field

Keep the **Properties** window open and click on the **Century** field in the **frmGallery : Form** window. Set the **Default Value** to **19**.

Use the same method to change the **Style** field's **Default Value** to **Impressionist**.

Switch back to **Form** view and press the **New Record** button again. This time the new defaults should be used, as shown in Figure 6.13.

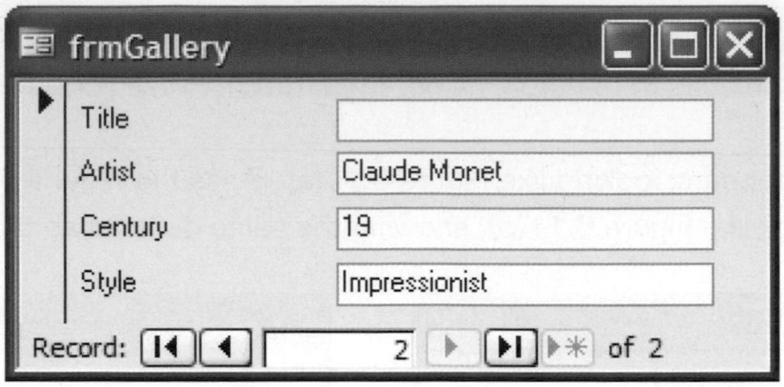

Figure 6.13: New default values

 Save and close the form and reopen the table **tblGallery**. Confirm that the default values for new records entered via the table have not changed: **20** and **Cubist**.

Input masks

Mandatory fields and default values go some way towards improving data integrity. However, as long as something is entered in each field, there is no check that what is entered is meaningful. The final two settings – **input masks** and **validation rules** – are useful when you need to restrict the type of data that can be held in a field.

An input mask controls which key presses are allowed, and in which order, when setting the value of a field.

> **Syllabus ref: AM5.1.1.5**
> Create, edit an input mask in a field, column.

Input masks in tables

> **Note!**
>
> The **Input Mask Wizard** may not be available if your copy of Access was installed with the **Typical Wizards** option (see page 10). If this is the case, Access will ask you to insert the Microsoft Office CD-ROM to install the wizard.

 To prevent problems later (see page 109), edit the **Century** for **The Scream**, typing it in again as **C19**.

 Switch to **Design** view for the table, select the **Century** field and click in the **Input Mask** property. Click the **...** button that appears to its right, as shown in Figure 6.14. The **Input Mask Wizard** appears.

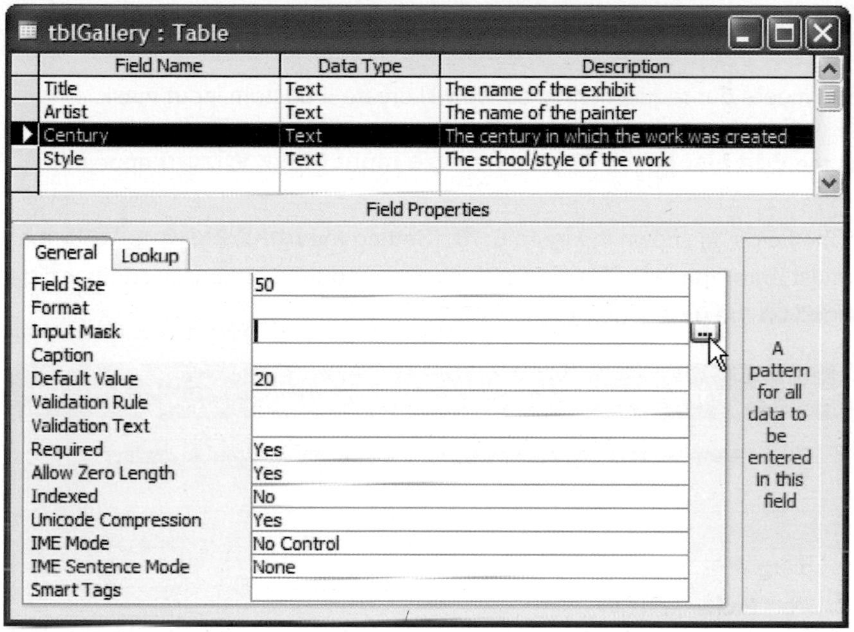

Figure 6.14: Adding an input mask for the Century field

We want to restrict the text input to just one or two digits for the century (typically it will be **19** or **20**, but it's possible that there might one day be some really old exhibits from the 9th Century or earlier). Before we set this up, let us try some of the built-in input masks.

With **Password** selected in the **Input Mask Wizard**, type some text in the **Try It** box. You should see a sequence of asterisks, as shown in Figure 6.15.

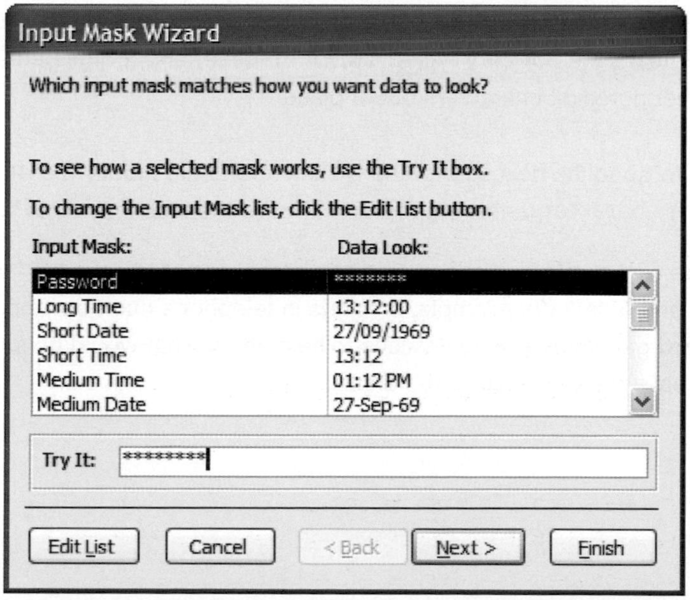

Figure 6.15: Trying a password in the Input Mask Wizard

Try each of the other mask types in turn to get a feel for how they respond.

None of these meets our requirements, so we will create a custom input mask.

 Press the **Edit List** button. The **Customize Input Mask Wizard** appears.

Fill in the fields as shown in Figure 6.16. (Setting the **Input Mask** to **\C09** means that the user must enter the letter **C** followed by a digit and then optionally another digit. This is explained on the next page.) Press **Close**.

Customize Input Mask Wizard		
Do you want to edit or add input masks for the Input Mask Wizard to display?		

Description:	Century (1 or 2 digits)	Help
Input Mask:	\C09	
Placeholder:	_	Close
Sample Data:	C20	
Mask Type:	Text/Unbound ▾	

Record: |◀ ◀ 1 ▶ ▶| ▶* of 1

Figure 6.16: Creating a custom input mask

Select **Century (1 or 2 digits)** in the **Input Mask Wizard** and test it by typing in the **Try It** box. Confirm that you can type 1-digit centuries (check that the wizard lets you press **Tab** to leave the box after typing **C9**, for example) and 2-digit centuries, but no letters or other non-digit characters out of place.

Press **Next** to go to the next step of the wizard. You could modify the **Input Mask** or the **Placeholder character** at this stage; we will leave them as they are. Press **Next**.

The next step of the wizard offers us the choice of whether or not to save the 'scaffolding' characters as part of the data (for example, brackets in telephone numbers and the letter **C** in our example). The wizard generates example values to help show what would be saved in each case. We will choose to save the **C** as well as the digits.

Input mask characters

Character	Description
0	Mandatory digit
9	Optional digit or space
#	Optional digit, space, + or –
L	Mandatory letter
?	Optional letter
A	Mandatory letter or digit
a	Optional letter or digit
&	Mandatory character
C	Optional character
. , : ; - /	Structural formatting placeholders (decimal point, thousands separator, date and time separators)
<	Convert characters that follow to lower case
>	Convert characters that follow to upper case
!	Fill input mask from right to left (normally left to right) when there are optional characters at the left end of the mask
\	Treat the next character literally (e.g. \0 must be a 0, not any digit). If you need to add several literal characters one after the other, you can enclose them in double inverted commas instead of having to use the backslash repeatedly.

Example input masks

Here are some examples of input masks

\x0000	A four-digit phone extension in the format **x1234**.
>L L<????????????????????	A single initial and a surname of up to 20 characters, for example **M Strawbridge**. The capitalisation is handled automatically.
\£999.00	A value in pounds up to a maximum of £999.99. The user can use **space** to skip past any of the whole pounds digits, but must enter values for the pence.
ISBN 000000000A	An international standard book number in the format **ISBN 1234567890** or **ISBN 123456789X**. (The last digit of an ISBN is either 0–9 or the letter X.)

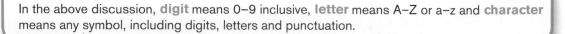

In the above discussion, **digit** means 0–9 inclusive, **letter** means A–Z or a–z and **character** means any symbol, including digits, letters and punctuation.

Select **With the symbols...**, as shown in Figure 6.17, and press **Next**.

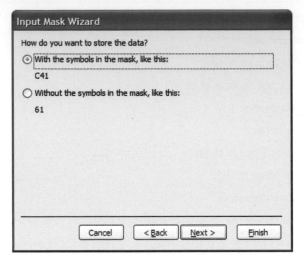

Figure 6.17: Opting to save the symbols in the mask

 Press **Finish**.

 Change the default value from **20** to **C20** to match the new input mask.

 Save the table and switch back to **Datasheet** view.

 Add a new record for **La Grande Jatte**, as shown in Figure 6.18.

Title	Artist	Century	Style
The Scream	Edvard Munch	C19	Expressionist
La Grande Jatte	Georges-Pierre Seurat	C19	Pointillist
		C20	Cubist

Record: |◄| ◄| 3 |►| |►|| |►*| of 3

Figure 6.18: Table after a new record has been added using the input mask

Suppose a rich patron of the gallery has agreed to donate one of his paintings, but has not yet told you which one it will be. You would like to create a placeholder record with **Unknown** in each of the four fields.

 Try to create this record now. The closest you will be able to get is **Unknown**, **Unknown**, **C20**, **Unknown** because the word **Unknown** does not match the input mask that we have set on the **Century** field.

Just as we did with default values, we can override a table's input masks by using a form.

Input masks in forms

 Close **tblGallery**.

 Create a new form with all of the fields from **tblGallery**. Call it **frmGalleryUnknown**.

 Switch the new form into **Design** view and look at the **Data** properties for the **Century** field. They should look like Figure 6.19.

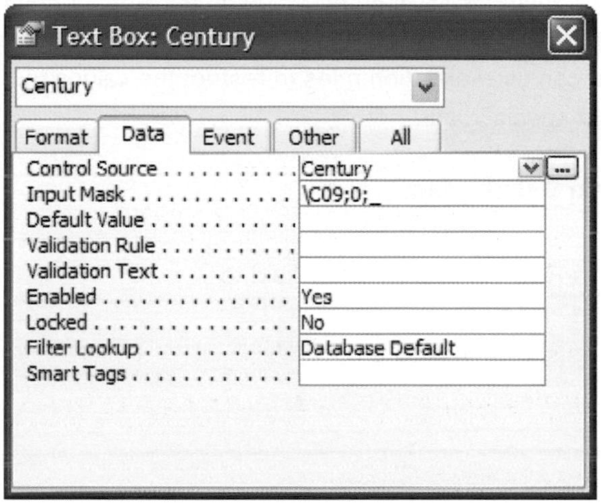

Figure 6.19: Properties for the Century field

 Select the contents of the **Input Mask** property and press the **Delete** key to blank it.

 Switch the form back to **Form** view. Press the **Last Record** button and change the Century to **Unknown**. This time it should work, as shown in Figure 6.20.

Last Record

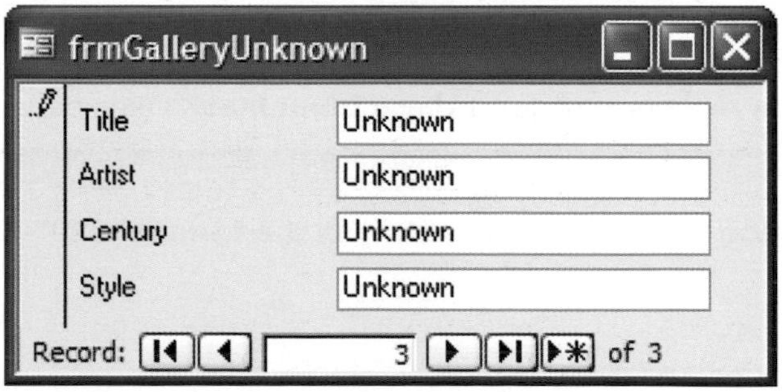

Figure 6.20: The blank input mask in the form overrides the one in the table

 Save and close **frmGalleryUnknown**.

Validation rules

Whereas an input mask checks an entry for validity as the user is typing, a validation rule is used to apply (possibly more complicated) checks after a user has finished typing but before the record is committed to the database.

> **Syllabus ref: AM5.1.1.4**
> Create, edit a validation rule in a field, column.

Validation rules in tables

At present you could enter a new work of art in the database with a century value of **C25** – one that is created in the future! This is clearly a mistake, but it fits the input mask that has been defined on the table. We can use validation rules to restrict the values to a maximum of **C21**, and allow **Unknown** as a special case.

 Open **tblGallery** in **Design** view.

 Set the **Validation Rule** for the **Century** field to
**Like "C#" Or Like "C1#" Or "C20" Or "C21"
Or "Unknown"**, as shown in Figure 6.21.

> **Note!**
>
> The **#** symbol matches any single digit when used with **Like**, so the validation rule will only pass for the following:
>
> - **C** + a digit (**C0**–**C9** inclusive); or
> - **C1** + a digit (**C10**–**C19** inclusive); or
> - **C20**; or
> - **C21**; or
> - **Unknown**.
>
> In a validation rule, the digit zero has no special meaning: Wildcard characters are different between **validation rules** (see page 111) and **input masks** (see page 105).

 Set the **Validation Text** to **Enter a century in the format "C20" or "Unknown"**

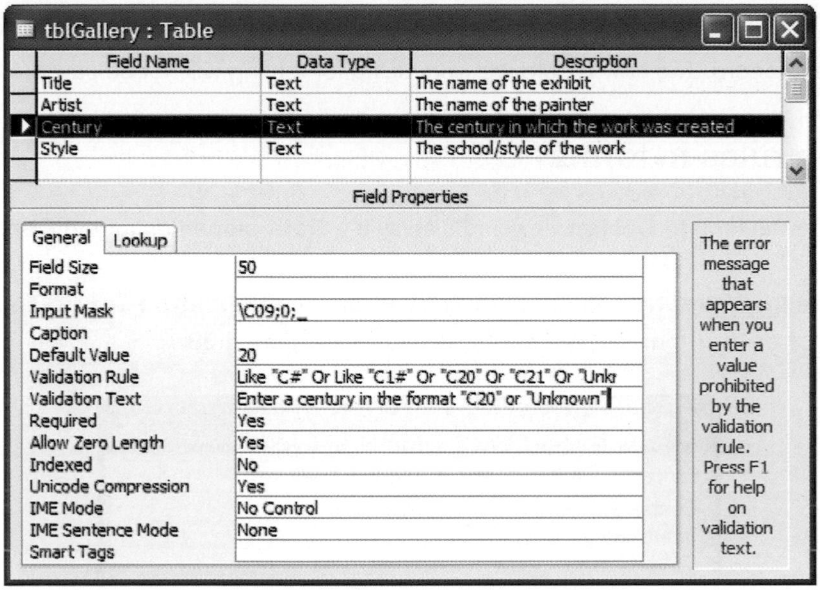

Figure 6.21: Setting a validation rule

🕐 Save and close the table. Press the **Yes** button when you are warned that the rules have changed. There should be no further warnings.

Note!

> If we had not updated The Scream's century (see page 102) from **19** to **C19** then we would have got an error here telling us that existing data contravened the validation rules.

🕐 Open **frmGalleryUnknown**. Press the **New Record** button.

▶* New Record

🕐 Confirm that you can enter the following **Century** items: **C9**, **C19**, **C20**, **C21**, **Unknown**. Each time, move to a different field to test the change, but do not move to a different record (we don't really want to save this new record).

🕐 Confirm that you cannot enter the following **Century** items: **C22**, **Don't know** (see Figure 6.22).

Figure 6.22: Testing the validation rules

Press the **Escape** key twice to clear the form (apart from the defaults) and move to a different record. The new record we were using for testing will not be saved.

Validation rules in forms

 Change the form to **Design** view and display the **Data** properties for the **Century** field.

 Change the **Validation Rule** to **"Unknown"** and the **Validation Text** to **This form is only for entering unknown dates**, as shown in Figure 6.23.

```
Text Box: Century                              [X]

 Format   Data    Event    Other    All

 Control Source . . . . . . . . . . Century
 Input Mask . . . . . . . . . . . .
 Default Value . . . . . . . . . . .
 Validation Rule . . . . . . . . . . "Unknown"
 Validation Text . . . . . . . . . . ng unknown dates
 Enabled . . . . . . . . . . . . . . Yes
 Locked . . . . . . . . . . . . . . . No
 Filter Lookup . . . . . . . . . . . Database Default
 Smart Tags . . . . . . . . . . . .
```

Figure 6.23: Overriding the table's validation rule in a form

Note!

If the validation rule set for a form is in conflict with the validation rule for the underlying table (for example, if we had set the only acceptable value to be **"Not known"** here), then the user will not be able to enter any records successfully using the form!

 Back in **Form** view, experiment with a new record again. If you try to set **Century** to any value other than **Unknown** you get an error message that this form is only for unknown dates.

 Press **Escape** twice when you have finished, save the form and switch to a record as before.

Validation rule syntax

Operator	Meaning	Examples
<	Less than	< 5
		< #16/03/2005#
<=	Less than or equal to	<= "Cunningham"
>	Greater than	> "Barnes"
>=	Greater than or equal to	>= 17
=	Equal to	= 5
<>	Not equal to	<> #25/12/2005#
IN	Match one of a list	IN ("SAT", "SUN")
BETWEEN	In the given range	BETWEEN 3 AND 9
		BETWEEN "A" AND "N"
LIKE	Match a pattern (see below)	LIKE "SW19 #??"
NOT	Reverse another comparison	NOT "Smith"
		NOT < 5
		NOT IN (3, 4, 5)
		NOT LIKE "A*"
IS NOT NULL	The field has a value	IS NOT NULL

> **TIP**
>
> Notice that dates must be surrounded by # symbols (see the example for < above), otherwise they will be interpreted as text strings.

Wildcard characters for LIKE

Wildcard	Meaning	Examples
?	One character	LIKE "SM???" (SMITH, SMART, etc.)
*	Zero or more characters	LIKE "S*" (S, Stuart, S123, etc.)
#	One digit	LIKE "UK#" (UK1, UK5, etc.)
[...-...]	Range of characters	LIKE "BOO[KT]" (BOOK or BOOT only)
		LIKE "UK[1-4]" (UK1, UK2, UK3 or UK4)
[!...-...]	Excluding range of characters	LIKE "BOO[!KT]" (BOON, BOOR, etc., but not BOOK or BOOT)

Conclusions

This exercise has demonstrated the following points.

 Table fields can be made **mandatory**, so that they cannot be left blank (null).

 You can assign a **default value** to a field in a table, and override that default in a form.

 You can assign an **input mask** to a field in a table, and override that mask in a form.

 You can assign a **validation rule** to a field in a table. You can override the rule in a form, but only to make it more restrictive (you cannot create a form that will permit data that contravenes the table's rules).

Test yourself

Auction database

1 Edit the **Lots** table, making the following fields mandatory: **Item**, **Auction** and **Lot number**. Try to add a new record to the table with blank (null) values for one or more of **Item**, **Auction** and **Lot number**: this should not be possible.

2 Modify the **Advance Bids** table to set the **Default Value** for **Auction** to **3**. Check that **3** is displayed in the bottom row of the grid when you view the table in **Datasheet** view.

3 Modify the **frmAdvanceBids** form to set the **Default Value** for **Date** to the formula **=Now()**. Check that the current date and time is used as the default for new records when you view the form in **Form** view (click ▶✳).

4 Modify the **Advance Bids** table to have an **Input Mask** of **00/00/0000\ 00:00:00;0;_** for the **Date** field. Set its **Format** property to **General Date**. Test the input mask by creating a new record in **Datasheet** view. Delete the new record again.

5 Modify the **frmAdvanceBids** form so that it uses an **Input Mask** which is the same as that used in Exercise 4 but with the first two digits of the year automatically set to **20**. Test the input mask by creating a new record using the form. Delete the new record again.

6 Modify the **Advance Bids** table, setting a **Validation Rule** that forces the **Paddle Number** to be positive. Add some suitable **Validation Text** (such as **Please enter a positive paddle number**). Check that you cannot now add a negative paddle number in a new record.

7 Modify the **frmAdvanceBids** form so that it has a **Validation Rule** to check that the **Date** is in 2006 or later (remember to use **#** symbols around the date – see page 111). Add suitable **Validation Text** and test the form: you should not be able to use the form to enter a new record with a **Date** earlier than 2006.

8 Create a query that uses wildcards (refer to the table on page 111) to find all of the records in the **Items** table where the **Description** contains two digits followed by **ct** (for example, the first matching record's **Description** is **18ct gold, sapphire and diamond ring**). This query should return 53 matching records, with a mixture of 14ct, 18ct and 22ct gold (**ct** stands for **carat**, a measure of the purity of gold: 24 carat gold is completely pure). Save the query as **qryHighCaratGold**.

7 Relationships & joins I

Introduction

In this chapter we will create some database tables to hold information about a library. We will use **relationships** to describe how the tables relate to one another. Relationships simplify the process of creating queries that consist of several joined tables, and form the basis for referential integrity (which we will cover in Chapter 8).

In this chapter, you will:

 create a simple **drop-down list with fixed values**

 create a **drop-down list with variable values**, obtained by a lookup in the database

 understand and use **one-to-one relationships**

understand and use **one-to-many relationships**

use a junction table to facilitate a **many-to-many relationship**

learn how to **modify existing relationships**

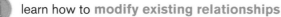 **join data when designing queries**, even where no relationship has been defined between the tables.

Lookups

You are familiar with drop-down lists – they are common in forms on the Internet, and you have been using them to set values while working through this book.

Sometimes it is useful to be able to make a field in a table act as a drop-down list, so that it is easier to set its value. There are two ways of setting the values that can appear: they can be hard-coded into the control, or they can be generated as the result of a **lookup** against a table or query. We will look at both types of drop-down list by creating a simple example.

Suppose that a library wants to keep a record of its books. Let's create two tables: **tblWorks** (to contain details about a published work, such as its author) and **tblBooks** (to contain a record for each physical book that the library owns, each of which will relate to one of the **tblWorks** records).

 Open the database **sandbox.mdb** if it isn't already open.

 Create a new table, called **tblWorks**, using the design in Figure 7.1. Just accept the default properties (not shown) for each field. Make **WorkID** a primary key.

Primary Key

	Field Name	Data Type	Description
🔑	WorkID	AutoNumber	Primary key
	Author	Text	Name of the author
	Title	Text	Title of the work

Figure 7.1: tblWorks design

 Add five records to **tblWorks**, as shown in Figure 7.2. Close the table when you have finished.

	WorkID	Author	Title
	1	Daniel Defoe	Robinson Crusoe
	2	Jane Austen	Pride and Prejudice
	3	H G Wells	The War of the Worlds
	4	Charles Dickens	A Christmas Carol
	5	Lewis Carroll	Alice's Adventures in Wonderland
▶	(AutoNumber)		

Record: |◄| |◄| 6 |▶| |▶I| |▶※| of 6

Figure 7.2: Initial data for tblWorks

 Create a second table, called **tblBooks**, using the design in Figure 7.3.

	Field Name	Data Type	Description
🔑	BookID	AutoNumber	Primary key
	Work	Number	Link to details about this book
	Condition	Text	State of repair of this book

Figure 7.3: tblBooks design

Creating a simple drop-down list

The condition of each book will be classified as **New**, **Good**, **Average** or **Poor**. We can encode this information in the **Condition** field itself.

 Select **Condition** and change the **Display Control** to **Combo Box** in the **Lookup** tab, as shown in Figure 7.4.

 Set the **Row Source Type** to **Value List** and the **Row Source** to **New;Good;Average;Poor**.

 Set **Limit To List** to **Yes**.

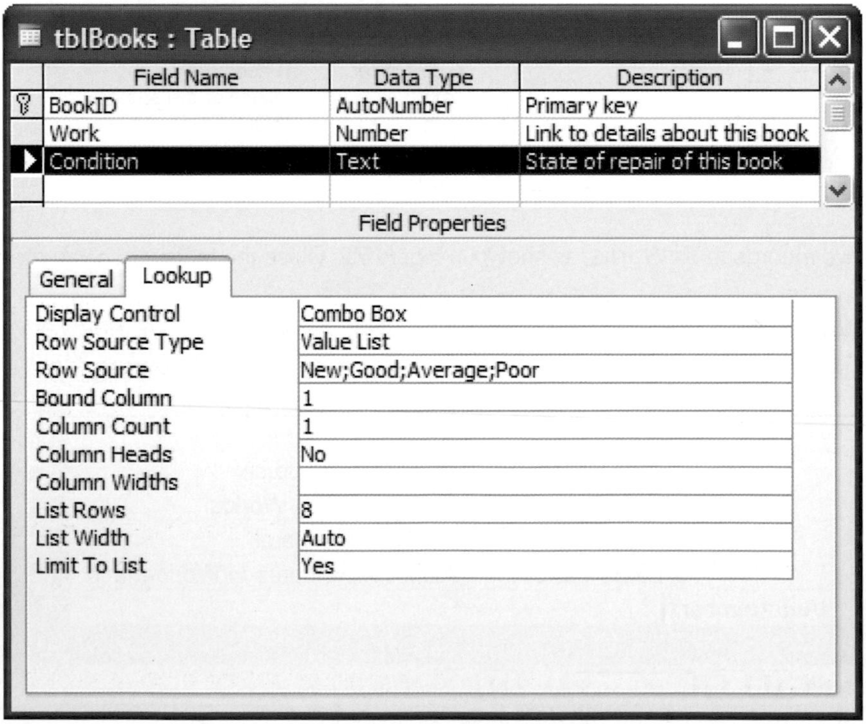

Figure 7.4: Setting a list of possible conditions for a book

Change to **Datasheet** view and test the **Condition** drop-down list as shown in Figure 7.5. **Do not actually select one of the values**, because we do not want to create any records yet – just click on the down arrow to show the choices, and click again to close the list.

Figure 7.5: Testing the simple drop-down list

Creating a lookup

Syllabus ref: AM5.1.1.3
Create, edit a lookup in a field, column.

In **Design** view, select the **Work** field on the **Lookup** tab. Change **Display Control** to **Combo Box**, as shown in Figure 7.6.

Make sure that **Row Source Type** is **Table/Query** and set **Row Source** to **tblWorks**. This tells Access that we want this field to act as a combo box which gets its list of values from the **tblWorks** table.

Make sure that **Bound Column** is **1**. We are linking to the **WorkID** field, which is the first field in **tblWorks**.

Set **Column Count** to **3**. This will allow us to show the user information from any of the first three fields in **tblWorks** – **WorkID**, **Author** and **Title** – even though we are only linking to the **WorkID**.

Make sure that **Column Heads** is **No**. The meaning of the information we will be displaying will be obvious without headings.

Set **Column Widths** to **1cm;0cm;4cm**. These three values give the widths that we wish to allocate to each of the three columns we chose by setting the **Column Count** field. Notice that by setting the second column's width to **0 cm** we will be hiding it completely.

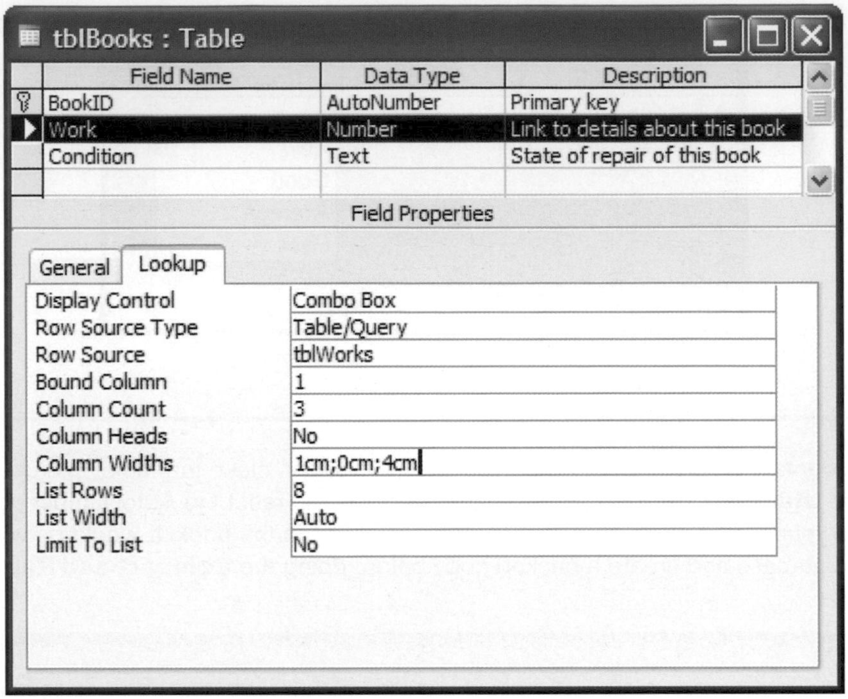

Figure 7.6: Adding a lookup to the Work field

Save the table and switch to **Datasheet** view. Resize the **Work** column until it is approximately three times the width of the **BookID** column.

Test the **Work** lookup by clicking on its arrow, as shown in Figure 7.7. Again, do not select any of the values yet, since it will mess up the AutoNumber field.

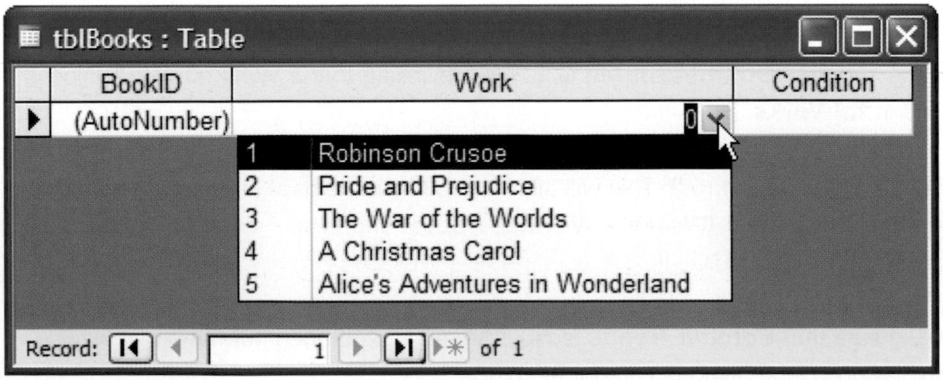

Figure 7.7: Testing the lookup field

Add three records to **tblBooks**, as shown in Figure 7.8.

tblBooks : Table

	BookID	Work	Condition
	1	2	Average
	2	4	Average
▶	3	4	New
*	(AutoNumber)	0	

Record: 3 of 3

Figure 7.8: Adding three records to tblBooks

Note!

In each case the **Work** number in **tblBooks** specifies the **WorkID** of a record in **tblWorks**. This is shown graphically in Figure 7.10.

Try changing the **Work** number for the first book from **2** to **99** by typing in the value. Access accepts this without complaint, even though there is no entry in **tblWorks** with a **WorkID** of **99**. Change the value back to **2** again.

Somehow we need to bind the tables more tightly so that the **Work** values in **tblBooks** must have a corresponding entry in **tblWorks**. We could change the **Limit To List** property of the **Work** field to **Yes**, but this would offer no protection against items being deleted from **tblWorks** and leaving orphaned references in **tblBooks**. To bind the tables more tightly we must declare a **relationship** between them.

Relationships

Syllabus ref: AM5.1.2.1
Understand the basis for creating a valid relationship.

Access, in common with most modern databases, is a **relational database management system** (**RDBMS**). In simple terms, an RDBMS is a database in which the data is stored as tables. Each table stores information about a single subject; in this sense a table is called a **relation**. The way in which two relations are related is called their **relationship**.

Relationships are used to ensure that information is stored in only one place – this is a good thing, since it prevents that information from getting out of sync.

In the example of our library database, we could have chosen just to put everything in a single table, as shown in Figure 7.9.

Author	Title	Condition
Jane Austen	Pride and Prejudice	Average
Charles Dickens	A Christmas Carol	Average
Charles Dickens	A Christmas Carol	New

Figure 7.9: We could have created a single table containing everything

Imagine this with a whole library full of books, and additional fields for other things that we might be interested in: the price we paid, who currently has it out on loan, when it's due back, and so on. This would quickly become difficult to manage, and the data is likely to get out of sync. For example, there would probably end up being a mixture of **Pride <u>and</u> Prejudice** and **Pride <u>&</u> Prejudice** entries.

Instead, we have split the information up into two **relations**, as shown in Figure 7.10.

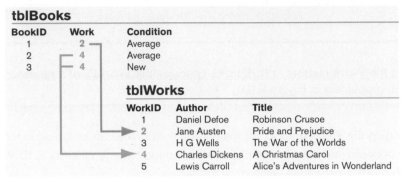

Figure 7.10: Informal relationship between two tables

Note!

Although the data in our tables follows this relationship, we have not yet formally defined the relationship between these two tables. We will do this later (see page 125).

TIP

Related fields must have the same **Data Type** and **Field Size**. The only exception is that you may relate a **Number** (**Long Integer**) field to an **AutoNumber** field.

Some definitions

A **one-to-many relationship** is a link from a unique value (typically a primary key) to zero or more references to it. We can define a one-to-many relationship from **tblWorks::WorkID** to **tblBooks::Work** (and we will – see page 125).

Note!

It may seem from Figure 7.10 that the relationship is really a **many-to-one relationship** from **tblBooks::Work** to **tblWorks::WorkID**. However, many-to-one relationships are always defined as the reverse one-to-many relationship, which is equivalent.

A **one-to-one relationship** links two fields in such a way that each joined value occurs at most once in each table. Suppose the library had a strict policy that they would only ever have one book of each possible type of work (so we would have to remove the third entry in **tblBooks** – see Figure 7.10). Then we could define a **one-to-one relationship** between **tblBooks::Work** and **tblWorks::WorkID**. It would be OK to have records of works for which the library held no books, but the library would not be able to add two entries to **tblBooks** with the same **Work** value.

A **many-to-many relationship** links two fields in such a way that the common value may occur several times on either side of the relationship. This needs special handling, as we will see later (page 128).

Do not worry if all this seems complicated. It should be easier to understand by actually creating an example of each of these types of relationship.

Setting the scene for a one-to-one relationship

Suppose the library needs to record the price it paid for each of the books. We could add an extra **Price** field to **tblBooks**. However, most of the time when dealing with the day-to-day running of the library (for example, when checking out a book that someone is borrowing), the original price paid for the books is not important. Another alternative is to create a new table to hold the prices.

 Create a new table using the design in Figure 7.11. Notice that you must make **Book** a primary key, but it is a **Number** field not an **AutoNumber**.

	Field Name	Data Type	Description
🔑	Book	Number	ID of the book
	Price	Currency	How much this book cost originally

Figure 7.11: Creating a table to hold the prices

Save the table as **tblAccounts** and add the values shown in Figure 7.12.

Book	Price
1	£5.00
2	£4.00
3	£8.00
0	£0.00

Record: |◀ ◀ | 4 ▶ ▶|

Figure 7.12: Prices originally paid for books in the library

It is important to know that we have not yet defined a formal relationship between this table and **tblBooks** – we have just used book numbers that happen to tie up. To see why relationships are useful, let us create a simple cross-table query that lists the condition and purchase price of every book in the library.

Close **tblAccounts**.

Select **Queries** in the **Objects** list of the **Database** window, then double-click **Create query in Design view**.

 In the **Show Table** dialogue box, select **tblBooks** and then press **Add**. Select **tblAccounts** and then press **Add** again. Finally, press **Close**.

 Double-click on the **Condition** and **Price** fields in turn. Each appears in the grid at the bottom of the window, as shown in Figure 7.13.

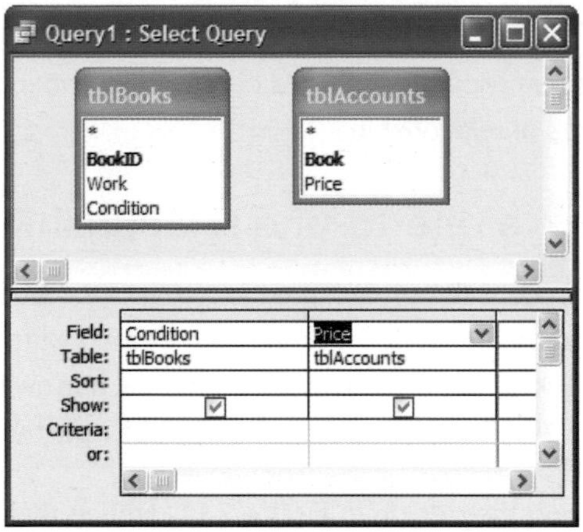

Figure 7.13: Creating a simple cross-table query

Run

 Press the **Run** button on the **Query Design** toolbar. The results shown in Figure 7.14 appear. At first glance these look promising: we wanted a list of condition against price, and that is what we have. However, there are only three books in **tblBooks**, so we should get three results; but we have nine!

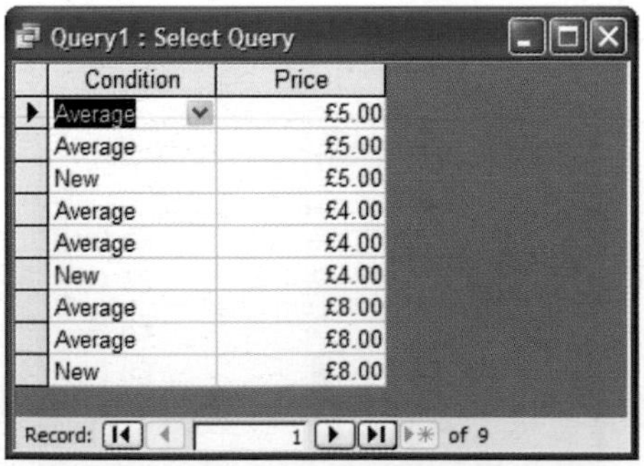

Figure 7.14: Results of querying condition against price, but there is a problem!

What is happening is that Access is creating a permutation of the two sets of data – every **Condition** is being paired with every **Price**. We need to join the tables together using their shared data.

 Switch back to **Design** view.

> **Syllabus ref: AM5.1.2.7**
> Relate/join data when designing queries.

Click on **BookID** and drag it over **Book**, as shown in Figure 7.15. A line appears between the two tables to show which fields are linked.

Drag from here...

...to

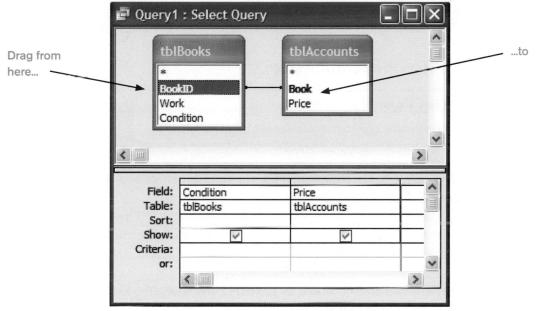

Figure 7.15: Joining two tables in a query

Run the query again. This time the three results we wanted appear, as shown in Figure 7.16.

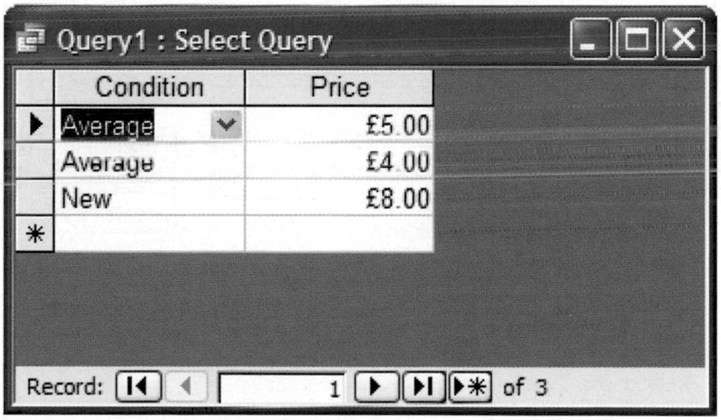

Figure 7.16: Result of running the query with the join

Our query is a success. However, the information that there is a connection between these two tables is stored only in this query.

Close the query without saving it.

Start to create a new query in **Design** view. Again, add the two tables **tblBooks** and **tblAccounts**.

The two tables appear, but the link between them has been lost. Ideally we want the information about how the tables are related to be stored centrally, so that Access can create the joins automatically whenever we construct a query. We can achieve this using **relationships**.

 Having seen that the link does not appear in the new query, close it without saving.

Creating a one-to-one relationship

> **Syllabus ref: AM5.1.2.2**
> Create, modify a one-to-one, one-to-many relationship between tables.

 From the menu, select **Tools**, **Relationships**. The **Relationships** and **Show Table** windows appear.

 Select **tblBooks** and press the **Add** button. Do the same for **tblAccounts**. Press **Close** to dismiss the **Show Table** dialogue box.

 Drag from **BookID** and drop on **Book**, as you did for the query. The **Edit Relationships** dialogue box appears, as shown in Figure 7.17.

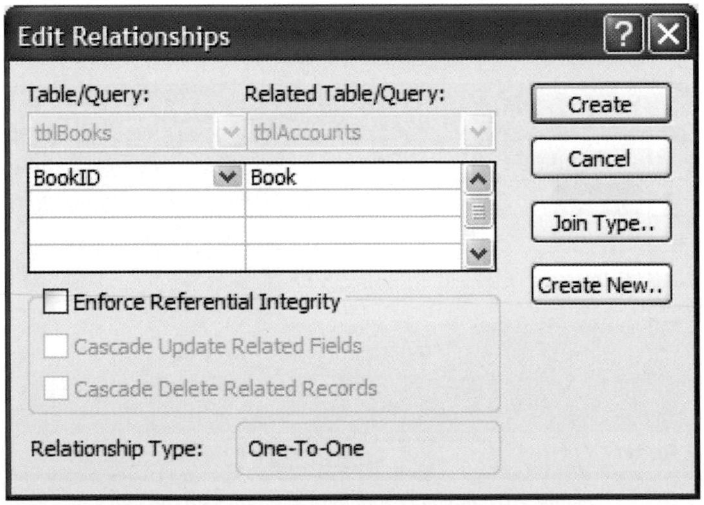

Edit Relationships

Table/Query:	Related Table/Query:
tblBooks	tblAccounts
BookID	Book

☐ Enforce Referential Integrity
☐ Cascade Update Related Fields
☐ Cascade Delete Related Records

Relationship Type: One-To-One

Buttons: Create, Cancel, Join Type.., Create New..

Figure 7.17: Creating a one-to-one relationship

Notice that the **Relationship Type** is set to **One-To-One**, which is what we want. Because both of the joined fields are primary keys, neither table can contain duplicate values, therefore Access knows it must be a one-to-one relationship.

 Press the **Create** button. A line appears in the **Relationships** window, joining **BookID** and **Book**, as shown in Figure 7.18.

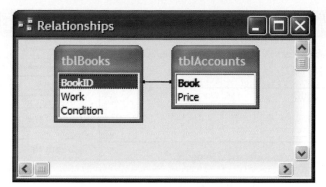

Figure 7.18: A relationship has been created

TIP

You can move the tables around by dragging them with your mouse. The links will reflow to the correct positions. When you close the **Relationships** window, and agree to save, the positions of the tables will be saved. The actual relationships you create are saved automatically as soon as you create them – manual saving is solely concerned with the relative positions of the tables in the **Relationships** window.

 Leave the **Relationships** window open, and again go through the process of designing a new query and adding the **tblBooks** and **tblAccounts** tables. This time you should find that the join is drawn automatically, based on the relationship that you have defined.

 Add the **Condition** and **Price** fields to your query and run it. Check that you get the same results as before (Figure 7.16).

 Save the query as **qryStock**.

Creating a one-to-many relationship

 Select the **Relationships** window.

 From the menu, select **Relationships**, **Show Table** to open the **Show Table** dialogue box. Add **tblWorks** and then close the dialogue box.

 Click **WorkID** and drag and drop it on to **Work**. The **Edit Relationships** dialogue box appears, as shown in Figure 7.19.

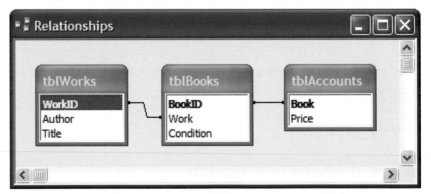

Figure 7.19: Creating a one-to-many relationship

Because **WorkID** is a primary key (and therefore all of its values are unique) but **Work** is not, Access correctly guesses that we are creating a one-to-many relationship.

 Press **Create**. The **Edit Relationship** dialogue box closes and a relationship line appears in the **Relationships** window. You might like to rearrange it as shown in Figure 7.20.

Relationships

tblWorks	tblBooks	tblAccounts
WorkID	**BookID**	**Book**
Author	Work	Price
Title	Condition	

Figure 7.20: A new relationship has been created

 Open **qryStock** in **Design** view. Let's add the book's title to the query.

From the menu, select **Query**, **Show Table**. Use the dialogue box that appears to add **tblWorks** to the query, then close the dialogue box.

Notice that a join is automatically created because of the one-to-many relationship we have defined.

Drag the **Title** field from the **tblWorks** list and drop it on the **Condition** column of the grid. This will insert the **Title** field before the **Condition** field in the query. Figure 7.21 shows this (the three tables have been reordered for clarity).

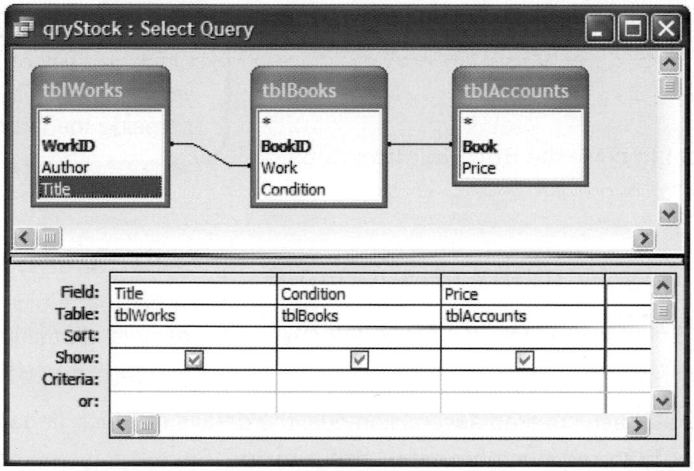

Figure 7.21: Adding the Title field to the query

Run the query. The result should look like Figure 7.22.

Title	Condition	Price
Pride and Prejudice	Average	£5.00
A Christmas Carol	Average	£4.00
A Christmas Carol	New	£8.00

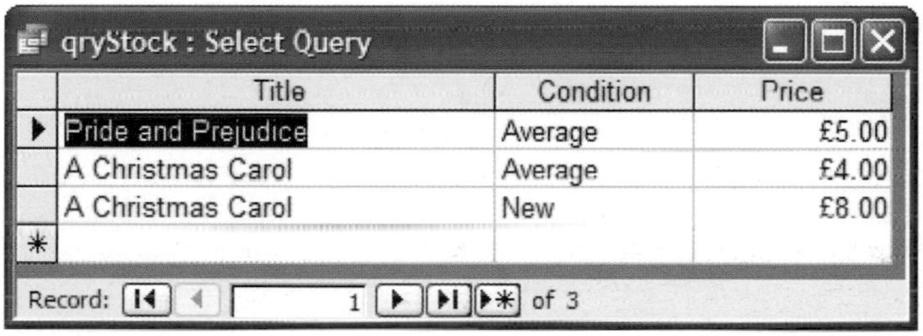

Figure 7.22: The result of running the query with the Title field added

Save and close **qryStock**.

Modifying relationships

Modifying an existing relationship is straightforward.

Click once on the line joining **tblWorks** and **tblBooks** in your **Relationships** window. It should become bold, as shown in Figure 7.23 (b). It can be difficult to get this selection to work: keep clicking until you manage it.

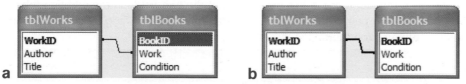

Figure 7.23: The relationship line (a) before and (b) after selecting it

Once the line is selected, choose **Relationships**, **Edit Relationship** from the menu (or double-click the selected line). The **Edit Relationships** dialogue box appears.

You can use this dialogue box to modify the relationship. We will cover referential integrity and join type in the next chapter.

TIP

Once you select a relationship line, you can delete the relationship by pressing the **Delete** key.

 Press **Cancel** to close the **Edit Relationships** dialogue.

Creating a many-to-many relationship

Syllabus ref: AM5.1.2.3
Understand and modify a many-to-many relationship between tables.

Let's start with a traditional example of a many-to-many relationship.

Suppose that this database covered several libraries, the details of which (locations, opening times, and so on) were stored in a table called **tblLibraries**. Each library can hold many works, and each work can exist in many libraries. If you wanted to find out which libraries had copies of a particular work, or to list all of the works held by a particular library, then you would need a many-to-many relationship between the two tables.

tblLibraries	many-to-many	**tblWorks**
LibraryID ←———	? ———→	WorkID
Name		Author
...		Title

Figure 7.24: How can we create this relationship

The missing link is that there is no record of which libraries hold which works. The trick is to add a **junction table** to hold this missing information, as shown in Figure 7.25. The two arrows indicate one-to-many relationships.

tblLibraries	**tblJunction**	**tblWorks**
LibraryID ——→	Library	
Name	Work ←———	WorkID
...		Author
		Title

Figure 7.25: Using a junction table to create a many-to-many relationship

TIP

It is often the case (although not in this example) that the two fields in the junction table are unique when taken as a pair. When this is true, it can be worth defining a primary key on the pair of fields in the junction table.

Note!

You can create relationships between tables even if neither table has a primary key or other unique index on the linked fields. However, you will not be able to turn on referential integrity for the relationship – see Chapter 8, page 144.

We will create a slightly more complicated example of a many-to-many relationship, linking members of the library with the books they have previously borrowed. It's slightly more complicated only because we can put extra information into our junction table.

 Create a new table as shown in Figure 7.26. Notice that **MemberID** is a **Number**, not an **AutoNumber** (see note below). Save the table as **tblMembers**.

	Field Name	Data Type	Description
🔑	MemberID	Number	Primary key
	Name	Text	Name of the member
	Date joined	Date/Time	The date when they became a member of the library

Figure 7.26: New table for members of the library

Add the data shown in Figure 7.27 and then close the table.

Note!

The main reason that **MemberID** is a **Number** field is so that we can change the numbers (you cannot edit an **AutoNumber**). In the next chapter, in the section on referential integrity, we will see what happens when you change an ID that is referred to from another table (see page 144). In a real library database, it may be more convenient to make this an **AutoNumber** field.

tblMembers : Table		
MemberID	Name	Date joined
1	Ahmed Arifi	10/01/2006
2	Ben Baker	12/01/2006
3	Christine Cooper	15/01/2006
0		

Record: ◄ ◄ 4 ► ►► ►* of 4

Figure 7.27: Adding data for tblMembers

Our junction table will need to have two numeric fields: one for the link to the **MemberID** and one for the link to the **BookID**. In effect, the junction table is a record of the library's loans, so we can add some other useful fields: the date the book was lent out, the date the book was due to be returned, and the date it was actually returned.

Create a new table for the loans, as shown in Figure 7.28. Save it as **tblLoans**. Notice that the combination of **Book** and **DateOut** has been made a primary key – the combination is unique if we know that a book cannot be lent out more than once on any given day. (Set this combination as a **joint primary key**: hold down the **Control** key while you click the grey square to the left of each of the two fields, and then press the **Primary Key** icon as usual.)

	Field Name	Data Type	Description
🔑	Book	Number	The book that was loaned
	Member	Number	The person who borrowed it
🔑	DateOut	Date/Time	When they borrowed it
	DateDue	Date/Time	When it was due back
	DateIn	Date/Time	When it was actually returned

Figure 7.28: New (junction) table for the loans

 Add the data shown in Figure 7.29 and then close the table.

Book	Member	DateOut	DateDue	DateIn
1	2	01/02/2006	28/02/2006	20/02/2006
1	3	25/02/2006	20/03/2006	28/02/2006
2	1	28/02/2006	24/03/2006	
1	1	28/02/2006	24/03/2006	
0	0			

Record: 4 of 4

Figure 7.29: Adding data for tblLoans

Use the **Relationships** window to create one-to-many relationships from **tblBooks:: BookID** to **tblLoans::Book** and from **tblLoans::Member** to **tblMembers::MemberID**, as shown in Figure 7.30. (Refer back to page 124 for instructions about adding tables to the **Relationships** window and creating relationships.)

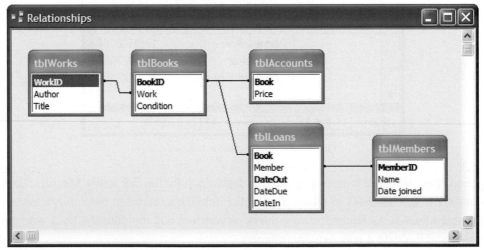

Figure 7.30: Adding relationships for the two new tables

Let's show that these relationships work by creating a simple query to list who has borrowed which works.

Create the query shown in Figure 7.31. The join lines should appear automatically.

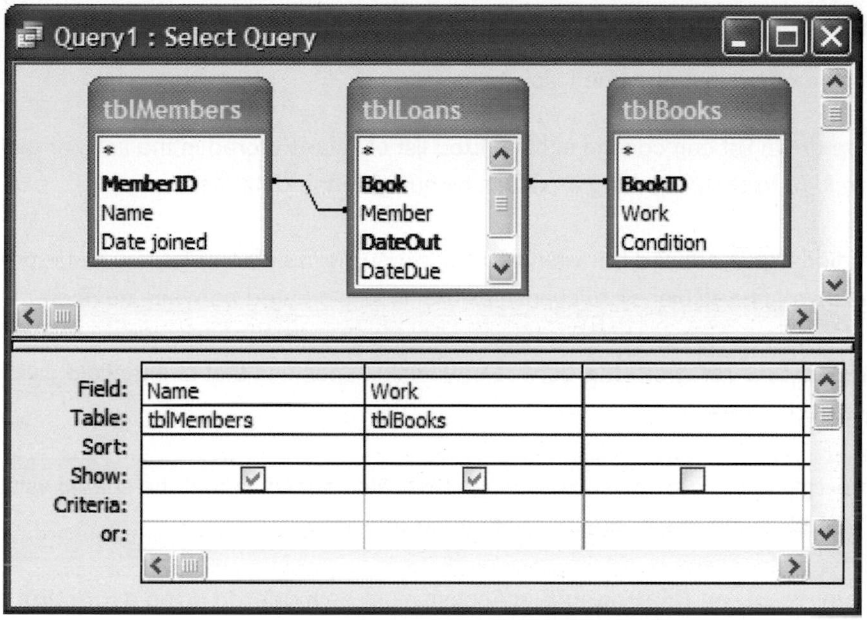

Figure 7.31: Creating a simple many-to-many query

Run the query. You should get the results shown in Figure 7.32.

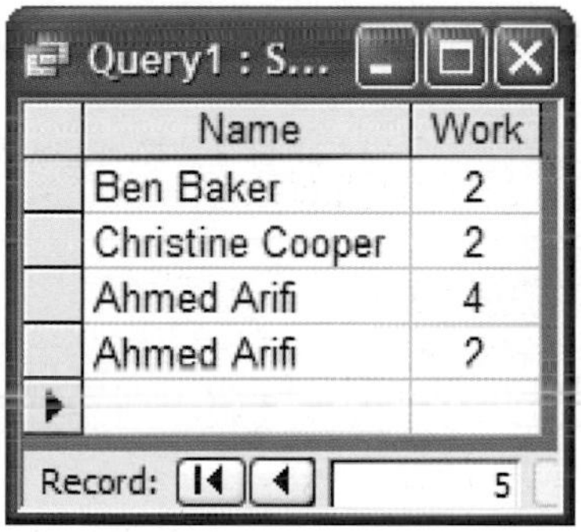

Figure 7.32: Result of running the query

This shows that Ben Baker has borrowed work 2 (Pride and Prejudice), Christine Cooper has also borrowed work 2, and Ahmed Arifi has borrowed both work 4 (A Christmas Carol) and work 2.

Save the query as **qryWhoHasBorrowedWhat**.

Conclusions

This exercise has demonstrated the following points.

 A drop-down list can contain either a fixed list of values stored in the field, or can be dynamic (a **lookup**), getting its values by querying the database.

 A relationship is created between two fields, usually in different tables, that represent the same thing. For efficiency, relationships are usually created between numbers.

 A **one-to-one relationship** between two fields specifies that neither field can hold duplicated values.

 A **one-to-many relationship** between two fields specifies that the shared value can be duplicated on the **many** side but not on the **one** side.

 A **many-to-many relationship** in Access must be modelled using a **junction table** that sits between two one-to-many relationships.

Test yourself

Sandbox database

We chose to store the **Author** as a string in **tblWorks**. If we wanted to store more information about each author then it would make sense to store this information in a separate table. Create a new table **tblAuthors** with **AuthorID**, **First Name** and **Last Name** fields. Add entries to the new table for the authors that are mentioned in **tblWorks**. Change the **Author** field in **tblWorks** to a **Number**, and edit the data to the appropriate **AuthorIDs**.

1 Create an appropriate one-to-many relationship between the **tblAuthors** and **tblWorks** tables.

2 Some books have more than one author. Create a new table called **tblWhoWroteWhat** and use it to allow you to create a many-to-many relationship between **tblAuthors** and **tblWorks**.

Auction database

3 Modify the **Advance Bids** table, changing the **Auction** field to a lookup into the first column of the **Auctions** table, as shown in Figure 7.33.

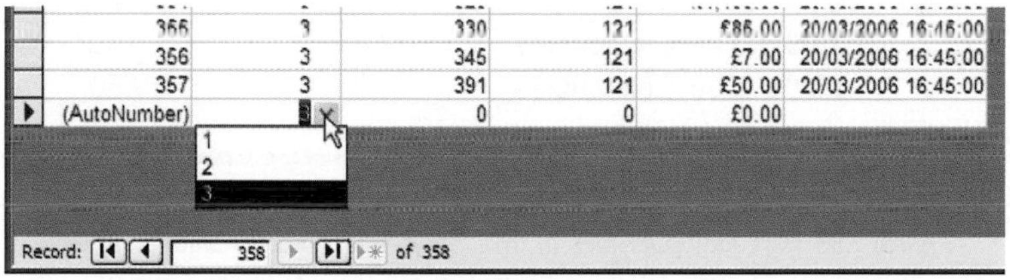

Figure 7.33: The Advance Bids table after completing Exercise 3

4 Modify the **Advance Bids** table again, changing the **Auction** field lookup so that it is still bound to the first column in the **Auctions** table, but actually displays the second column (the date) as shown in Figure 7.34.

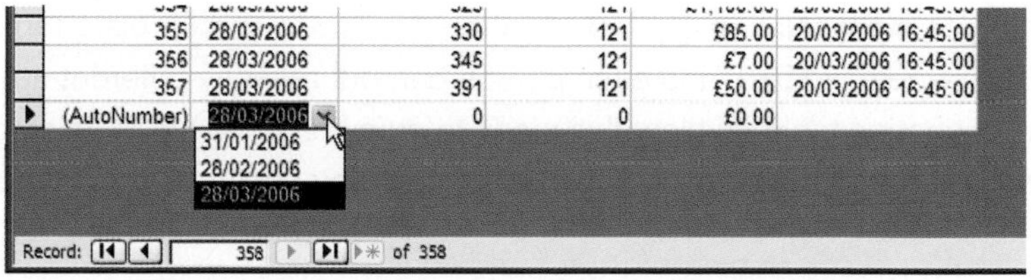

Figure 7.34: The Advance Bids table after completing Exercise 4

5 Create a new query to show sales information for auction catalogues, as shown in Figure 7.35(a). The three tables are not yet related, so you must join them in the query using drag and drop. When you run the query, you should get the results shown in Figure 7.35(b). Save the query as **qryCatalogueSales**.

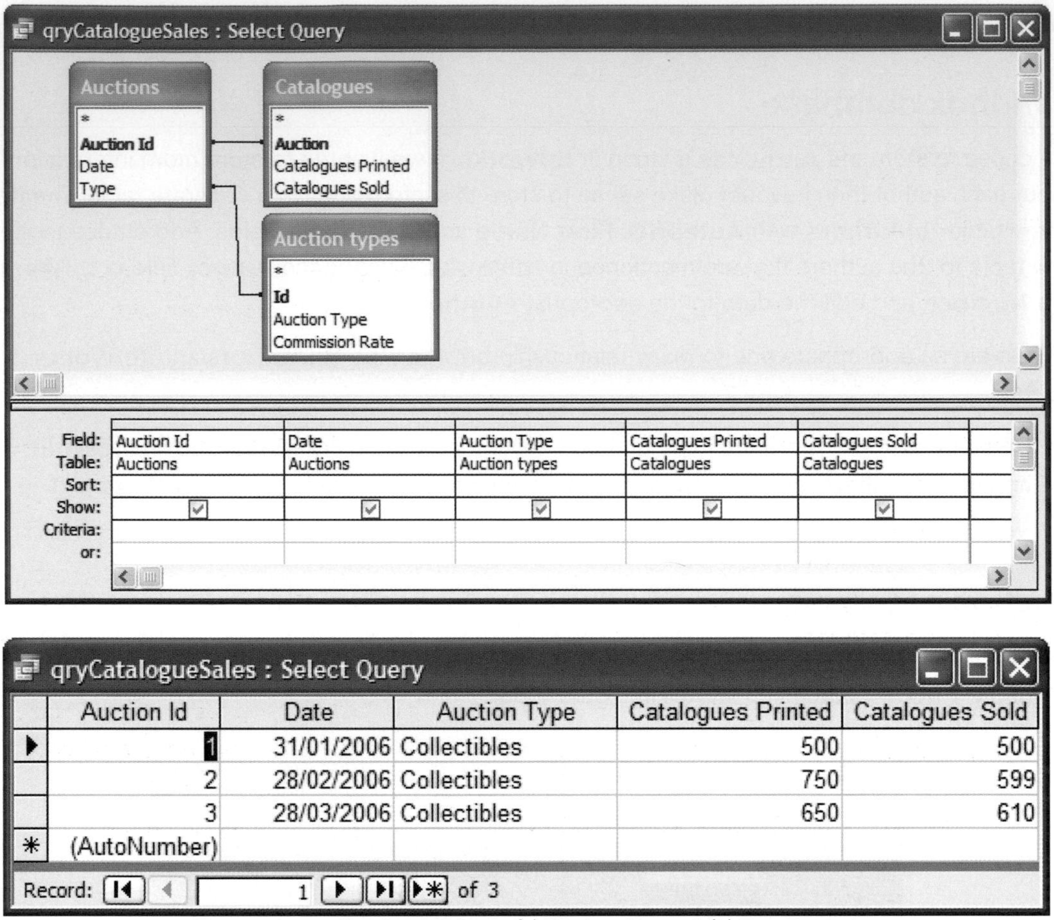

	Auction Id	Date	Auction Type	Catalogues Printed	Catalogues Sold
▶	1	31/01/2006	Collectibles	500	500
	2	28/02/2006	Collectibles	750	599
	3	28/03/2006	Collectibles	650	610
*	(AutoNumber)				

Record: 1 of 3

Figure 7.35: qryCatalogueSales in (a) Design view and (b) Datasheet view

6 Open the **Relationships** window and add the tables **Auction types** and **Catalogues**. Create a **one-to-one** relationship between **Catalogues::Auction** and **Auctions::Auction Id**. Create a **one-to-many** relationship between **Auction types::Id** and **Auctions::Type**. Save the relationships.

7 There is a many-to-many relationship between the **Auctions** and **People** tables: each auction can have many people bidding, and each person can bid at many different auctions. Which table acts as a junction table to allow this many-to-many relationship? Which other joining tables are there in the database, and which many-to-many relationships do they facilitate?

Note!

The relationships have referential integrity turned on (see Chapter 8). For now, all you need to know about this is that symbols on the relationship show you what type it is: a one-to-one relationship has a **1** at each end, and a one-to-many relationship has a **1** at the **one** end and an **infinity symbol** at the **many** end.

8 Relationships & joins II

Introduction

In this chapter we will look at join types and referential integrity.

We will use a simple example of people's favourite types of music to show the difference between an **inner join**, a **left outer join** and a **right outer join**. Then we will use the Royal Family's family tree to provide an example as to where a **self join** is necessary.

Then we will return to the library example we started in the previous chapter, experimenting with the various options provided by **referential integrity** to enforce the consistency of data between related tables.

In this chapter, you will:

i create a query that uses an **inner join** between two tables (only records with shared values in both tables will appear in the results)

i create a query that uses **outer joins** between two tables (the query will return all of the records from one of the tables, and any records with matching values from the other table)

i create a query that uses **self joins** to traverse a more complicated data structure – a family tree

i use **referential integrity** to enforce consistency of data between related tables

i create a query that returns **unmatched values** between two tables

i use **Cascade Update Related Fields** to flow data changes between related tables

i use **Cascade Delete Related Records** to enforce consistency by deleting all of the records that reference a record when that record is deleted.

Joins

We used joins in the previous chapter. A join is the link in a query that controls how two or more tables are related to one another. A join is created automatically for any relationships that have already been defined.

There are several different types of join. We'll put together a couple of straightforward examples to demonstrate the differences between them.

Preparing the first example: Music Fans

For the first example we will create two tables. The first will hold a list of music styles, and the second will pair people together with their favourite styles of music.

 Open your database **sandbox.mdb** if it is not already open.

 Use the **Create table by entering data** option to create the table shown in Figure 8.1.

> **TIP**
>
> Remember that you can double-click the column headings to set their names.

	Style	Name
	1	Pop
	2	Rock
	3	Blues
	4	Jazz
	5	Rap
	6	Reggae
	7	Country
	8	Soul
	9	Classical
▶	10	Zydeco

Figure 8.1: Table listing music styles

 Save the table as **tblMusicStyles** without assigning a primary key. Close the new table.

 Use the same option to create the table shown in Figure 8.2. Leave the **Favourite Music** for **Fiona** blank (she doesn't like any type of music). Save the table as **tblMusicFans** without assigning a primary key. Close the new table.

tblMusicFans : Table

Person	Favourite Music
Andy	4
Betty	8
Charles	2
Dianne	2
Ed	9
Fiona	

Record: 6

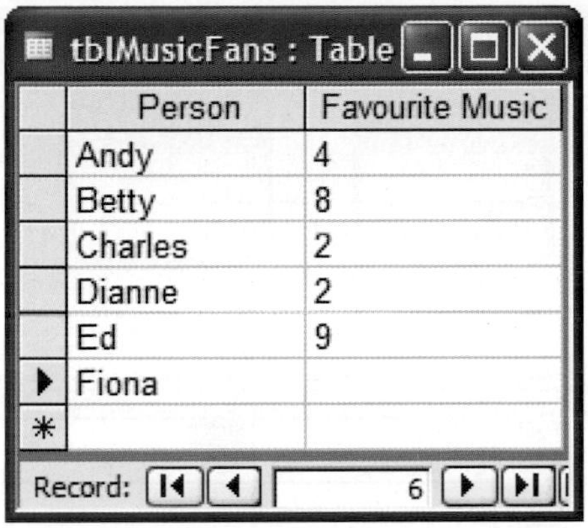

Figure 8.2: Table pairing people with their favourite types of music

The **Favourite Music** column refers to the **Style** number in the other table. Therefore Andy's favourite music is Jazz, and so on down the list.

Notice that not every person has a favourite style of music, and not every style of music is someone's favourite. This is the sort of situation in which different types of join can be useful.

Inner join

A query using an inner join between two tables will display those results where the joined field has a shared value in both of the tables. It will skip any records with values in this field that do not appear in the other table. This is the default type of join (which you have already used).

- Create a new query in **Design** view. Choose to display the **tblMusicFans** and **tblMusicStyles** tables.

- Click and drag from **tblMusicFans::Favourite Music** to **tblMusicStyles::Style** to create an inner join between these two fields.

- Double-click **tblMusicFans::Person** and **tblMusicStyles::Name** in turn to add these two fields to the query, as shown in Figure 8.3.

Figure 8.3: Creating a query with a standard join

Run

 Run the query. You should get the results shown in Figure 8.4.

Figure 8.4: Result of running the query

This is a useful query for finding out who likes which style of music. Notice, however, that wherever there is not a perfectly matched pair (that is, for any values in either table that do not have a corresponding value in the other table) then nothing appears in the results.

Save the query as **qryMusicInnerJoin**.

Left outer joins

An **outer join** will return all of the records from one of the tables (let's call this the main table) and all of the matching values from the other table (the subsidiary table). Null values are returned for fields from the subsidiary table for records that exist only in the master table.

A **left outer join** has the master table first and the subsidiary table second; a **right outer join** has the tables the other way round. The following examples should make this clear.

> **Syllabus ref: AM5.1.2.4**
> Apply inner, outer and self joins.

Change the query back into **Design** view.

Click the join line to select it (it should go bold), then double-click it. The **Join Properties** dialogue box appears.

Select option **2**, as shown in Figure 8.5, then press **OK**.

Figure 8.5: Changing the type of a join

As explained in the dialogue box, join type **2** includes all of the records from the first table, whether or not there are any matching records in the second table. This is a **left outer join**, although the dialogue doesn't call it this directly. Notice that the join has changed to show an arrow pointing from the first to the second table, as shown in Figure 8.6.

Options **1**, **2** and **3** are **inner joins**, **left outer joins** and **right outer joins** respectively.

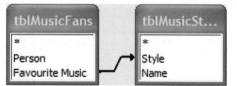

Figure 8.6: Left outer join displayed as an arrow

From the menu, select **File**, **Save As**. Save the modified query as **qryMusicLeftOuterJoin**.

Run the query. The result should look like Figure 8.7.

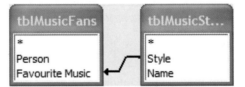

Figure 8.7: Result of running the query with a left outer join

Notice that Fiona has appeared in the list, even though she does not have a favourite style of music.

Right outer joins

A right outer join, as you might expect, will show all of the records from the second table even if they do not have matching records in the first table. Let's modify the query again.

 Edit the query, changing the join to type **3**: a right outer join. The arrow changes direction, as shown in Figure 8.8.

Figure 8.8: Right outer join displayed as an arrow

 Use **File, Save As** to save the modified query as **qryMusicRightOuterJoin**.

 Run the modified query. The result should look like Figure 8.9.

Figure 8.9: Result of running the query with a right outer join

Every style of music appears at least once, even if nobody has chosen it as their favourite. Fiona is no longer in the results because these are now 'driven' by the right-hand table, and she does not have a favourite type of music so no entry in the right-hand table refers back to her. Dianne and Charles are both in the results, even though they both like the same type of music.

Self joins

A **self join** can be useful when you need to extract information from a set of data that refers back to itself: typically a tree or web structure. We will use the Royal Family's family tree to show how this works.

 Using the **Create table by entering data** option, create the table shown in Figure 8.10. Save it as **tblRoyalFamily** without assigning a primary key (which would add an extra column).

ID	Name	Mother	Father
1	Elizabeth		
2	Philip		
3	Charles	1	2
4	Diana		
5	Anne	1	2
6	Mark		
7	Andrew	1	2
8	Sarah		
9	Edward	1	2
10	Sophie		
11	William	4	3
12	Harry	4	3
13	Peter	5	6
14	Zara	5	6
15	Beatrice	8	7
16	Eugenie	8	7
17	Louise	10	9

Record: [◄◄] [◄] 17 [►] [►►] [►*] of 17

Figure 8.10: Royal Family's family tree

 Switch to **Design** view and now make **ID** a primary key. This is good practice, since the tree-like structure means that there will be lots of lookups against the **ID** field.

 Save and close the table.

Let's create a query that lists the mothers and fathers of the members of the Royal Family. We will need to use two self joins for this.

 Use **Create query in Design view** to create a new query. Use the **Show Table** dialogue box to add the table **tblRoyalFamily** to the query three times. Resize the table windows at the top so that you can see their full names. Initially, the query should look like Figure 8.11.

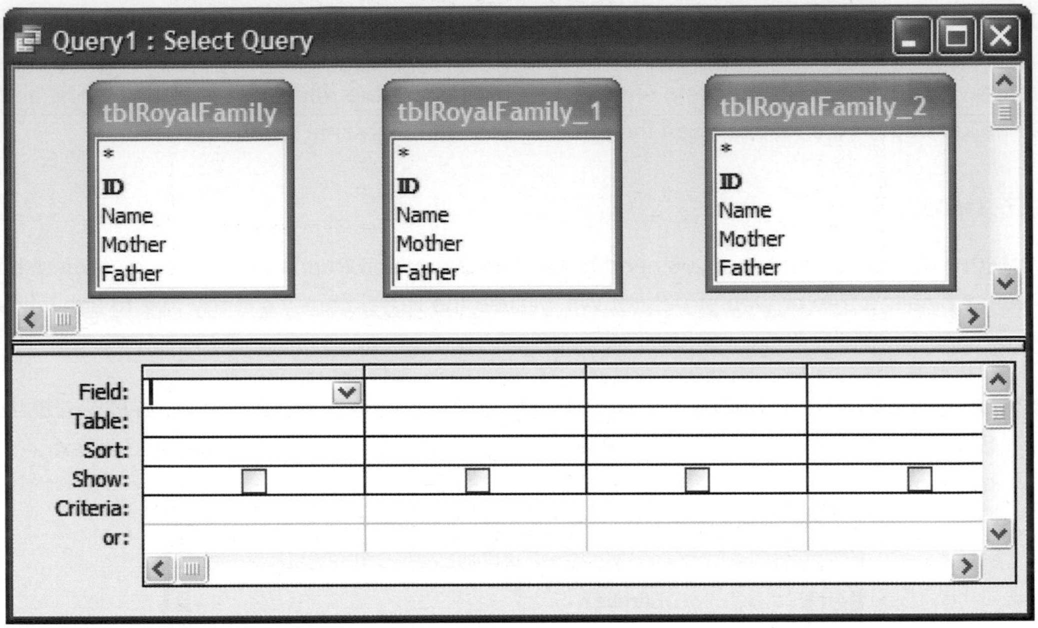

Figure 8.11: The starting point for a query using self joins

Click on the horizontal dividing line that runs across the middle of the window and drag it down so that the top portion is about twice its original height. You may need to resize the whole window so that you can still see the grid.

Arrange the three tables as shown in Figure 8.12. The main table is at the bottom, with the two top tables representing that person's mother and father. Create links from the **Mother** and **Father** fields of the main table to the **ID** fields of the other two tables, as shown in Figure 8.12.

Double-click on the **Name** field from the bottom table to add it to the query. Do the same with the **Name** field from the left-hand and right-hand table, in that order. Manually edit the top row of the grid to rename the second and third columns **Mother Is** and **Father Is** using colons to separate the names from the fields, as shown in Figure 8.12 (which should then match your query).

> **TIP**
>
> It is useful to be able to change the name of a column without affecting the field in any way. This is exactly what this syntax does – just add the new name followed by a colon, before the field name.

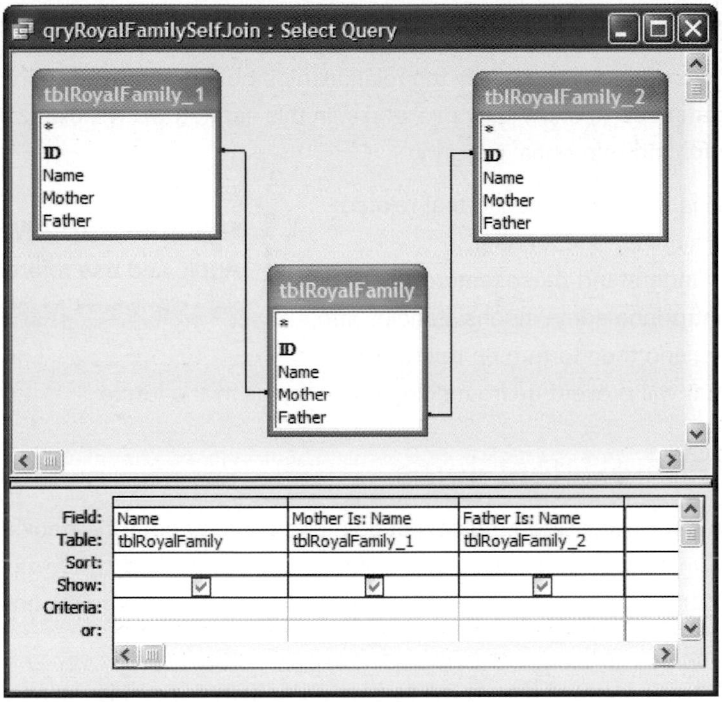

Figure 8.12: Adding self joins to the table

Run the query. You should get the results shown in Figure 8.13.

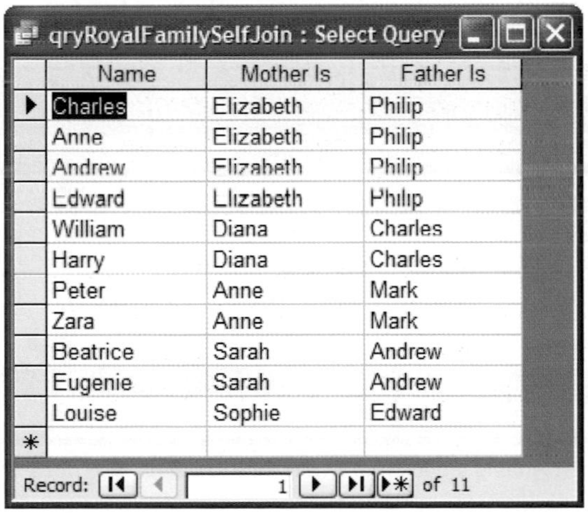
qryRoyalFamilySelfJoin : Select Query

Name	Mother Is	Father Is
Charles	Elizabeth	Philip
Anne	Elizabeth	Philip
Andrew	Elizabeth	Philip
Edward	Elizabeth	Philip
William	Diana	Charles
Harry	Diana	Charles
Peter	Anne	Mark
Zara	Anne	Mark
Beatrice	Sarah	Andrew
Eugenie	Sarah	Andrew
Louise	Sophie	Edward

Record: 1 of 11

Figure 8.13: Result of running the query – mother and father names are listed

Save the query as **qryRoyalFamilySelfJoin**.

Referential integrity

In the last chapter we saw how to specify the relationships between tables. Remember that we used a library database to show how this works. In this section we will extend the power of relationships by enforcing referential integrity.

Referential integrity is a way of ensuring that related tables are kept in sync with one another. The easiest way to understand these features is to deliberately try to introduce some inconsistencies into the library database, and then to turn on referential integrity features that will prevent us from doing these things in the future.

> **Syllabus ref: AM5.1.2.5**
> Apply and use referential integrity.

Referencing non-existent items

Remember that we have two related tables that hold information about the books themselves: **tblWorks** lists information about books that the library might have, and **tblBooks** lists the actual physical volumes that it holds on its shelves. We created a one-to-many relationship between **tblWorks** and **tblBooks**.

Every record in **tblBooks** should have a link to a record in **tblWorks**. However, at present it is possible to add a book before the work record has been created, as we will demonstrate.

There are only five works listed in **tblWorks**. Add a new record to **tblBooks** with a reference to the non-existent work **6**, as shown in Figure 8.14.

	BookID	Work	Condition
+	1	2	Average
+	2	4	Average
+	3	4	New
+	4	6	New
	(AutoNumber)	0	

Record: 5 of 5

Figure 8.14: Adding a book with a reference to a work that does not exist

Remember that we created a query to list all of the books owned by the library. Let's run this again now.

Run **qryStock**. Even though there are now four books in the library, the query only reports three of them, as shown in Figure 8.15. This is because **qryStock** uses an **inner join**, and the fourth book has no corresponding work.

qryStock : Select Query		
Title	**Condition**	**Price**
▶ Pride and Prejudice	Average	£5.00
A Christmas Carol	Average	£4.00
A Christmas Carol	New	£8.00
＊		

Record: ◄◄ ◄   1   ► ►► ►＊ of 3

Figure 8.15: The new book does not appear in the query results

 Close the query.

We really want to prevent people adding books to the database until the work has been added. We can use referential integrity to enforce this.

 Select **Tools**, **Relationships** to display the **Relationships** window.

Click the relationship between **tblWorks** and **tblBooks** to select it, and then double-click it to display the **Edit Relationships** dialogue box.

Tick the **Enforce Referential Integrity** box, as shown in Figure 8.16.

Edit Relationships   [?][X]

Table/Query:	Related Table/Query:	
tblWorks ⌄	tblBooks ⌄	OK
WorkID ⌄	Work ⌃	Cancel
		Join Type..
	⌄	Create New..

☑ Enforce Referential Integrity
☐ Cascade Update Related Fields
☐ Cascade Delete Related Records

Relationship Type: One-To-Many

Figure 8.16: Trying to enforce referential integrity

 Press **OK**. Oops – we have a problem! The error message shown in Figure 8.17 appears.

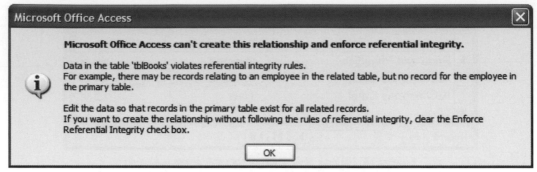

Figure 8.17: Access cannot enforce referential integrity

The reason that Access cannot enforce referential integrity is that we deliberately broke it when we created a record in **tblBooks** without a corresponding record in **tblWorks**. We will have to fix the existing referential integrity before we can get Access to enforce it for us.

 Press **OK** to close the error dialogue box.

Press **Cancel** to close the **Edit Relationships** dialogue box.

We happen to know where the problem lies in this case, but in a real-life situation we would probably have to construct a query to find out. Let's do that anyway, since it's a convenient point to find out how this is done.

> **Syllabus ref: AM5.2.3.2**
> Show unmatched values.

(You are feeling sleepy, very sleepy. Clear your mind. You've forgotten which book does not have a matching work!) It's lucky that Access has a wizard that you can use to find unmatched values.

New

 Make sure you are in the **Queries** section of the **Database** window and then press the **New** button at the top of the **Database** window. The **New Query** dialogue box opens.

>
>
> The **Find Unmatched Query Wizard** may not be available if your copy of Access was installed with the **Typical Wizards** option (see page 10). If this is the case, Access will ask you to insert the Microsoft Office CD-ROM to install the wizard.

Select **Find Unmatched Query Wizard**, as shown in Figure 8.18, and press **OK**. The **Find Unmatched Query Wizard** appears.

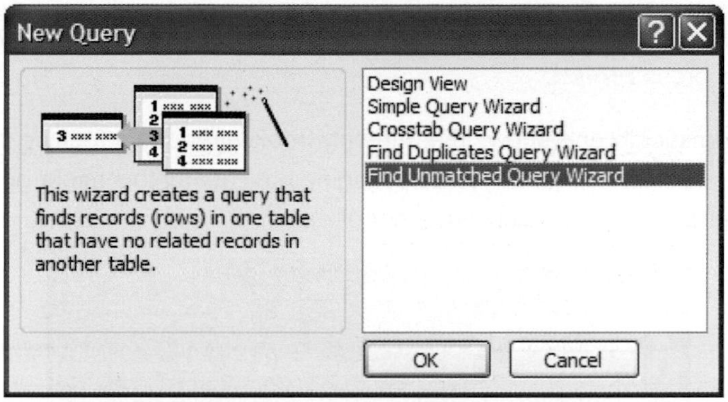

Figure 8.18: Creating a new query using a wizard

We need to select the two linked tables. The order is important: first we must select the 'from' table (in this case **tblBooks**) and then the 'to' table (**tblWorks**).

 Select **Table: tblBooks** and then press **Next**. This is the 'from' table.

 Select **Table: tblWorks** and then press **Next**. This is the 'to' table – the one that contains the related records.

 Because we have set up a relationship between these two tables, Access already knows what piece of information is in both tables (**Work** and **WorkID**). Press **Next**.

 With **BookID** selected, press **>** to move it into the **Selected fields** box, as shown in Figure 8.19. Because the IDs are unique, this will be sufficient for us to identify the problem record(s). Press **Next**.

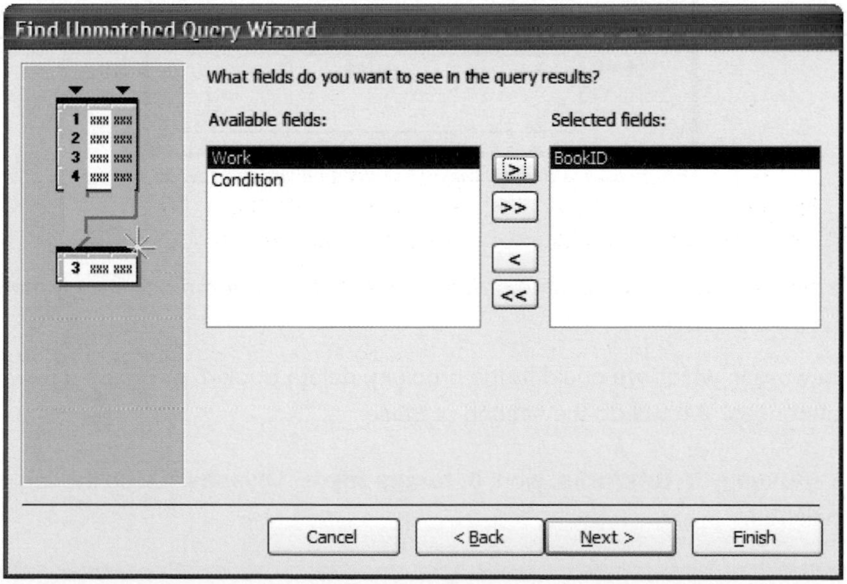

Figure 8.19: Choosing a field to display in the query

147

Change the query name to **qryBooksWithoutWorks**, to be in keeping with our other queries, then press **Finish**.

The query runs automatically and shows that the only book without a matching work is book **4** (Figure 8.20). Well, we knew that, but you can imagine how useful this might be if you wanted to find record mismatches across a much larger set of data.

Figure 8.20: Result of running the query – book 4 has no matching work

For the inquisitive reader, Figure 8.21 shows what this query looks like in **Design** view. Notice that there is a **left outer join** between the tables, and the **Criteria** for **WorkID** is **Is Null**.

Figure 8.21: What the wizard has done behind the scenes

 Close the query.

(*Click! Wide awake now. Of course, the problem was that book 4 did not have a matching work. You knew that all the time.*)

There are two ways in which we could fix the problem: delete book 4, or create a new record for the work it references. We will do the second of these.

 Add a sixth entry to **tblWorks**: work **6**, **James Joyce**, **Ulysses**. Close the table when you have finished.

 Run **qryBooksWithoutWorks** again. This time there should be no results returned.

Now we can try again to enforce referential integrity.

 Back in the **Relationships** window, highlight the link between **tblWorks** and **tblBooks** and then double-click on it.

 Tick the **Enforce Referential Integrity** box (but not the others – we will cover these next) and press **OK**.

This time it works! Notice that the style of the relationship has changed (Figure 8.22), with **1** and **infinity** symbols showing that this is a one-to-many relationship with referential integrity enforcement.

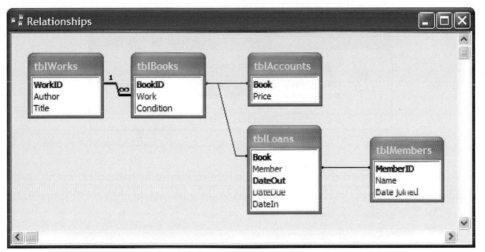

Figure 8.22: Updated relationships diagram

So, what does this mean? All of the records in **tblBooks** must refer to an existing record in **tblWorks**.

Referential integrity at the relationship source

 Open **tblBooks** and try to change the **Work** for the last book from **6** to **7**, which does not exist in **tblWorks**. You will be able to type in the **7** (of course, it does not appear in the drop-down list), but as soon as you click on a different record you should get the error message shown in Figure 8.23.

Figure 8.23: Error when trying to break referential integrity

 Press the **OK** button and then press the **Escape** key to undo the edit. You should now be able to move to another record.

Referential integrity at the relationship target

There are also some restrictions about what you will now be able to do at the other end of the relationship.

 Close **tblBooks** and open **tblWorks**.

Click in the grey box to the left of the first data row (the row with a **WorkID** of **1**) and press the **Delete** key. The confirmation dialogue box from Figure 8.24 appears – Access is quite happy to let you delete this record because none of the records in **tblBooks** refer to this work.
Press **No** to cancel the deletion.

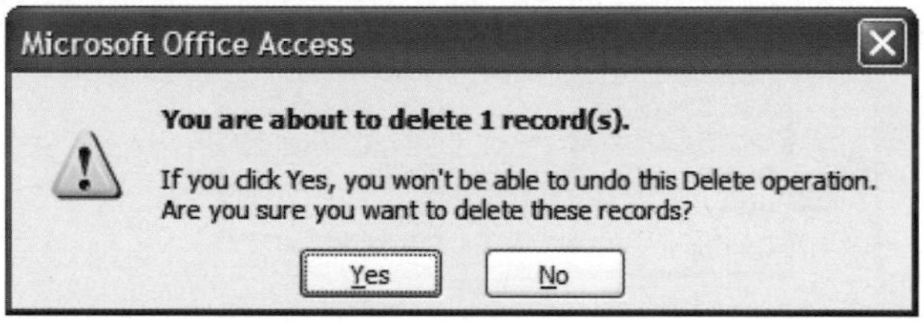

Figure 8.24: Access will let you delete a record if it is not linked to

Try to delete the second data row (which is referred to from **tblBooks**) in the same way. This time you could not proceed – you get the error message shown in Figure 8.25. Press **OK** to dismiss the dialogue.

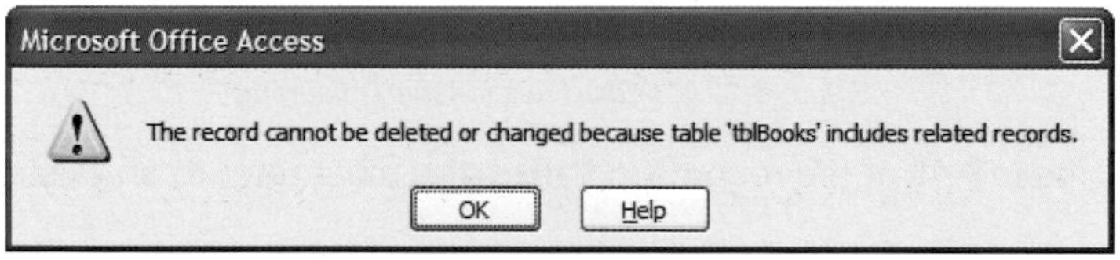

Figure 8.25: Access will not let you delete a record if it is linked to

Note!

WorkID is an AutoNumber, so you cannot modify it anyway. If it were a plain number then you would find that you could not change any values that were referenced from elsewhere (for example, **2**) but you could change the others (for example, you could change **1** to **7**).

We do have one relationship in our database that does not involve an AutoNumber: the link between **tblLoans::Member** and **tblMembers::MemberID**. Let's enforce referential integrity for this relationship and then see what happens when we try to change the **MemberID** values.

Enforce the referential integrity of the link between **tblLoans::Member** and **tblMembers::MemberID** as before. It should work because all of the loan records refer to valid members. The **1** and **infinity** symbols appear on the new link.

As the database currently stands, all of the members have borrowed at least one book, as shown in Figure 8.26 (there are only three members).

Figure 8.26: The tblLoans table as it currently stands

Let's add a new member. Suppose Danny Davis joined on 20/01/2006.

 Add the new record to **tblMembers**. Afterwards, the table should look like Figure 8.27.

		MemberID	Name	Date joined
	+	1	Ahmed Arifi	10/01/2006
	+	2	Ben Baker	12/01/2006
	+	3	Christine Cooper	15/01/2006
	+	4	Danny Davis	20/01/2006
▶		0		

Record: 5 of 5

Figure 8.27: The tblMembers table with the new member

We have already seen that you cannot delete a record that is referred to elsewhere via a relationship with enforced referential integrity. In other words, we could delete the record for the new member (since Danny Davis has never borrowed any books) but we could not delete any of the other three records.

 Change the **MemberID** for **Danny Davis** from **4** to **5** and select a different record to commit the change. Access makes no complaint about this.

 Change the **MemberID** for **Christine Cooper** from **3** to **6** and select a different record to commit the change. This time, the same error message we saw when we tried to delete a referenced record (Figure 8.25) appears.

 Press **OK** to dismiss the dialogue box and press the **Escape** key to undo the edit. Now you should be able to select a different record.

This behaviour is good, since it prevents us from leaving a 'dangling reference' in the **tblLoans** table – the **3** there would no longer refer to Christine Cooper. An alternative approach is to get Access to change both tables at the same time. This is easy to set up.

 Close all open tables.

Edit the relationship between **tblMembers::MemberID** and **tblLoans::Member** again. This time, tick the **Cascade Update Related Fields** box, as shown in Figure 8.28. Press **OK** to confirm the change.

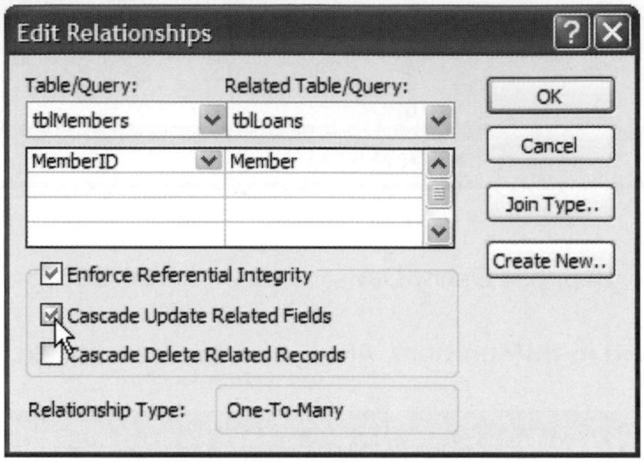

Figure 8.28: Cascading updated fields

Open both **tblMembers** and **tblLoans** and resize and arrange them so that you can see both on the screen at the same time.

Take note of the second row of the **tblLoans** table references member **3** – Christine Cooper. Keep your eye on this as you perform the following step.

Change the **MemberID** for **Christine Cooper** from **3** to **6**, as before. Change to a different row to commit the change. This time there is no complaint. Access has changed both tables together see (Figure 8.29) so the potential corruption has been avoided.

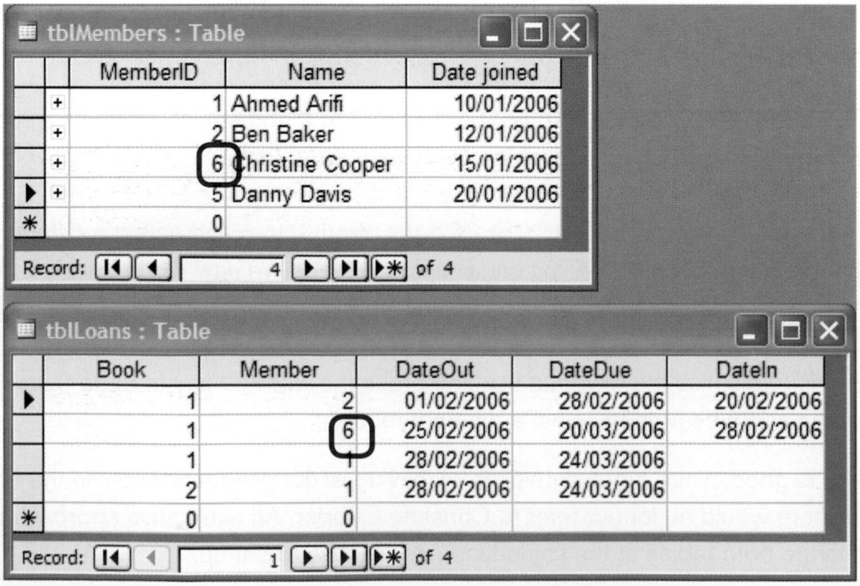

Figure 8.29: Access has cascaded the change between tables

You probably noticed a third checkbox on the **Edit Relationships** dialogue box: **Cascade Delete Related Records**. This works in much the same way as the cascaded update we have just demonstrated, but is more destructive!

 Close both tables (you cannot update relationships for open tables).

> **Syllabus ref: AM5.1.2.6**
> Apply automatic deletion of related records.

Edit the relationship again, and this time tick the **Cascade Delete Related Records** box (there is no need to deselect **Cascade Update Related Fields**).

Open both tables and again arrange them so that you can see both of them.

Click in the grey box to the left of the **tblMembers** record for **Christine Cooper**, to select the whole row. (Since the renumbering, this will be the bottom non-empty row.) Press the **Delete** key.

The dialogue box shown in Figure 8.30 appears, warning us that this delete will affect other tables as well.

Microsoft Office Access ☒

⚠ **Relationships that specify cascading deletes are about to cause 1 record(s) in this table and in related tables to be deleted.**

Are you sure you want to delete these records?

[Yes] [No] [Help]

Figure 8.30: Warning about cascaded delete

Press **Yes**. The warning dialogue box closes and the record for Christine Cooper is deleted from **tblMembers**. More interesting is the fact that the related record in **tblLoans** is also deleted, as shown in Figure 8.31.

tblLoans : Table

	Book	Member	DateOut	DateDue	DateIn
▶	1	2	01/02/2006	28/02/2006	20/02/2006
	#Deleted	#Deleted	#Deleted	#Deleted	#Deleted
	1	1	28/02/2006	24/03/2006	
	2	1	28/02/2006	24/03/2006	
✱	0	0			

Record: ◄◄ ◄ 1 ► ►► ►✱ of 4

Figure 8.31: The corresponding record in tblLoans has been deleted

Close and re-open **tblLoans**. Confirm that there are now only three records in the table.

Close your **Relationships** window, saving if prompted.

153

Note!

Something to be aware of if you create very large, complex databases in Access: Access imposes a limit of 32 indexes per table. Each relationship with enforced referential integrity creates an extra index in each of the tables involved; these do count towards the overall limit.

Conclusions

This exercise has demonstrated the following points.

 If a query uses an **inner join** between two tables, it will return only those records for which a shared value is present in both tables.

 If a query uses an **outer join** then it will return all of the records from one of the tables, and all of the matching records from the other table. A **left outer join** returns all of the records from the left-hand table in the join and a **right outer join** returns all of the records from the right-hand table.

 You can use **self joins** in queries on structured data that references itself, such as a tree or a web that has been flattened into a single table.

 When **referential integrity** is enforced on a **one-to-one** relationship, you cannot add a value to the right-hand table in the relationship unless it already exists in the left-hand table (although note that we didn't actually cover this scenario).

When **referential integrity** is enforced on a **one-to-many** relationship, you cannot add a value at the **many** end of the relationship until that value has been created at the **one** end and you cannot change or delete values that are referred to from elsewhere (unless you enable the Cascade options).

You can use **Cascade Update Related Fields** to flow data changes between related tables. Access warns you before completing the update.

You can use **Cascade Delete Related Records** to enforce consistency by deleting all of the records that reference a record when that record is deleted. Access warns you before completing the deletion.

Test yourself

Auction database

1   At present there are three entries in the **Auctions** table that tie up with three entries in the
    Catalogues table. Create a query, using an **inner join**, which shows the **Auction Id**, **Date**,
    Catalogues Printed and **Catalogues Sold** for the three auctions, as shown in Figure 8.32.
    Save the query as **qryAuctionCatalogues**.

Auction Id	Date	Catalogues Printed	Catalogues Sold
1	31/01/2006	500	500
2	28/02/2006	750	599
3	28/03/2006	650	610
(AutoNumber)			

Figure 8.32: A simple query using an inner join

2   Change the **Catalogues** table, editing the record for auction **1** so that it says **4** instead.
    How many results would you expect **qryAuctionCatalogues** to return now? Run it again
    to see if you are right (there should be two results, relating to auctions 2 and 3).

3   Edit the properties of the join in the query, making it an **outer join** that returns all of the
    records from **Auctions**. Run your query again: it should now look like Figure 8.33.

Auction Id	Date	Catalogues Printed	Catalogues Sold
1	31/01/2006		
2	28/02/2006	750	599
3	28/03/2006	650	610
(AutoNumber)			

*Figure 8.33: An outer join showing all of the records from the Auctions table, whether
or not they have matching entries in the Catalogues table*

4   Edit the properties of the join again, this time so that it becomes an **outer join** that returns all of the records from the **Catalogues** table. Run your query again: it should now look like Figure 8.34.

Figure 8.34: An outer join showing all of the records from the Catalogues table, whether or not they have matching entries in the Auctions table

5   Some of the items in the auction do not sell, either because there are no bids at all or because they fail to reach their reserve price. Use a **self join** to create a query to list those items that did not sell in the first auction they were entered into, but have sold at a later auction. Figure 8.35 shows both the design and the expected results (two items have sold after originally failing to sell). Save the query as **qryRelistedSales**.

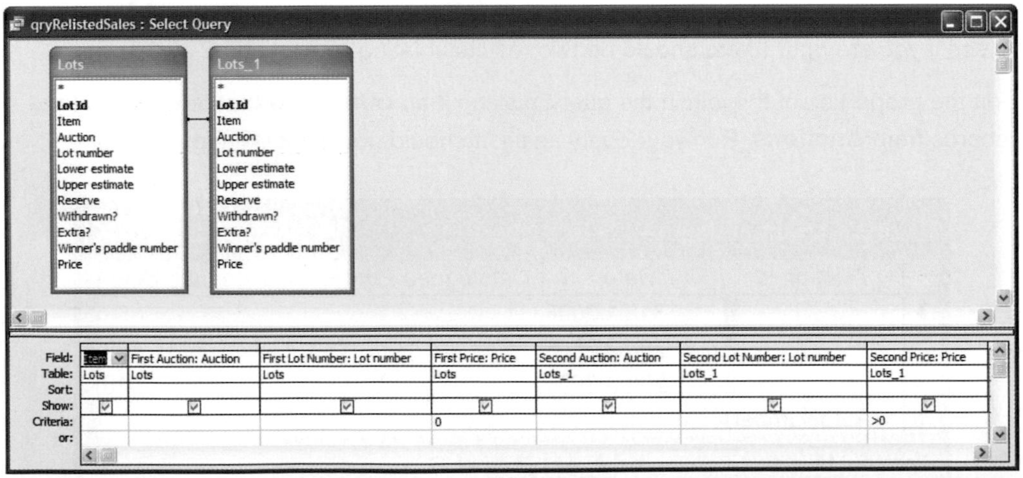

a

b

Figure 8.35: qryRelistedSales in (a) Design view and (b) Datasheet view

Referential integrity

Close all open tables and queries, saving if prompted, and then try to enforce referential integrity for the relationship between **Auctions::Auction Id** and **Catalogues::Auction**. You should get an error message stating that some of the data 'violates referential integrity rules'.

6   Create a query, using the **Find Unmatched Query Wizard**, that shows auctions without matching catalogues. This should return a single result (Auction 4). Create a similar query that shows catalogues without a matching auction. This should return a different single result (Auction 1).

Change the **Auction** id from **4** back to **1** in the **Catalogues** table and then close it.
Now you should be able to enforce referential integrity on the relationship. Create a new entry in the **Auctions** table (**Auction Id: 4, Date: 25/04/2006, Type: 1**) and then a new entry in the **Catalogues** table (**Auction: 4, Catalogues Printed: 650, Catalogues Sold: 600**).

7   Make sure that **Cascade Update Related Fields** is enabled for the relationship between **Auctions::Auction Id** and **Catalogues::Auction**. Change the **Auction** number from **4** to **5** in the **Auctions** table. Show that this change is reflected in the **Catalogues** table.

8   Make sure that **Cascade Delete Related Fields** is enabled for the relationship between **Auctions::Auction Id** and **Catalogues::Auction**. Delete the record for auction **5** from the **Auctions** table, and confirm that the related record is automatically deleted from the **Catalogues** table.

9   Create **one-to-many** relationships from **Auctions::Auction Id** to **Lots::Auction** and from **Auctions::Auction Id** to **Registered Bidders::Auction**. Enable referential integrity in each case.

9 Queries I

Introduction

In this chapter we will type in or import a set of athletics results and use them as a set of data to query in a variety of ways. We will use grouping and expressions to extract information from the data. We will also use different types of query – **update**, **make-table**, **append** and **delete** – to automate some database administration tasks.

In this chapter, you will:

- use an **update query** to automatically modify the data in a table

- use **grouping** and **grouping functions** to summarise data in a query

- use **expressions** to perform calculations on the fields in a query

- create a **make-table query** to save the results of a query as a new table

- create an **append query** to add the results of a query to the end of an existing table

- create a **delete query** to delete the matching records in bulk.

Queries that update data

You are already familiar with queries that find records matching certain criteria and display them on the screen. However, queries can do much more than that. If you need to modify several records at once, you may find that this can be done quickly and consistently with an **update query**.

There are several different types of update query. You can create an update query to update the data in a table, to delete selected records, or to export data to another table (either as a new table, or by appending it to the end of an existing table). We will look at each of these in turn.

Creating the data we will be querying

To give us some suitable data to work with, we will create a new table that lists athletics results for two events over two years. The same techniques could be applied to a much larger table listing all of the results for all of the years that the competition had been running.

Open **sandbox.mdb** if it isn't already open.

Use the **Create table by entering data** option to create the table shown in Figure 9.1.

Note!

If you don't want to type all this in, this table is available from the publisher's website (http://www.payne-gallway.co.uk/ecdl) in a format suitable for importing, together with other resources for this book.

TIP

You can use the shortcut key **Ctrl+'** (apostrophe) to copy data from the cell above. This speeds thing up when you have lots of repeated data, as in columns two and four.

Table1 : Table				
Athlete	Event	Time	Date	
Willie Beatyou	Sprint	11.54	27/08/2005	
Peter Est	Sprint	11.68	27/08/2005	
Harry Quickly	Sprint	11.90	27/08/2005	
Doug Inspikes	Sprint	11.49	27/08/2005	
Justin Front	Sprint	11.42	27/08/2005	
Adam Beaten	Sprint	12.23	27/08/2005	
Aaron Alott	200 metres	23.65	27/08/2005	
Howard Liketowin	200 metres	23.41	27/08/2005	
Victor Ealap	200 metres	25.00	27/08/2005	
Rod Runner	200 metres	24.88	27/08/2005	
Arthur Lapp	200 metres	24.65	27/08/2005	
Alf Inish	200 metres	23.67	27/08/2005	
Ray Singh	Sprint	11.46	28/08/2004	
Jay Smee	Sprint	11.83	28/08/2004	
Dean Umberwun	Sprint	11.41	28/08/2004	
Dustin Second	Sprint	11.59	28/08/2004	
Mark Setgo	Sprint	12.11	28/08/2004	
Ron Andron	Sprint	12.67	28/08/2004	
Cory Squick	200 metres	23.48	28/08/2004	
Noel Ooser	200 metres	24.16	28/08/2004	
Owen Again	200 metres	24.09	28/08/2004	
Hugo First	200 metres	25.23	28/08/2004	
Miles Ahead	200 metres	24.37	28/08/2004	
Gus Fast	200 metres	24.86	28/08/2004	

Record: 25 of 25

Figure 9.1: Athletics results table

Save the table as **tblAthleticsResults** without a primary key and then close it.

Using a query to update data

Let's create a query to update **Sprint** to **100 metres** in this table.

Use **Create query in Design view** to create a new query. Add only **tblAthleticsResults**.

> **Syllabus ref: AM5.2.1.1**
> Create and use a query to update data in a table.

First, we need to create a standard query that returns only the records we wish to change – those matching **Sprint**.

Double-click **Athlete** and **Event** in turn to add them to the query. Set the **Criteria** for **Event** to **"Sprint"**. Your query should look like Figure 9.2.

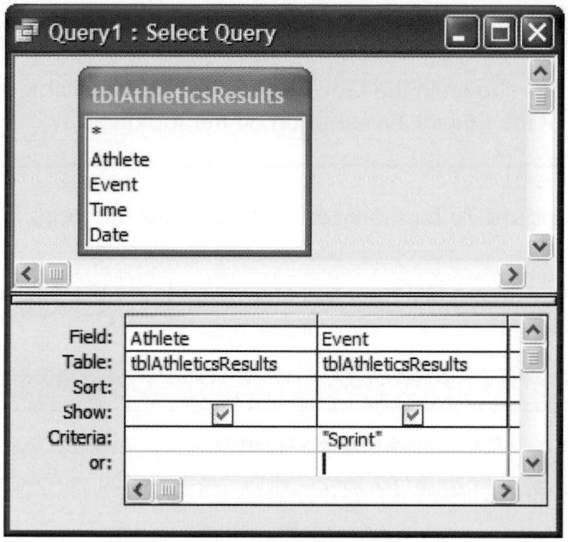

Figure 9.2: Finding only sprint records

Note!

We don't strictly need to include the **Athlete** field in the query, but it will help to confirm that we are picking out the right records.

Run the query. The results should look like Figure 9.3.

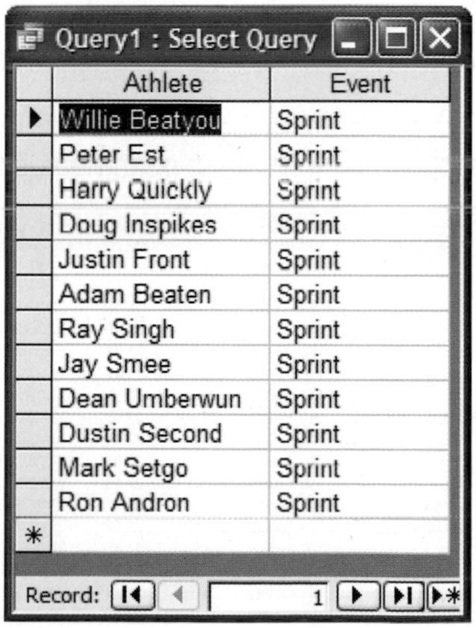

Figure 9.3: All of the sprint records

These are indeed the records that we want to modify.

Switch back to **Design** view and, from the menu, select **Query**, **Update Query**.
Notice that a new row for **Update To** has appeared in the grid at the bottom of the query.

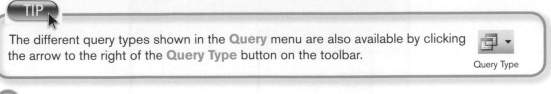

TIP

The different query types shown in the **Query** menu are also available by clicking the arrow to the right of the **Query Type** button on the toolbar.

Query Type

Set the value of **Update To** for the **Event** field to **"100 metres"**.

Run the query. The warning dialogue box shown in Figure 9.4 appears. Check that it says you are about to update **12** rows, then press **Yes**.

Microsoft Office Access

You are about to update 12 row(s).

Once you click Yes, you can't use the Undo command to reverse the changes. Are you sure you want to update these records?

Yes   No

Figure 9.4: Warning about the update

Save your query as **qupdAthleticsSprintTo100m** and then close it.

Note!

We are highlighting this as an update query by using **qupd** instead of **qry** at the beginning of the name. It will also appear with a different icon in the list of queries.

Update Query

Open **tblAthleticsResults** and confirm that all of the **Sprint** entries have been changed to **100 metres**, as shown in Figure 9.5. Close the table again.

Athlete	Event	Time	Date
Willie Beatyou	100 metres	11.54	27/08/2005
Peter Est	100 metres	11.68	27/08/2005
Harry Quickly	100 metres	11.90	27/08/2005
Doug Inspikes	100 metres	11.49	27/08/2005
Justin Front	100 metres	11.42	27/08/2005
Adam Beaten	100 metres	12.23	27/08/2005
Aaron Alott	200 metres	23.65	27/08/2005
Howard Liketowin	200 metres	23.41	27/08/2005
Victor Ealap	200 metres	25.00	27/08/2005
Rod Runner	200 metres	24.88	27/08/2005
Arthur Lapp	200 metres	24.65	27/08/2005
Alf Inish	200 metres	23.67	27/08/2005
Ray Singh	100 metres	11.46	28/08/2004
Jay Smee	100 metres	11.83	28/08/2004
Dean Umberwun	100 metres	11.41	28/08/2004
Dustin Second	100 metres	11.59	28/08/2004
Mark Setgo	100 metres	12.11	28/08/2004
Ron Andron	100 metres	12.67	28/08/2004
Cory Squick	200 metres	23.48	28/08/2004
Noel Ooser	200 metres	24.16	28/08/2004
Owen Again	200 metres	24.09	28/08/2004
Hugo First	200 metres	25.23	28/08/2004
Miles Ahead	200 metres	24.37	28/08/2004
Gus Fast	200 metres	24.86	28/08/2004

Record: 1 of 24

Figure 9.5: Updated table

Using a query to save selected information as a table

Let's design a query to create a new table, **tblAthleticsRecords**, that holds the fastest times for each event listed in **tblAthleticsResults**. To achieve this we will have to use **grouping** – other than that, the technique is very similar to what we have just done for the update.

 Create a new query in **Design** view and add the **tblAthleticsResults** table to it.

Grouping

We will work our way towards the query we want to use to pick out the fastest times, by looking at how grouping works.

Syllabus ref: AM5.2.2.1
Group information in a query.

 Double-click the **Event** field to add it to the query.

 Click the **Totals** button on the toolbar. It becomes highlighted and **Total** row appears in the grid. The value for **Event** is defaulted to **Group By**.

Σ

Totals

 Run the query. The results should look like Figure 9.6.

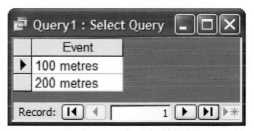

Figure 9.6: Result of running the simple grouped query

This query is grouping together all of the matching values into a single row. Therefore, there are only two rows in the results – one for each of the unique values in the **Event** field in the table.

When you group data in a query, you can only display values calculated from the entire group and not bits and pieces from the individual records. For example, you could not display the **Time** field because each group is a bundle of lots of times; however, you could display the minimum time, since this will have a unique value for the group.

 Back in **Design** view, double-click on the **Time** field to add it to the query. Change its **Total** value to **Avg** (average).

Syllabus ref: AM5.2.2.2
Use functions in a query: sum, count, average, max, min.

 Run the query again. You should get the results shown in Figure 9.7.

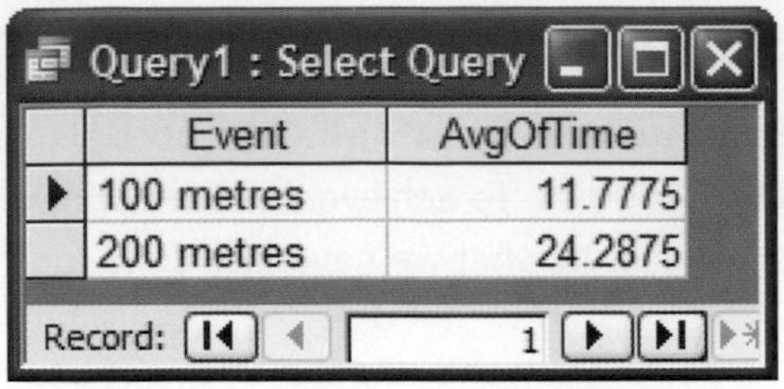

Query1 : Select Query

Event	AvgOfTime
100 metres	11.7775
200 metres	24.2875

Record: 1

Figure 9.7: Average times for each event

This is useful information – it's telling us the average time for each group (that is, the average time for each event). So we now know that the average 100 metres time is 11.7775 seconds and the average 200 metres time is 24.2875 seconds.

The other functions work in the same sort of way. We will add them all so you can see for yourself.

Back in **Design** view, add the **Time** field four more times to the query. Set the **Total** property to **Min**, **Max**, **Sum** and **Count** for these four new fields, as shown in Figure 9.8.

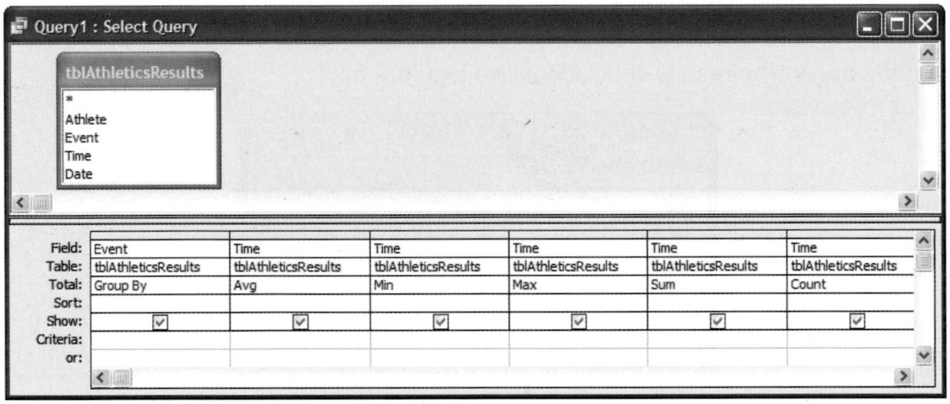

Figure 9.8: Using functions on grouped data

Run the query again. The results should look like Figure 9.9.

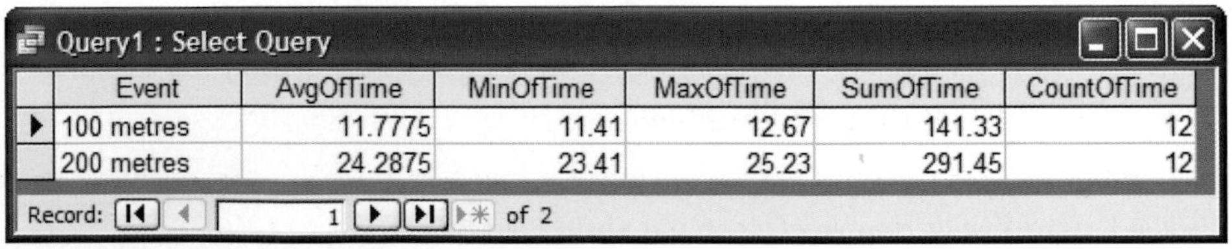

Query1 : Select Query

Event	AvgOfTime	MinOfTime	MaxOfTime	SumOfTime	CountOfTime
100 metres	11.7775	11.41	12.67	141.33	12
200 metres	24.2875	23.41	25.23	291.45	12

Record: 1 of 2

Figure 9.9: Lots of statistics about the race times

So, taking the 100 metres, we now also know that the times range from a minimum of 11.41 seconds to a maximum of 12.67 seconds. We also know that all of the times added together come to 141.33 seconds (not very useful in this example, but very important in some situations). Finally, the count tells us that there were 12 results in this group.

It's possible to group by more than one field, as the following steps demonstrate.

Back in **Design** view, drag the **Date** field and drop it on top of the first of the **Time** columns. A **Date** column appears between **Event** and the first **Time**. Leave its **Total** property as **Group By**.

Run the query. It should produce the results shown in Figure 9.10.

Event	Date	AvgOfTime	MinOfTime	MaxOfTime	SumOfTime	CountOfTime
100 metres	28/08/2004	11.845	11.41	12.67	71.07	6
100 metres	27/08/2005	11.71	11.42	12.23	70.26	6
200 metres	28/08/2004	24.365	23.48	25.23	146.19	6
200 metres	27/08/2005	24.21	23.41	25	145.26	6

Record: 1 of 4

Figure 9.10: Grouping by two fields

This query is now grouping results by **Event** and then by **Date** within each **Event**.

Using expressions in a query

We can do calculations on the other fields by using an **Expression** total type. First we need to give each column that we wish to refer to a unique name.

Back in **Design** view, add names to the min and max columns by using a colon as before: change the **Field** that does the **Min** total to **MinTime: Time** and the **Field** that does the **Max** total to **MaxTime: Time**.

Now we can add the **Expression**.

In the seventh column (the first blank column) enter a name and calculation of **Range: [MaxTime]-[MinTime]** and set the **Total** to **Expression**, as shown in Figure 9.11.

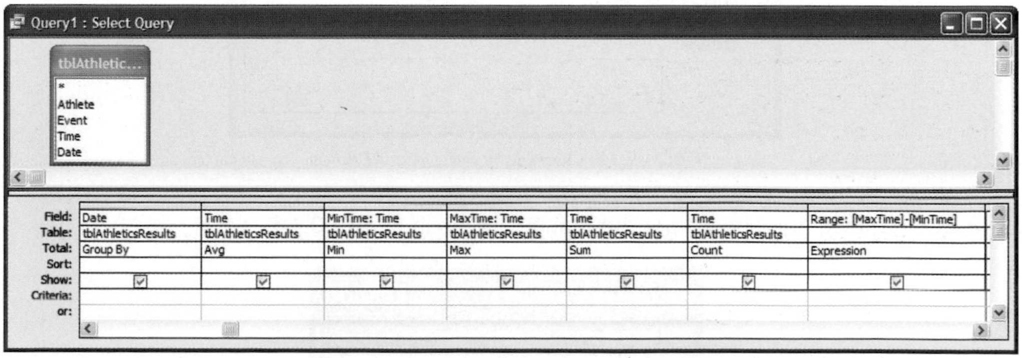

Field:	Date	Time	MinTime: Time	MaxTime: Time	Time	Time	Range: [MaxTime]-[MinTime]
Table:	tblAthleticsResults	tblAthleticsResults	tblAthleticsResults	tblAthleticsResults	tblAthleticsResults	tblAthleticsResults	
Total:	Group By	Avg	Min	Max	Sum	Count	Expression
Sort:							
Show:	☑	☑	☑	☑	☑	☑	☑
Criteria:							
or:							

Figure 9.11: Adding a calculated expression to the query

Run the query. You should get the results shown in Figure 9.12.

Query1 : Select Query

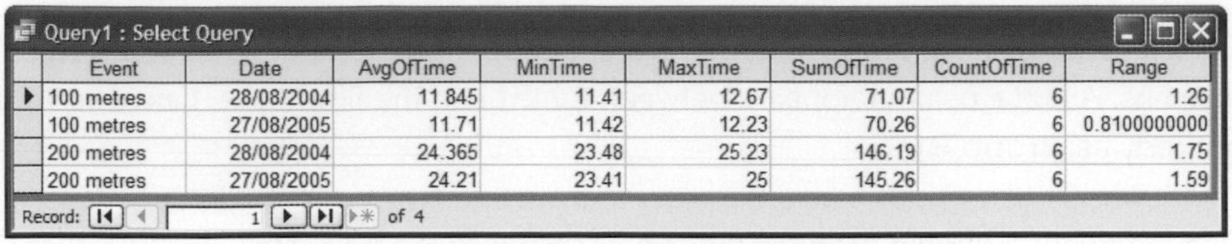

	Event	Date	AvgOfTime	MinTime	MaxTime	SumOfTime	CountOfTime	Range
▶	100 metres	28/08/2004	11.845	11.41	12.67	71.07	6	1.26
	100 metres	27/08/2005	11.71	11.42	12.23	70.26	6	0.8100000000
	200 metres	28/08/2004	24.365	23.48	25.23	146.19	6	1.75
	200 metres	27/08/2005	24.21	23.41	25	145.26	6	1.59

Record: 1 of 4

Figure 9.12: Query results including new calculated Range

The difference between the minimum and maximum values (**Range**) is calculated automatically.

Returning to the query we first thought of

I hope you enjoyed this excursion into how groups work. Now is the time to revert our query to the form we originally wanted: the minimum times for each event.

- Delete all of the fields apart from **Event** and **MinTime: Time**. (In **Design** view click on the thin grey heading of each field you wish to delete and then press the **Delete** key.)

- Rename **MinTime: Time** to **Record: Time**. The query should now look like Figure 9.13.

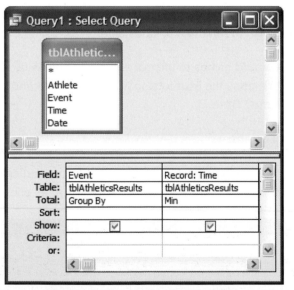

Figure 9.13: Query to find the record times

- Run the query. You should get the results shown in Figure 9.14.

Query1 : Select ...

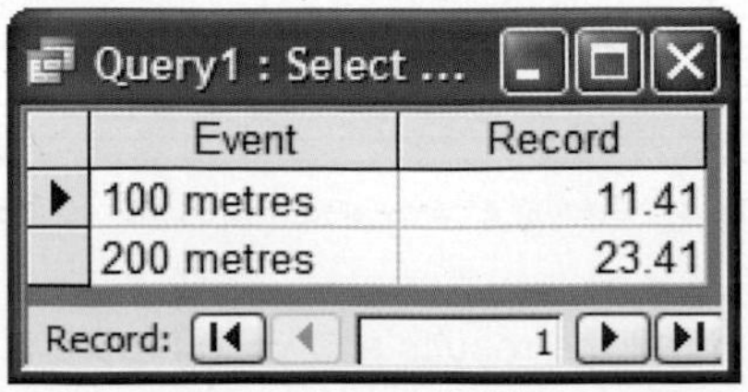

	Event	Record
▶	100 metres	11.41
	200 metres	23.41

Record: 1

Figure 9.14: The record times for the 100 metres and 200 metres

We now want to make the query automatically create a table to hold this information each time it is run.

Creating a table from a query

 Back in **Design** view, select **Query**, **Make-Table Query** from the menu. The **Make Table** dialogue box appears.

> **Syllabus ref: AM5.2.1.3**
> Create and use a query to save the selected information as a table.

 Type the **Table Name** as **tblAthleticsRecords**, as shown in Figure 9.15, then press **OK**.

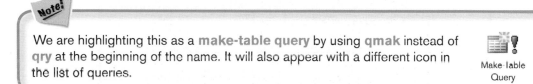

Figure 9.15: Assigning a table name

 Save the query as **qmakAthleticsRecords**.

> **Note!**
>
> We are highlighting this as a **make-table query** by using **qmak** instead of **qry** at the beginning of the name. It will also appear with a different icon in the list of queries.
>
> Make-Table
> Query

 Run the query. The warning dialogue box shown in Figure 9.16 may appear.

Microsoft Office Access

⚠ **You are about to run a make-table query that will modify data in your table.**

Are you sure you want to run this type of action query?
For information on how to prevent this message from displaying every time you run an action query, click Help.

[Yes] [No] [Help]

Figure 9.16: Warning that you are about to create a table

 Press **Yes**. Another warning dialogue box appears, as shown in Figure 9.17.

Figure 9.17: Warning that you are pasting records into the new table

 Press **Yes** again. Find and open the new table **tblAthleticsRecords** (this table was created and populated by the query **qmakAthleticsRecords**). The data should look like the query result did (Figure 9.14). Close the table again.

Using a query to append records to an existing table

Suppose that you only want the most recent results in your **tblAthleticsResults** table, and you have another table – **tblAthleticsArchive** – that you use for all the old results. We will create two queries, one to copy the records from **tblAthleticsResults** to **tblAthleticsArchive** and one to delete the records from **tblAthleticsResults** afterwards.

 Use the **Create table by entering data** option to create the table shown in Figure 9.18 (you can type dummy data if you are pressed for time – this isn't important).

Athlete	Event	Time	Date
Ted Heat	100 metres	12.01	30/08/2003
Ian Dalead	100 metres	11.59	30/08/2003
Aidan O'Howtastop	100 metres	11.87	30/08/2003
Darren Ofislife	100 metres	11.49	30/08/2003
Ed Start	100 metres	12.16	30/08/2003
Isaac Race	100 metres	11.48	30/08/2003
Ivan Twin	200 metres	24.44	30/08/2003
Kenny Winnett	200 metres	24.56	30/08/2003
Max Speed	200 metres	25.02	30/08/2003
Scott Legges	200 metres	23.99	30/08/2003
Luca Mie	200 metres	24.51	30/08/2003
Evan Chooley	200 metres	24.88	30/08/2003

Record: 13 of 21

Figure 9.18: Table of previous results

 Save the table as **tblAthleticsArchive** without a primary key and then close it.

Create a query that finds all of the 2004 results from the **tblAthleticsResults** table. It should look like Figure 9.19.

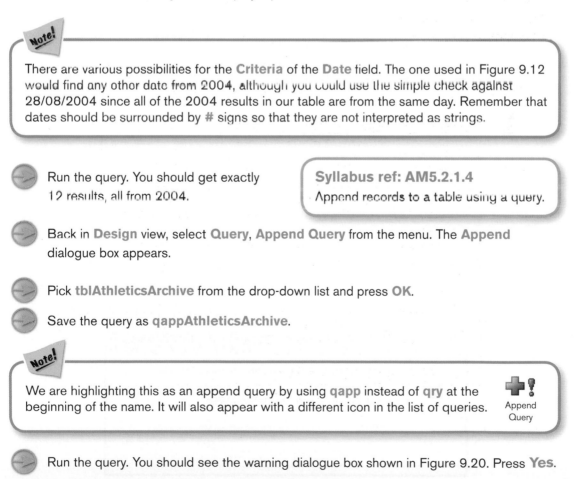

Figure 9.19: A query to pick out the results from 2004

There are various possibilities for the **Criteria** of the **Date** field. The one used in Figure 9.12 would find any other date from 2004, although you could use the simple check against 28/08/2004 since all of the 2004 results in our table are from the same day. Remember that dates should be surrounded by **#** signs so that they are not interpreted as strings.

Run the query. You should get exactly 12 results, all from 2004.

> **Syllabus ref: AM5.2.1.4**
> Append records to a table using a query.

Back in **Design** view, select **Query, Append Query** from the menu. The **Append** dialogue box appears.

Pick **tblAthleticsArchive** from the drop-down list and press **OK**.

Save the query as **qappAthleticsArchive**.

We are highlighting this as an append query by using **qapp** instead of **qry** at the beginning of the name. It will also appear with a different icon in the list of queries.

Append
Query

Run the query. You should see the warning dialogue box shown in Figure 9.20. Press **Yes**.

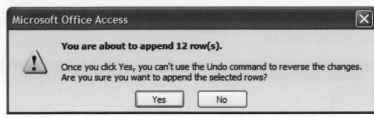

Figure 9.20: Warning that you are about to append 12 rows to a different table

 Close the query and open **tblAthleticsArchive**. It should now contain 24 records: the original 12 from 2003 and the appended 12 from 2004. Close the table again.

Using a query to delete data

The only thing that remains for us to do is to delete the records for 2004 from the **tblAthleticsResults** table. We can adapt the query that we have just used (which already picks out the right records), changing it from an append query to a delete query.

 Open the **qappAthleticsArchive** query in **Design** view: be careful not to run the query by mistake! The easiest way to open it in **Design** view is to right-click on it and select **Design View** from the menu that appears.

> **Syllabus ref: AM5.2.1.2**
>
> Create and use a query to delete records in a table.

From the menu, select **Query**, **Delete Query**.

Use **File**, **Save As** to save the query as **qdelAthleticsOldResults**.

> **Note!**
>
> We are highlighting this as a delete query by using **qdel** instead of **qry** at the beginning of the name. It will also appear with a different icon in the list of queries.
>
>
> Delete Query

Run the query. The warning dialogue box shown in Figure 9.21 appears. Press **Yes**.

Figure 9.21: Warning that you are about to delete 12 records

Close the query and open **tblAthleticsResults**. Only the 12 results from 2005 should now remain, as shown in Figure 9.22.

Athlete	Event	Time	Date
Willie Beatyou	100 metres	11.54	27/08/2005
Peter Est	100 metres	11.68	27/08/2005
Harry Quickly	100 metres	11.90	27/08/2005
Doug Inspikes	100 metres	11.49	27/08/2005
Justin Front	100 metres	11.42	27/08/2005
Adam Beaten	100 metres	12.23	27/08/2005
Aaron Alott	200 metres	23.65	27/08/2005
Howard Liketowin	200 metres	23.41	27/08/2005
Victor Ealap	200 metres	25.00	27/08/2005
Rod Runner	200 metres	24.88	27/08/2005
Arthur Lapp	200 metres	24.65	27/08/2005
Alf Inish	200 metres	23.67	27/08/2005

Record: 12 of 12

Figure 9.22: The results from 2004 have been deleted from the table

Conclusions

This exercise has demonstrated the following points.

Several types of 'active' query exist: **update**, **make-table**, **append** and **delete**.

When designing one of these 'active' queries, it is a good idea to create a standard query first. You can test the query without modifying the data it is querying, and when you are happy that the correct records are being returned, you can change the query type.

You can use **grouping** to find out information about subsets of data. The **sum**, **count**, **average**, **min** and **max** functions allow you to get information about a group of records.

You can use **expressions** to perform calculations in a query.

It is often useful to supply an alternative name for a field in a query. You do this by supplying the name, followed by a colon, at the beginning of the **Field** parameter.

Test yourself

Auction database

1   Create an **update query** to update the **Items** table, changing each **SILVER & GOLD** entry in the **Type** field to **GOLD & SILVER**. Run the query and save it as **qupdGoldSilver**.

2   Create a **make-table query** that creates a new table called **Central Lotbury** and adds all of the records from the **People** table where the **Postal Code** starts **LB1** (Tip: use **Like** in the **Criteria** – there should be 118 matching records). Run this query and then save it as **qmakCentralLotbury**.

3   Create an **append query** that appends to the **Central Lotbury** table all those records from the **People** table where the **Postal Code** starts **LB2** or **LB3** (there should be 119 matching records). Run this query and then save it as **qappCentralLotbury**. The **Central Lotbury** table should now have 237 records.

4   Create a **delete query** that deletes those records from the **Central Lotbury** table (not the **People** table) where the **Postal Code** starts **LB3** (there should be 56 matching records). Run this query and then save it as **qdelCentralLotbury**. The **Central Lotbury** table should now have 181 records.

10 Queries II

Introduction

In this chapter we will use sales data from a shop that sells stationery to explore some of the more advanced topics relating to queries.

In this chapter, you will:

create a query to **find duplicate values** in a set of data

use a **crosstab query** to summarise data across categories

understand how to search for **null** and **not null** values using a query

perform calculations using **arithmetic and logical expressions** in a query

create a query that uses a **parameter** to prompt the user, whenever the query is run, for one of the search criteria

tell Access to **truncate** the query and return only a specified maximum number of results.

Creating a table to query

In this chapter we will use the example of a small shop that sells pens, paper and other types of stationery. First we will create a simple table listing some of the sales they have made and then we will create some useful queries to tell us about the data.

 Open your database **sandbox.mdb** if it isn't already open.

 Use **Create table by entering data** and type in the headings and data shown in Figure 10.1. Save the table as **tblStationerySales** without a primary key.

Date	Customer	Item Type	Amount	Discount
09/01/2006	Carter	Pens	£8.95	
09/01/2006	Carter	Utensils	£14.95	
09/01/2006	Reynolds	Utensils	£9.50	
09/01/2006	Wilson	Paper	£3.95	
09/01/2006	Wilson	Pens	£2.95	
10/01/2006	Peterson	Utensils	£12.75	5%
10/01/2006	Peterson	Paper	£8.00	5%
10/01/2006	Smith	Pens	£1.50	
10/01/2006	Lee	Utensils	£16.00	
10/01/2006	Patel	Pens	£12.95	8%
11/01/2006	Carter	Pens	£3.50	
11/01/2006	Peterson	Paper	£4.75	5%
11/01/2006	Jones	Paper	£15.00	
11/01/2006	Cooper	Pens	£0.75	
11/01/2006	Cooper	Paper	£1.95	

Record: 15 of 21

Figure 10.1: Creating a table to record the stationery shop's sales

Note!

Of course, a real stationery shop would sell many more items over these three days. However, 15 records is just enough to show the different types of query we need to cover without taking you too long to type.

Note also that some customers have discounts. These are applied to the amounts, so the actual income of the stationery shop is less than the sum of the raw amounts in the table.

Finding duplicate values

Suppose that the shop would like to encourage its customers to buy in bulk. It would be useful to find out which of their customers have bought the same type of item more than once. Let's create a query to find out.

Syllabus ref: AM5.2.3.1
Show duplicates.

With **Queries** selected from the **Objects** list in the **Database** window, press the **New** button. The **New Query** dialogue box appears.

> **Note!**
>
> The **Find Duplicates Query Wizard** may not be available if your copy of Access was installed with the **Typical Wizards** option (see page 10). If this is the case, Access will ask you to insert the Microsoft Office CD-ROM to install the wizard.

Select **Find Duplicates Query Wizard** and press **OK**. The **Find Duplicates Query Wizard** appears.

Select **Table: tblStationerySales** and press **Next**.

We want to find all of the records where the **Customer** and **Item Type** fields are both duplicated (that is, where the same customer bought the same type of item).

Select **Customer** and press > to transfer it to the list on the right. Do the same for **Item Type**. The wizard should now look like Figure 10.2. Press **Next**.

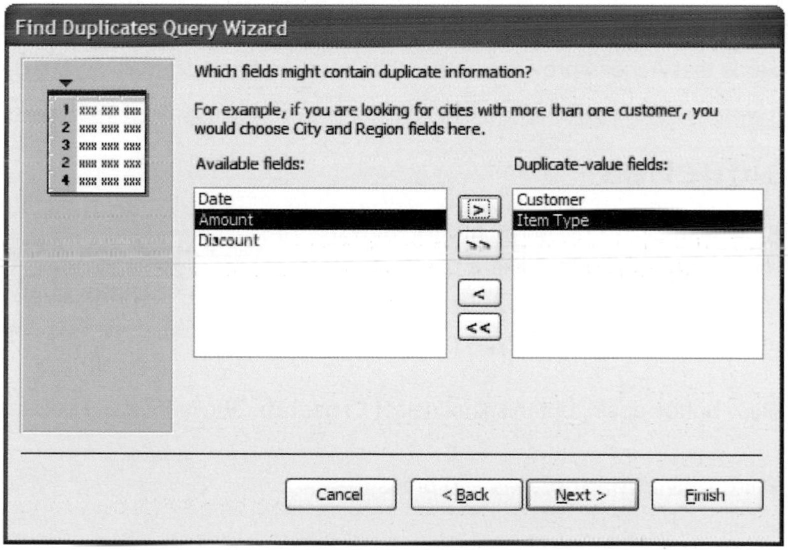

Figure 10.2: Choosing which fields to search for duplicates

The next step of the wizard allows us to add other fields that will appear in the results but which do not have to match for records to be considered duplicates.

Add the **Date** and **Amount** fields, but not **Discount**, using the > button as before. Press **Next**.

Name the query **qryStationerySalesDuplicates** and press **Finish**.

The results should look like Figure 10.3. This tells us that two customers have bought the same type of item more than once: **Carter** has bought **Pens** twice and **Peterson** has bought **Paper** twice.

Customer	Item Type	Date	Amount
Carter	Pens	11/01/2006	£3.50
Carter	Pens	09/01/2006	£8.95
Peterson	Paper	11/01/2006	£4.75
Peterson	Paper	10/01/2006	£8.00

Figure 10.3: Two customers have bought the same type of item twice

Therefore, it might be worth asking customers Carter and Peterson whether they would like to buy a bulk lot of stationery.

Note!

If you look at the new query in **Design** view, you will see the following complicated criterion: **In (SELECT [Customer] FROM [tblStationerySales] As Tmp GROUP BY [Customer],[Item Type] HAVING Count(*)>1 And [Item Type] = [tblStationerySales].[Item Type]).**

You do not need to understand this; however, it does demonstrate why it can be much quicker to use the wizards that Access provides, rather than trying to hand-craft all of your queries.

Crosstab queries

A crosstab query allows you to generate an overview of the information held in a table, rather like a pivot table in a spreadsheet. Let's generate a crosstab to show how much each customer spends on each type of stationery.

Syllabus ref: AM5.2.2.3
Use a crosstab query.

New

Use the **New** button again, but this time select **Crosstab Query Wizard** before pressing **OK**.

Select **Table: tblStationerySales** and press **Next**.

Click **Customer** and press > to select this field as the row heading. Press **Next**.

Click **Item Type** to select this field as the column headings. Press **Next**.

Note!

Notice that you can select many row headings but only a single column heading.

Select **Amount** in the list of **Fields** and **Sum** in the list of **Functions**, as shown in Figure 10.4. Make sure that **Yes, include row sums** is ticked – this will show the total spent by each customer. Press **Next**.

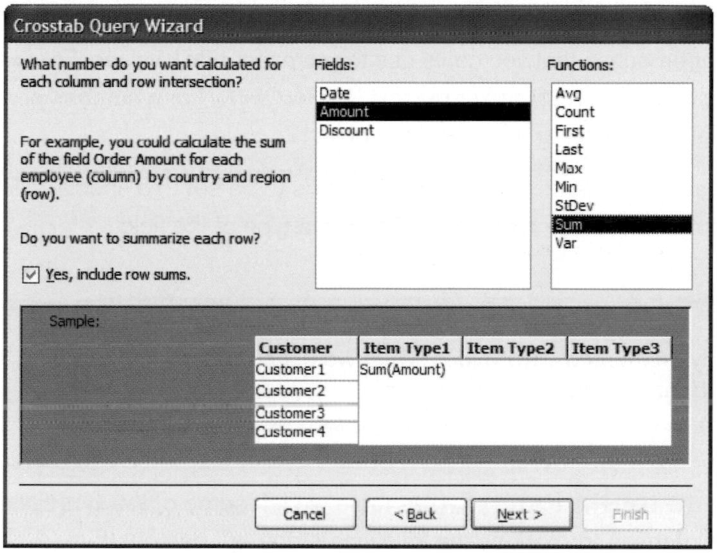

Figure 10.4: Selecting the field and function to use for
the value shown in the body of the crosstab query

Name the query **qxtbStationerySales** and press **Finish**.

> **Note!**
>
> We are highlighting this as a crosstab query by using **qxtb** instead of **qry** at the beginning of the name. It will also appear with a different icon in the list of queries.
>
> Crosstab Query

The result of running the crosstab should look like Figure 10.5. The first line, for example, tells us that customer Carter has spent £27.40 in total, made up of £12.45 spent on Pens and £14.95 spent on Utensils (the category that the shop uses for things like staplers).

qxtbStationerySales : Crosstab Query

Customer	Total Of Amount	Paper	Pens	Utensils
Carter	£27.40		£12.45	£14.95
Cooper	£2.70	£1.95	£0.75	
Jones	£15.00	£15.00		
Lee	£16.00			£16.00
Patel	£12.95		£12.95	
Peterson	£25.50	£12.75		£12.75
Reynolds	£9.50			£9.50
Smith	£1.50		£1.50	
Wilson	£6.90	£3.95	£2.95	

Record: |◄ ◄ 1 ► ►| ►* of 9

Figure 10.5: Result of running the crosstab query

Null values

It is often necessary to create a record in a database when not all of the fields have known values. For example, if you split an address into a field for each line then some of the later fields may need to be blank because not all addresses are the same length.

There are various approaches that you could use to represent blank values. For example, if the field is a string then you could use a **space** or the text **UNKNOWN**. For a number, perhaps you could use a **0**. But what about a date, or an embedded object?

All relational database management systems allow fields to be set to a special value, called **null**, if they are truly empty. This is true regardless of the data type of the field.

> **Note!**
>
> We have already mentioned **null** values when we used outer joins
> – see Chapter 8, page 138.

When we created the **tblStationerySales** table we left some of the **Discount** values blank. Access has set all of these to **null**, as the following steps will demonstrate.

Create a new query in **Design** view to show customers and their discounts, as shown in Figure 10.6.

> **Syllabus ref: AM5.2.3.5**
> Refining queries using Null and NOT values.

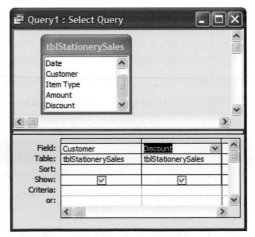

Figure 10.6: Simple query to list customers and their discounts

Run the query. The results should look like Figure 10.7.

Figure 10.7: Customers and their discounts

Note!

If customers have bought more than one item then they appear more than once in the results. This doesn't matter. (A real shop would do better to have two separate tables: one to hold the customer details – such as address and discount – and another table to hold the sales records.)

We can limit the results to just those customers with discounts by using the criterion **Is Not Null**. This will limit the records to those for which values have been set.

In **Design** view, set the **Criteria** for **Discount** to **Is Not Null**.

Run the query again. This time it should be limited to those customers who have been awarded discounts – Peterson and Patel – as shown in Figure 10.8.

Figure 10.8: List of customers who receive discounts

TIP

If you wanted to show each customer only once, you could edit the query in **SQL** view (by selecting **View, SQL View** from the menu) and add the keyword **DISTINCT** before **tblStationerySales.Customer**.

The keyword **Is** may only be used before **Null** or **Not Null**. However, the **Not** keyword can be used in any expression to reverse a true or false expression (for example, **Not Between 5 And 10** matches values less than 5 or more than 10). The syntax is the same as for the validation rules; see the table on page 111 for more examples.

To find all of the other records (those with null values) instead, use **Is Null** instead of **Is Not Null**, as follows.

 In **Design** view, change the **Criteria** for **Discount** to **Is Null**.

 Run the query again. This time you should get a list of all of the customers who do not get discounts, as shown in Figure 10.9.

Customer	Discount
Carter	
Carter	
Reynolds	
Wilson	
Wilson	
Smith	
Lee	
Carter	
Jones	
Cooper	
Cooper	

Record: ◄◄ ◄ 1 ► ►► ►*

Figure 10.9: All of the customers who do not qualify for discounts

In the next section we will be performing calculations using the discounts. This will be easier if they are set to **0%** instead of **null**. Let's change our query into an **update query** that changes all of the **null** discounts to **0%**.

 In **Design** view, select **Query, Update Query** from the menu.

 Change the **Update To** property for **Discount** to **0**, as shown in Figure 10.10. (We don't need the percentage sign because this is a number field that is formatted to display with a percentage sign.)

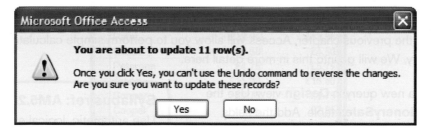

Figure 10.10: Changing this to an update query

 Run the query. The warning message shown in Figure 10.11 appears. Press **Yes**.

Microsoft Office Access

⚠ **You are about to update 11 row(s).**

Once you click Yes, you can't use the Undo command to reverse the changes.
Are you sure you want to update these records?

[Yes]   [No]

Figure 10.11: Warning that you are updating 11 rows

 Open **tblStationerySales**. It should look like Figure 10.12. Close the table and close the query without saving it (we only needed to run it once).

Note!

This isn't a maths test, so do not worry too much if you are a bit shaky about how percentages work or why this formula gives the VAT. The important thing is that you know how to get the expression into the query.

- Right-click anywhere in the third column and select **Properties** from the menu that appears. The **Field Properties** dialogue box appears. In the **General** tab, change **Format** to **Currency** and then close the dialogue box.

- Run the query. You should get the results shown in Figure 10.15.

Query1 : Select Query

Customer	Amount	VAT
Carter	£8.95	£1.33
Carter	£14.95	£2.23
Reynolds	£9.50	£1.41
Wilson	£3.95	£0.59
Wilson	£2.95	£0.44
Peterson	£12.75	£1.90
Peterson	£8.00	£1.19
Smith	£1.50	£0.22
Lee	£16.00	£2.38
Patel	£12.95	£1.93
Carter	£3.50	£0.52
Peterson	£4.75	£0.71
Jones	£15.00	£2.23
Cooper	£0.75	£0.11
Cooper	£1.95	£0.29

Record: 1 of 15

Figure 10.15: Calculating the VAT component of the amount

So, for example, the first amount was £8.95. The VAT was £1.33, so the price before VAT was (£8.95 – £1.33 =) £7.62.

Note!

In the following, **integer** just means **whole number**.

You can use the following arithmetic operators in expressions. Suppose that a sofa is 2.15 m long, 0.93 m deep and 0.90 m high and a chair is 1.4 m long, 1.0 m deep and 0.8 m tall. You plan to put them in a square room where every wall is 3 m long.

+ (addition)	TotalLength: [SofaLength] + [ChairLength] (TotalLength = 2.15 + 1.4 = 3.55)
− (subtraction)	SpaceBesideSofa: [WallLength] − [SofaLength] (SpaceBesideSofa = 3 − 2.15 = 0.85)
* (multiplication)	SofaVolume: [SofaLength] * [SofaDepth] * [SofaHeight] (SofaVolume = 2.15 * 0.93 * 0.9 = 1.8 (approx.))
/ (division)	ChairsPerSofa = [SofaLength] / [ChairLength] (ChairsPerSofa = 2.15 / 1.4 = 1.54)
\ (integer division)	ChairsThatCouldFit = [WallLength] \ [ChairLength] (ChairsThatCouldFit = 2 \ 1 = 2)
^ (raising to a power)	FloorArea: [WallLength] ^ 2 (FloorArea = 3^2 = 9 m²)
Mod (modulus, remainder after division)	Space: [WallLength] Mod [SofaLength] (Space = 3 Mod 2.15 = 3 Mod 2 = 1, where this is the space, to the nearest whole metre, after you have added as many sofas as possible side-by-side).

Note!

The \ operator rounds both of its arguments to integers and then truncates the result without rounding it. So, for example

3.4 \ 1.4 = 3 \ 1 = 3   3.4 \ 1.5 = 3 \ 2 = 1.5 = 1   3.5 \ 1.4 = 4 \ 1 = 4   3.5 \ 1.5 = 4 \ 2 = 2

The **Mod** operator also rounds both of its arguments before calculating the remainder.

11 Mod 3.4 = 11 Mod 3 = 2 (because 11 / 3 leaves 2 spare)
11 Mod 3.5 = 11 Mod 4 = 3 (because 11 / 4 leaves 3 spare)

Logical expressions

A **logical** (or **Boolean**) expression is one that must evaluate to either **true** or **false**. For example, the expression [**SellPrice**] > [**BuyPrice**] will return **true** if the selling price is higher than the buying price, otherwise it will return **false**.

Logical expressions can be combined using the **And** and **Or** operators. For example, a check might be [**SellPrice**] > 0 And [**BuyPrice**] > 0. Figure 10.16 shows the values of **A And B** and **A Or B** for the four possible combinations of **A** and **B**.

A	B	A And B	A Or B
false	false	false	false
false	true	false	true
true	false	false	true
true	true	true	true

Figure 10.16: A logic table

Let's try some logical expressions.

 In **Design** view, type the following for the **Field** in the fourth column:
Pens?: [Item Type]="Pens".

This creates an expression called **Pens?** and sets it to **true** if the **Item Type** is **Pens** and sets it to **false** otherwise.

 Run the query. You should get the results shown in Figure 10.17. These look rather strange because **true** is represented by **−1** and **false** is represented by **0**.

Customer	Amount	VAT	Pens?
Carter	£8.95	£1.33	-1
Carter	£14.95	£2.23	0
Reynolds	£9.50	£1.41	0
Wilson	£3.95	£0.59	0
Wilson	£2.95	£0.44	-1
Peterson	£12.75	£1.90	0
Peterson	£8.00	£1.19	0
Smith	£1.50	£0.22	-1
Lee	£16.00	£2.38	0
Patel	£12.95	£1.93	-1
Carter	£3.50	£0.52	-1
Peterson	£4.75	£0.71	0
Jones	£15.00	£2.23	0
Cooper	£0.75	£0.11	-1
Cooper	£1.95	£0.29	0

Record: 1 of 15

Figure 10.17: Query showing true and false values as numbers (−1 and 0 respectively)

 In **Design** view, right-click on the new **Field** and select **Properties** from the menu that appears. Change the **Format** to **Yes/No** by typing it in, as shown in Figure 10.18.

TIP

Not all of the available formats appear in the drop-down list, but you can type them in instead. Alternative ways of displaying logical results are **True/False** and **On/Off**.

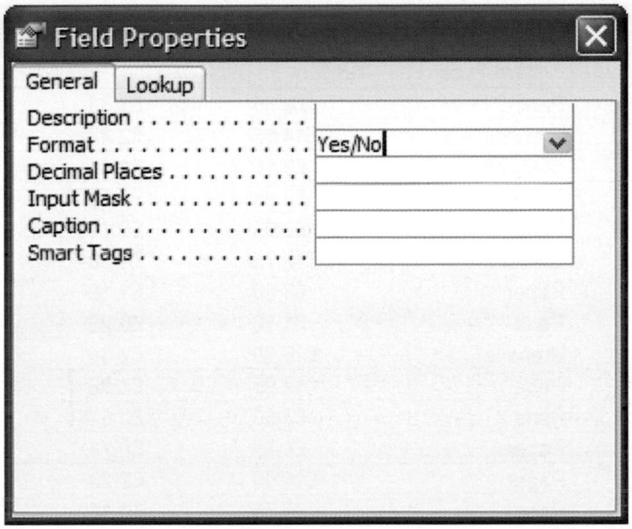

Figure 10.18: Changing the format of a logical field to display Yes or No

Run the query again. This time you get **Yes** and **No** instead of **-1** and **0**.

Suppose that we want to highlight any transactions for £5 or more of paper or £10 or more of utensils.

In **Design** view, drag the **Item Type** field from the table on to the **Amount** column. It appears between the **Customer** and **Amount** columns.

Change the **Field** for what is now the fifth column as follows:
Target Transaction: ([Item Type]="Utensils" And [Amount]>=10) Or ([Item Type]="Paper" And [Amount]>=5).

Run the query. You should get the results shown in Figure 10.19.

Query1 : Select Query				
Customer	Item Type	Amount	VAT	Target Transaction
Carter	Pens	£8.95	£1.33	No
Carter	Utensils	£14.95	£2.23	Yes
Reynolds	Utensils	£9.50	£1.41	No
Wilson	Paper	£3.95	£0.59	No
Wilson	Pens	£2.95	£0.44	No
Peterson	Utensils	£12.75	£1.90	Yes
Peterson	Paper	£8.00	£1.19	Yes
Smith	Pens	£1.50	£0.22	No
Lee	Utensils	£16.00	£2.38	Yes
Patel	Pens	£12.95	£1.93	No
Carter	Pens	£3.50	£0.52	No
Peterson	Paper	£4.75	£0.71	No
Jones	Paper	£15.00	£2.23	Yes
Cooper	Pens	£0.75	£0.11	No
Cooper	Paper	£1.95	£0.29	No

Record: |◄| ◄ | 1 | ► | ►| | ►* | of 15

Figure 10.19: A more complicated logical expression

TIP

There are some powerful functions related to logical expressions. You are unlikely to need these in your course, but might wish to use them in your future work. If you are interested you could look up the following functions in the online help: **Choose**, **IIf**, **IsArray**, **IsDate**, **IsEmpty**, **IsError**, **IsMissing**, **IsNull**, **IsObject**, **StrComp**, and **Switch**.

Parameter queries

Let's change our query to display the best customers for a particular type of item: **Pens**.

 Edit the query so that the **Criteria** for the **Item Type** column is **"Pens"**.

 Run the query. The results should look like Figure 10.20.

Query1 : Select Query				
Customer	Item Type	Amount	VAT	Target Transaction
Carter	Pens	£8.95	£1.33	No
Wilson	Pens	£2.95	£0.44	No
Smith	Pens	£1.50	£0.22	No
Patel	Pens	£12.95	£1.93	No
Carter	Pens	£3.50	£0.52	No
Cooper	Pens	£0.75	£0.11	No

Record: |◄| ◄ | 1 | ► | ►| | ►* | of 6

Figure 10.20: Showing only the transactions that were pen sales

It would be useful to be able to choose which of **Pens**, **Paper** or **Utensils** to display. We can use a **parameter query** to do this.

Syllabus ref: AM5.2.3.4
Allow query input from a data prompt (parameter query).

⊝ In **Design** view, change the **Criteria** for **Item Type** to [Type: Pens, Paper or Utensils?].

Note!

If you create a variable (by putting it in square brackets) that Access does not recognise as a field name then Access will ask you to supply a value when you run the query.

⊝ Run the query. A dialogue box titled **Enter Parameter Value** appears, containing the text that you put in square brackets and a text input box. Type **Paper** as shown in Figure 10.21 and then press **OK**.

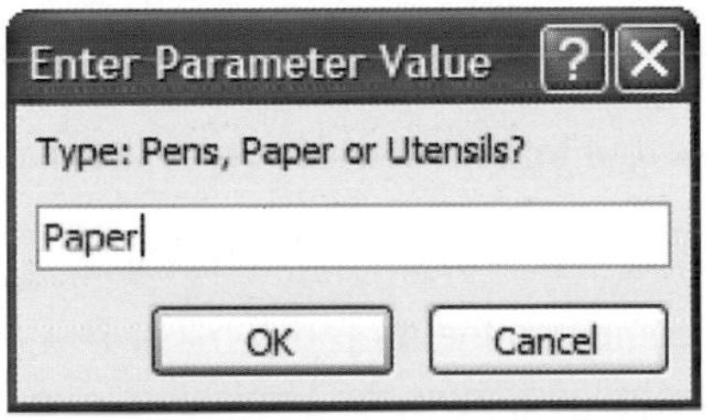

```
┌────────────────────────────────────────┐
│ Enter Parameter Value        [?][X]     │
├────────────────────────────────────────┤
│ Type: Pens, Paper or Utensils?          │
│ ┌────────────────────────────────────┐  │
│ │Paper│                              │  │
│ └────────────────────────────────────┘  │
│        [   OK   ]   [  Cancel  ]         │
└────────────────────────────────────────┘
```

Figure 10.21: Typing a value for a parameter query

You should get the results shown in Figure 10.22. These are the same as you would have got by setting the **Item Type** to **Paper** in **Design** view.

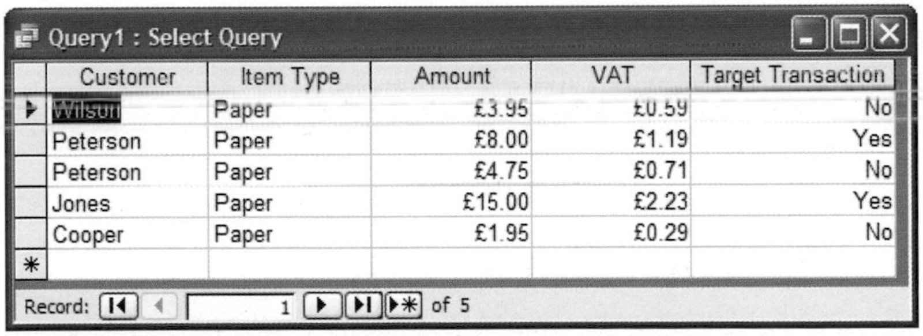

Customer	Item Type	Amount	VAT	Target Transaction
Wilson	Paper	£3.95	£0.59	No
Peterson	Paper	£8.00	£1.19	Yes
Peterson	Paper	£4.75	£0.71	No
Jones	Paper	£15.00	£2.23	Yes
Cooper	Paper	£1.95	£0.29	No

Record: [I◀] [◀] 1 [▶] [▶I] [▶*] of 5

Figure 10.22: Results of running the query and typing in Paper as the parameter

Truncating queries

Usually, you will want a query to return all of the matching results. However, sometimes you know in advance that you will only be interested in some of them. In this case it can be more efficient, particularly if there would otherwise be lots of results, to tell Access to return only some of the results.

Syllabus ref: AM5.2.3.3
Show highest, lowest range of values in a query.

Let's modify the query so that only the two highest amounts are returned.

In **Design** view, change **Sort** for **Amount** to **Descending**. This will reorder the results so that the highest amounts come first.

The **Top Values** control in the toolbar will say **All** by default. We can change this to return only a percentage or fixed number of results.

 Click the button to the right of the **Top Values** control. This displays a list of standard values that you might want to choose, as shown in Figure 10.23.

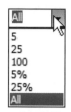

Figure 10.23: The Top Values control

We only want the top two values, but that it not an option in the list. We will have to type it in instead.

 Click the arrow again to compress the drop-down list. The value in the control will remain selected. Press **2**. The control will show the first value from the list that starts with a **2**: in this case **25**. Press **Delete** to delete the **5**, then press **Enter**. The control is left with the value **2**.

> **TIP**
>
> To return the lowest range of values in a query, simply reverse the sort order so that the **Top Values** control works from the other end of the sorted list.

 Run the query again, typing **Utensils** when prompted. This time it should return only the two highest amounts paid in utensil transactions, as shown in Figure 10.24.

Query1 : Select Query

Customer	Item Type	Amount	VAT	Target Transaction
Lee	Utensils	£16.00	£2.38	Yes
Carter	Utensils	£14.95	£2.23	Yes

Record: 1 of 2

Figure 10.24: The query now returns only two values

 Save the query as **qryTopTwoSales**.

Wildcards in queries

Chapters 9 and 10 have given you plenty of experience of using expressions in the criteria of queries. You need to be aware that you can use the **LIKE** keyword in these expressions to search for matches using wildcards.

> **Syllabus ref: AM5.2.2.4**
> Use wildcards in a query.

The syntax for using wildcards in queries is the same as for specifying validation rules (see pages 108–111).

Conclusions

This exercise has demonstrated the following points.

 You can use the **Find Duplicates Query Wizard** to simplify the creation of queries to identify duplicated data.

 A **crosstab query** is rather like a pivot table in a spreadsheet. You can use it to summarise data across categories. You can have many row headings but only a single column heading.

A field in a database may have a **null** value, indicating that its true value is not known. You can use **Is Null** and **Is Not Null** as search criteria in queries when you need to take account of null values.

You can use **arithmetical and logical expressions** to perform calculations in a query. These can be used just like any other fields in your query.

 If you refer to a field (by enclosing it in square brackets in the **Criteria** property of a query) that does not exist, Access will treat it as a **parameter** and will prompt the user for its value whenever the query is run.

Use the **Top Values** control to restrict the number of values that a query will return. Make sure that the query sorts the results in the order you require, so that it is the least useful results that are truncated.

Test yourself

Auction database

1 Use the **Find Duplicates Query Wizard** to list all of the records from the **Lots** table that share the same **Item** (that is, items that failed to sell in one auction so were relisted). Save the query as **qryRelistedSales2** and compare its results (there should be 4) with those from **qryRelistedSales** created in Exercise 5 in Chapter 8 (page 156).

2 Create a crosstab query, based on **qryTypesAndPrices**, to show the average price for which items sold across the three auctions, broken down by the type of item, as shown in Figure 10.25. Save the query as **qryTypesAndPrices_Crosstab**.

qryTypesAndPrices_Crosstab : Crosstab Query

Type	Total Of Price	1	2	3
BOOKS	£34.11	£66.00	£18.67	£29.75
COLLECTIBLES	£48.67	£70.47	£32.72	£42.62
FURNITURE	£210.08	£260.46	£173.11	£196.29
GLASS	£56.50	£31.00	£74.11	£48.75
JEWELLERY	£258.15	£253.85	£255.88	£264.73
MISCELLANY	£71.04	£69.72	£93.36	£46.71
POTTERY & PORCELAIN	£80.41	£83.50	£80.65	£78.07
SILVER & GOLD	£93.02	£76.57	£94.49	£106.81
TOYS	£31.75	£33.80	£27.60	£31.80
WATCHES & CLOCKS	£278.21	£332.61	£148.83	£287.24

Record: 1 of 10

Figure 10.25: A crosstab query showing the average price that items sold for in various categories

3 Create the grouped query shown in Figure 10.26(a). When you run it you should get the results shown in Figure 10.26(b).

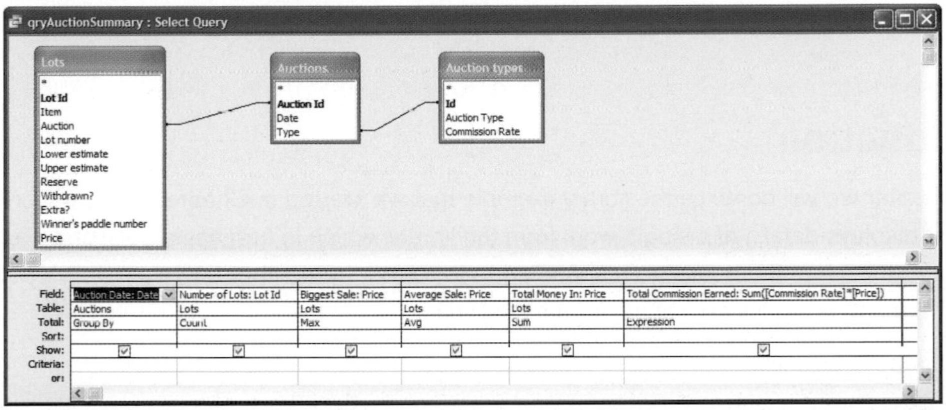

a

b qryAuctionSummary : Select Query

Auction Date	Number of Lots	Biggest Sale	Average Sale	Total Money In	Total Commission Earned
31/01/2006	399	£3,400.00	£164.71	£65,721.00	£6,572.10
28/02/2006	400	£1,800.00	£121.70	£48,678.00	£4,867.80
28/03/2006	420	£3,600.00	£136.72	£57,423.00	£5,742.30

Record: 1 of 3

Figure 10.26: Auction summary query

4 The **People** table has null values for **Telephone** and **Email** where these are unknown. Create a query that lists all of the people for whom neither a telephone number nor an email address is known (there should be eight) and save it as **qryPeopleDifficultToContact**.

5 Create a query that lists all of the records from the **Items** table that match a **Type** entered by the user when the query is run. Test the query, typing **FURNITURE** at the prompt – there should be 373 matching records. Save the query as **qryItemsMatchingType**.

6 Modify **qryItemsMatchingType** so that it returns only the first 10 matching records, ordered by **Insurance** value from highest to lowest. The results for **FURNITURE** should look like Figure 10.27.

qryItemsMatchingType : Select Query

Item Id	Type	Description	Seller	Date received	Date taken	Insurance value
241	FURNITURE	Good Victorian mahogany dining table	35	13/01/2006	09/02/2006	£4,500.00
761	FURNITURE	George III mahogany bowfronted sideboard	163	16/02/2006	06/03/2006	£3,800.00
933	FURNITURE	Good early 19th century oak dresser	10	09/03/2006	29/03/2006	£3,300.00
220	FURNITURE	George III mahogany roll-top desk	41	13/01/2006	31/01/2006	£3,000.00
90	FURNITURE	Good late 19th century figured mahogany sideboard	16	06/01/2006	07/02/2006	£2,300.00
1125	FURNITURE	Set of six Victorian balloon-back dining chairs	90	16/03/2006	05/04/2006	£1,800.00
1100	FURNITURE	Set of eight Continental mahogany-framed spoon-back salon chairs	5	15/03/2006	28/03/2006	£1,800.00
376	FURNITURE	Regency mahogany fold-over-top card table	43	20/01/2006	10/02/2006	£1,800.00
841	FURNITURE	Early 19th century mahogany secretaire bookcase	76	06/03/2006	28/03/2006	£1,800.00
373	FURNITURE	Late Victorian oak dining table	16	20/01/2006	09/02/2006	£1,500.00
(Number)			0			£0.00

Record: 1 of 10

Figure 10.27: The 10 most valuable pieces of furniture

11 Subforms

Introduction

In this chapter we will continue the library example that we started in Chapter 7. We will create a form that displays details of a single work from the library, which in turn has a **subform** displaying details about each of the books corresponding to that work (remember that a **work** is a published title and a **book** is a physical volume on the shelves).

In this chapter, you will:

 create a subform and link it to a parent form

 use a subform to edit linked records

 change a subform to use an **alternate source of records**.

Creating a form with a subform

Creating the main form

 Open the **sandbox.mdb** database if it is not already open.

 Select **Forms** in the **Database** window and then double-click **Create form by using wizard**. The **Form Wizard** appears.

Select **Table: tblWorks** from the drop-down list and then press the **>>** button to select all of the fields, as shown in Figure 11.1.

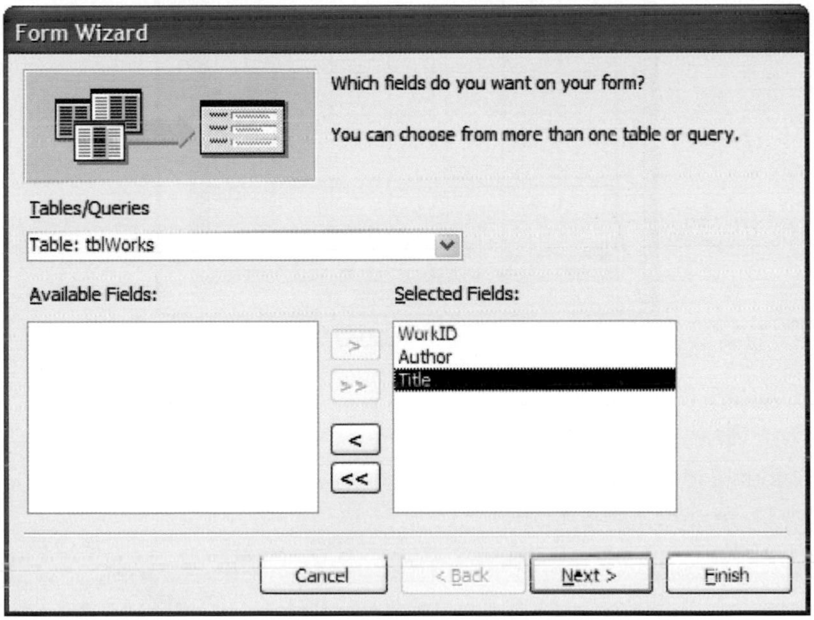

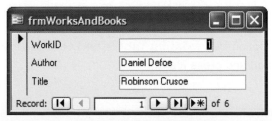

Figure 11.1: Choosing which fields to add to the form

Press **Next**. In the next two steps of the wizard, select **Columnar** layout and **Standard** style. Finally, name the form **frmWorksAndBooks** and press **Finish**.

The form opens, looking like Figure 11.2. At the moment, it shows details for the works. We want to add a subform that will list all of the books that the library owns for the currently displayed work.

Figure 11.2: The initial form

Creating a subform

Switch to **Design** view and increase the height of the form by clicking and dragging the top edge of the **Form Footer** bar downwards. Resize the form so that it looks like Figure 11.3.

Figure 11.3: Resized form

Syllabus ref: AM5.3.2.1
Create a subform and link to parent.

Note!

The **SubForm Wizard** may not be available if your copy of Access was installed with the **Typical Wizards** option (see page 10). If this is the case, Access will ask you to insert the Microsoft Office CD-ROM to install the wizard.

Note!

If you need a reminder about how **tblBooks** and **tblWorks** are related, refer back to Figure 7.10 on page 120.

Subform/
Subreport

Click the **Subform/Subreport** tool and then click and drag a large rectangle that almost covers the grey area at the bottom of the form. The **Subform Wizard** appears.

Make sure that the option **Use existing Tables and Queries** is selected (the selection in the list doesn't matter) and press **Next**.

From the **Tables/Queries** drop-down list, select **Table: tblBooks**. Add the two fields **BookID** and **Condition** in the usual way, so that the wizard looks like Figure 11.4.

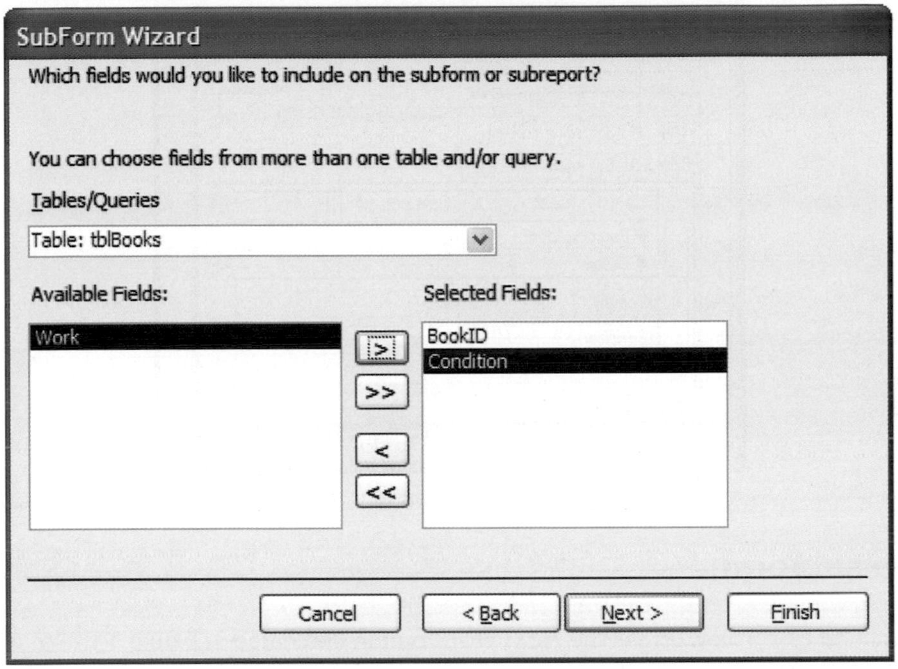

SubForm Wizard

Which fields would you like to include on the subform or subreport?

You can choose fields from more than one table and/or query.

Tables/Queries

Table: tblBooks

Available Fields:

Work

Selected Fields:

BookID
Condition

[Cancel]   [< Back]   [Next >]   [Finish]

Figure 11.4: Choosing which fields to add to the subform

Press **Next**. The next step of the **Subform Wizard** allows us to define how the subform is linked to the main form.

Note!

Because we have created a relationship between the two tables **tblWorks** and **tblBooks**, Access knows how the form and the subform should be linked (via the **WorkID** field). If we had not done this, we could choose the **Define my own** option to specify which fields between the two tables should be linked.

With **Show tblBooks for each record in tblWorks using WorkID** selected, press **Next**.

Name the form **fsubBooks** and press **Finish**.

Tidy up the subform by renaming its label from **fsubBooks** to **Books for this work**, and arranging the subform control and its label as shown in Figure 11.5. It is probably a good idea to save again at this stage.

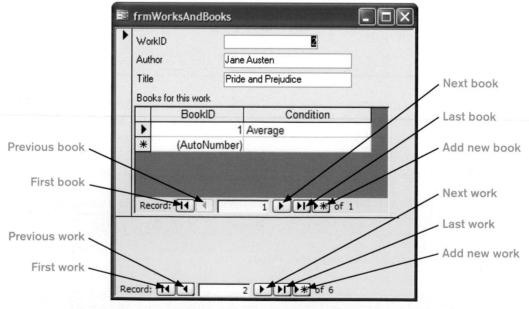

Figure 11.5: Rearranged form design

Using a subform

Switch to **Form** view. Press the **Next work** button (indicated in Figure 11.6) to move from **Robinson Crusoe** to **Pride and Prejudice**.

Figure 11.6: A form with a subform

This tells us straight away that the library has one copy of *Pride and Prejudice*, which is in average condition.

Note!

The buttons for navigating between books are only needed when there are more books than there is space in the subform to display them.

Suppose that a new copy of *Pride and Prejudice* has been bought. We can use the subform to add it.

Change the **Condition** drop-down on the second row of the subform to **New**.
This creates a new record, representing a copy of *Pride and Prejudice* in new condition, as shown in Figure 11.7.

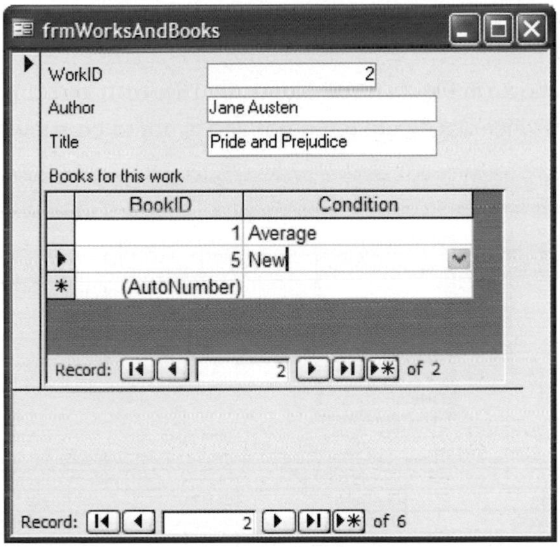

Figure 11.7: Using the subform to add a record

Notice that **BookID**, because it is an AutoNumber, has been filled in automatically. But has the link between the tables been preserved?

Close the **frmWorksAndBooks** form and open the **tblBooks** table. Notice that the new record (highlighted in Figure 11.8) has its **Work** field set to **2**. The **WorkID** for *Pride and Prejudice* is **2**, so this ties up correctly! Close the table again.

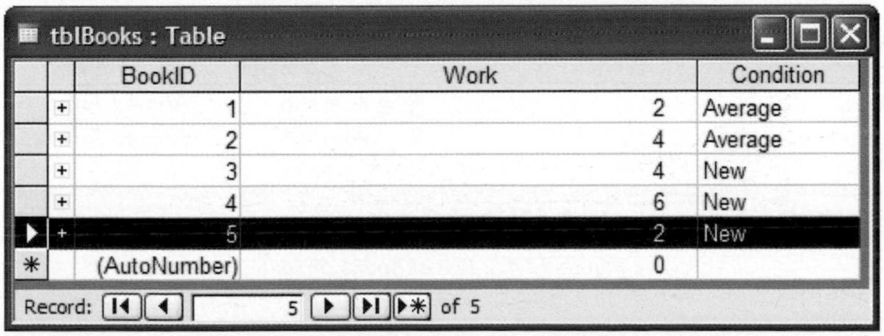

tblBooks : Table

	BookID	Work	Condition
+	1	2	Average
+	2	4	Average
+	3	4	New
+	4	6	New
+	5	2	New
*	(AutoNumber)	0	

Record: 5 of 5

Figure 11.8: The record has been created with the correct Work number

TIP

We could even choose to omit both the **WorkID** and the **BookID** from the form. Because these fields are AutoNumbers, they will be set automatically for any new works and books that are added.

Changing which records are displayed by a subform

Creating an alternate source of records

We can change the subform so that, instead of showing all of the books for the selected work, it shows only those that are currently loaned out.

 Create the query shown in Figure 11.9. Notice that **DateIn** is restricted to **null** records (this field is only filled in when books are returned) and is not to be shown as part of the query.

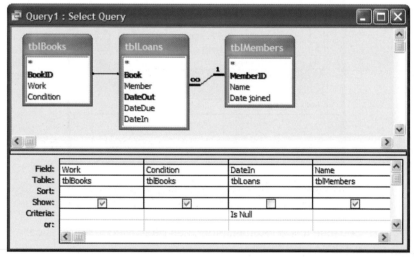

Figure 11.9: Design for a query to return a list of books on loan

 Run the query. Only two books are currently being borrowed, both by Ahmed Arifi, as shown in Figure 11.10.

Figure 11.10: List of books on loan

 Save the query as **qryBooksOnLoan** and close it.

Changing the source of records in the subform

Now we can modify our subform to take its data from **qryBooksOnLoan** instead of **tblBooks**.

Syllabus ref: AM5.3.2.2
Modify the subform to change records displayed.

Display **frmWorksAndBooks** in **Design** view.

Right-click on the subform and select **Subform in New Window** from (towards the bottom of) the menu that appears. The subform **fsubBooks** opens in a window of its own.

Note!

If you are using an earlier version of Access then the **Subform in New Window** command may not be available. This is not a problem: you can still edit the subform inside the main form, but it will be a bit more cramped.

If the properties window is not already on display, right-click the new window's title bar and select **Properties** from the menu that appears.

The drop-down list in the properties window should be set to **Form** – change it to this if it is something else.

Make sure that the **Data** tab is selected. The **Record Source** should be set to **tblBooks**. Change this to **qryBooksOnLoan** (you can use the drop-down list for this) as shown in Figure 11.11.

```
Form                                              ⊠

 Form                                         ⌄

 Format   Data   Event   Other     All
 Record Source . . . . . . . . . . .qryBooksOnLoan  ⌄ …
 Filter . . . . . . . . . . . . . . . .
 Order By . . . . . . . . . . . . . .
 Allow Filters . . . . . . . . . . . .Yes
 Allow Edits . . . . . . . . . . . . .Yes
 Allow Deletions . . . . . . . . . .Yes
 Allow Additions . . . . . . . . . .Yes
 Data Entry . . . . . . . . . . . . .No
 Recordset Type . . . . . . . . . .Dynaset
 Record Locks . . . . . . . . . . . .No Locks
 Fetch Defaults . . . . . . . . . . .Yes
```

Figure 11.11: Changing the Record Source for a subform

Remember that the query returns values for **Work**, **Condition** and **Name** (refer back to Figure 11.10). At the moment, the subform displays **BookID** and **Condition**. Let's delete the **BookID** field and add a new field for **Name**. We do not need to display the **Work** field; this is just how we are linking to the main form.

Click the **BookID** field and then press the **Delete** key. The field is removed from the form.

Resize the form so that there is some space below the **Condition** field.

ab|

Text Box

Select the **Text Box** tool and then click on the form below the **Condition** field. The form should now look like Figure 11.12.

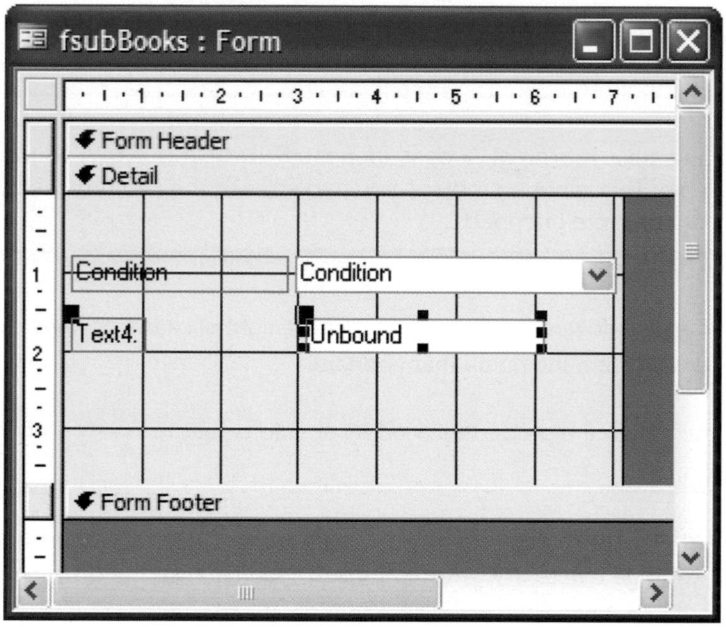

Figure 11.12: New field added to the form

Use the properties dialogue box to change the **Control Source** for the new control to **Name**, in much the same way as you just changed the **Record Source** for the whole subform.

Edit the text of the corresponding label to **Borrower**.

Your form should now look something like Figure 11.13. It doesn't matter if it is not very tidy, because the records will not appear in this format in the subform; they will be in a grid, so the positions of the fields are not important, only their order.

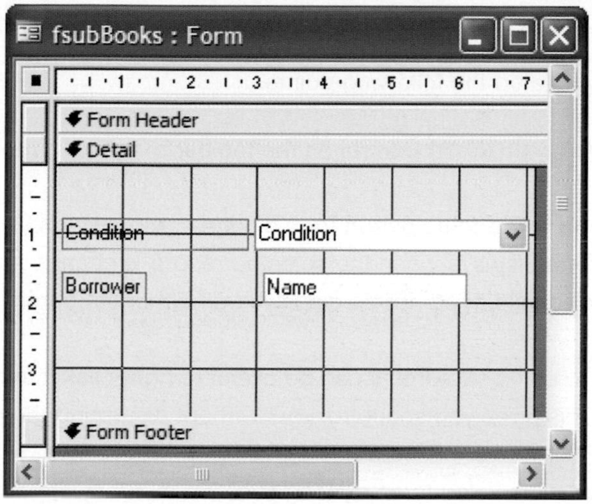

Figure 11.13: Form with its new control

Save and close the subform.

Switch the main form into **Form** view.

The subform now shows who has borrowed which books. Scroll through the records and check that Ahmed Arifi has borrowed *Pride and Prejudice* and *A Christmas Carol* (see Figure 11.14).

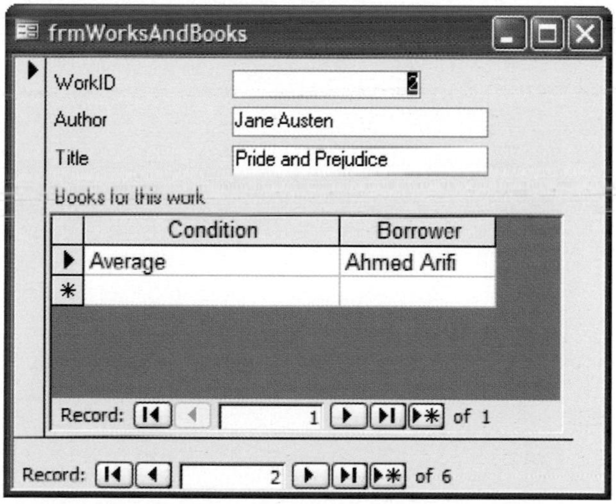

Figure 11.14: A record showing that Ahmed Arifi has borrowed a copy of Pride and Prejudice

Save and close the form.

Find the form **frmWorksAndBooks** in the **Forms** list in the **Database** window, right-click on it and select **Rename** from the menu that appears. Rename the form to **frmWorksAndBorrowers** to reflect its new contents more accurately.

Conclusions

This exercise has demonstrated the following points.

Subform/
Subreport

Use the **Subform/Subreport** control on the toolbar to create a new subform.

A subform must be linked to its parent form by one or more fields (this controls which records the subform displays when the selected record is changed in the parent form). However, this linked field need not be displayed on either the parent form or the subform.

When you need to edit a subform, it can be useful to right-click it and select **Subform in New Window**. This gives you space to work without disrupting the parent form.

If you need to add extra fields to an existing subform, but they are not part of the original table that was used as the record source for the subform, you must create a new query that contains all of the fields you need and then change the **Record Source** property of the subform from the original table to the new query.

Test yourself

Auction database

In this exercise you will create a form that the auctioneer could use while the auction is in progress. It will list just the information that the auctioneer requires in order to be able to control the bidding: minimal details about the current lot, its estimate and reserve and any advance bids that have been placed. To achieve this, you will build up a form within a form within a form.

1   Use the **Form Wizard** to create a simple form, based on the **Lots** table, containing the fields **Lot number**, **Lower estimate**, **Upper estimate** and **Reserve**. Call this form **fsubLotsAndBids** (since we will eventually be using this as a subform). In **Design** view, rearrange the controls and resize the form so that it looks like Figure 11.15.

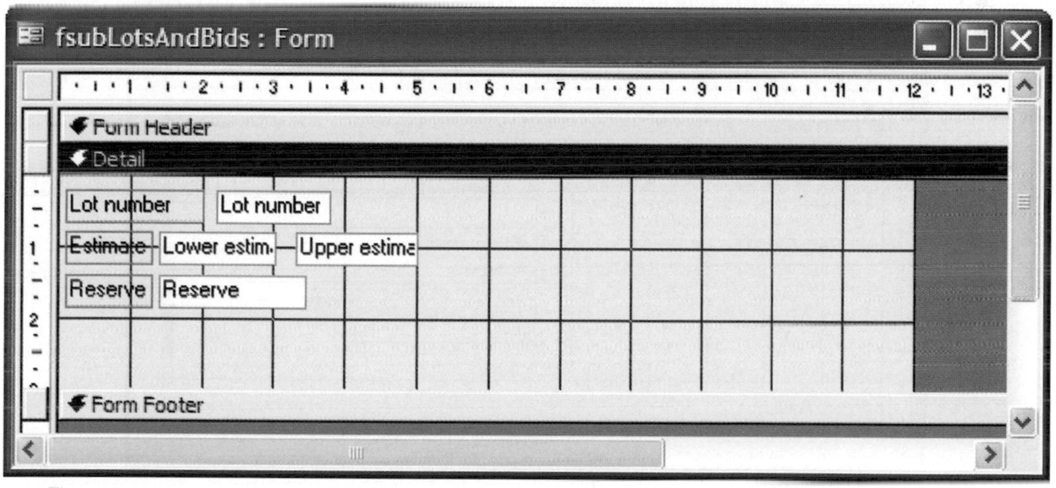

Figure 11.15: Start of the middle form – this will have a subform component, and the whole thing will act as a subform to another form

For each lot, we want the form to display all of the advance bids that have been placed on that lot. We can use a subform for this.

2   Add a subform to the right-hand side of **fsubLotsAndBids**: use the existing table **Advance Bids**, adding the **Lot**, **Auction**, **Paddle** and **Bid** fields. Define your own links between the main form and the subform, linking **Auction** to **Auction** and **Lot number** to **Lot**. Name the new subform **fsubAdvanceBids**. Delete the **Lot** and **Auction** fields from **fsubAdvanceBids** (these were only needed for linking to the main form). Edit the properties of the form in the subform: set both **Record Selectors** and **Navigation Buttons** to **No**, as shown in Figure 11.16 (this produces a cleaner look). Similarly, set **Allow Additions** (on the **Data** tab) to **No**. Tidy up the form so that it looks like Figure 11.17. View the form in **Form** view: record 1001 should look like Figure 11.18.

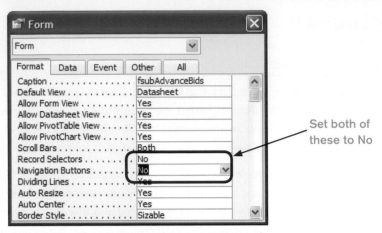

Figure 11.16: Cleaning the look of the form

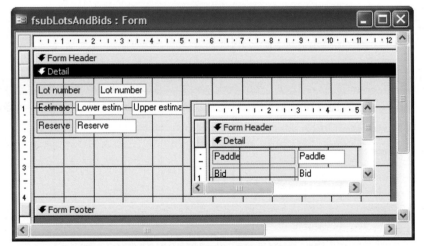

Figure 11.17: fsubLotsAndBids with a subform of its own

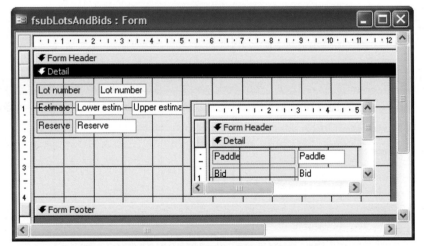

Figure 11.18: fsubLotsAndBids showing the two advance bids for lot 202 (record 1001)

It would be better if the advance bids were ordered with the highest first: the auctioneer is really only interested in the top two bids, since the live bidding can start just above the second-highest bid. One way to achieve this would be to get the subform's data from a query, and set this up to sort – Exercise 4 shows something very similar. For Exercise 3, we'll just tweak the **Record Source** to do the sorting for us.

3   Add **ORDER BY Bid DESC , Date** just before the final semicolon in the **Record Source** for
    the subform's form (so the whole **Record Source** becomes **SELECT [Advance Bids].Lot,**
    [Advance Bids].Auction, [Advance Bids].Paddle, [Advance Bids].Bid FROM [Advance
    Bids] ORDER BY Bid DESC , Date;). View the form in **Form** view and confirm that the
    order of the two advance bids has swapped compared with that given in Figure 11.18.

> **ORDER BY Bid DESC, Date** tells Access to sort the results in descending order of bid
> and then in ascending order of date (so that earlier bids come before later bids where the
> bid amounts are equal).

It would be useful to show a description of the item on the form. However, we cannot easily add
this field because the data source for **fsubLotsAndBids** is the **Lots** table, and the description is
stored in the **Items** table. Instead, we will create a query that contains all of the fields we want to
display and then change the form to get its data from this query.

4   Create a query that takes the **Auction, Lot number, Lower estimate, Upper estimate,**
    and **Reserve** fields from the **Lots** table and the **Description** field from the **Items** table.
    Set it to sort by **Auction** and then **Lot number**. When you run the query, it should look like
    Figure 11.19. Save the query as **qryLotsAndDescriptions**. Change the **Record Source** for
    fsubLotsAndBids from **Lots** to **qryLotsAndDescriptions** – at this stage you should find
    that the form works exactly as it did before. Add a new text box bound to the **Description**
    field, as shown in Figure 11.20, and test the form.

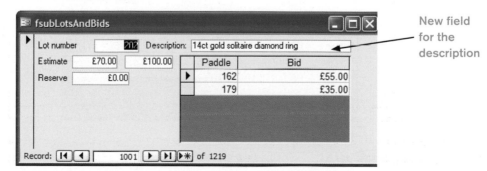

Figure 11.19: A query pulling together details from Lots and Items

Figure 11.20: fsubLotsAndBids with a new Description field

As a final step, we will wrap a main form around **fsubLotsAndBids** to allow the auctioneer to change the auction currently being viewed.

5   Save and close any open forms. Design a new form, based on the **Auctions** table, as shown in Figure 11.21. Add **fsubLotsAndBids** as a subform, linking it to the main form via the auction IDs. Save the form as **frmAuctioneerPrompt**. Test the form in **Form** view by selecting auction 3 and then lot 202, as shown in Figure 11.22.

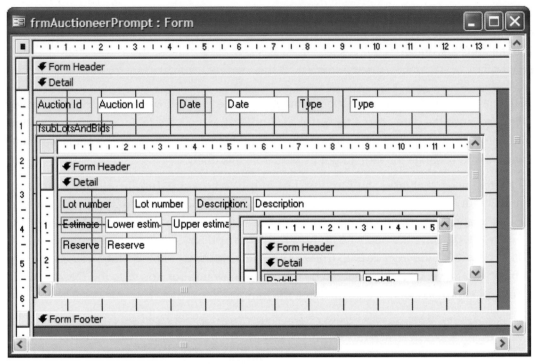

Figure 11.21: frmAuctioneerPrompt in Design view

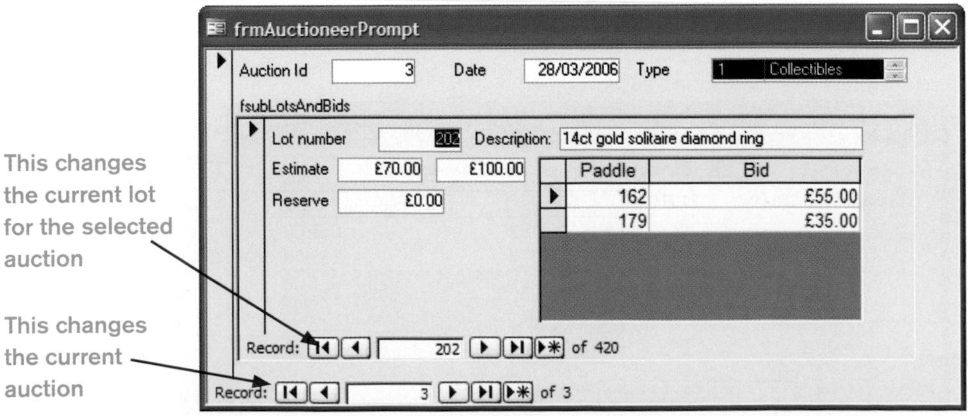

This changes the current lot for the selected auction

This changes the current auction

Figure 11.22: frmAuctioneerPrompt in Form view

12 Reports

Introduction

In this chapter we will be generating reports that would be useful to the owner of two rented properties. We will start by creating a list of the owner's income and expenses for the year, and will then use this as the basis for a report that uses grouping to separate out the income and expenses for each property, and shows useful information such as a running cash flow.

In this chapter, you will:

 add **grouping** to a report to provide summary data for groups of related records

 add **grand totals** to a report

 calculate **percentage contributions** of subtotals to the total and display these in the report

 change a field in a report into a **running sum** (running total)

 add a **page break** between each group of records.

Creating an example table

We will start by creating the data that will form the basis of our report: a list of the owner's income and outgoings for 2005.

 Open the database **sandbox.mdb** if it is not already open.

Use the **Create table by entering data** option to create the table shown in Figure 12.1.

> **TIP**
>
> If you wish to save yourself some typing, this table is available for import from the publisher's website: www.payne-gallway.co.uk/ecdl.

Date	Property	Description	Income	Expense
31/01/2005	1	Rent paid	800	0
31/01/2005	2	Rent paid	1200	0
28/02/2005	1	Rent paid	800	0
28/02/2005	2	Rent paid	1200	0
31/03/2005	1	Rent paid	800	0
31/03/2005	2	Rent paid	1200	0
21/04/2005	1	Renovations before new tenants move in	0	650
30/04/2005	2	Rent paid	1200	0
31/05/2005	1	Rent paid	900	0
31/05/2005	2	Rent paid	1200	0
20/06/2005	2	Repairs	0	425
30/06/2005	1	Rent paid	900	0
30/06/2005	2	Rent paid	1200	0
05/07/2005	2	New fridge	0	185
31/07/2005	1	Rent paid	900	0
31/07/2005	2	Rent paid	1200	0
31/08/2005	1	Rent paid	900	0
31/08/2005	2	Rent paid	1200	0
30/09/2005	1	Rent paid	900	0
30/09/2005	2	Rent paid	1200	0
31/10/2005	1	Rent paid	900	0
31/10/2005	2	Rent paid	1200	0
30/11/2005	1	Rent paid	900	0
30/11/2005	2	Rent paid	1200	0
31/12/2005	1	Rent paid	900	0
31/12/2005	2	Rent paid	1200	0

Record: 26 of 26

Figure 12.1: Table showing the income and expenses for the landlord of two properties in 2005

Save the table as **tblPropertyRentals** without a primary key, and then close it.

Creating a report

Creating a simple report

We will ease in gently by creating a simple report that lists all the information from the table we just created. Then we will go on to add in the advanced features that you need to know about.

 Select **Reports** in the **Objects** list in the **Database** window and then double-click on **Create report by using wizard**. The **Report Wizard** appears.

 From the drop-down list, select **Table: tblPropertyRentals**. Press **>>** to select all of the fields, as shown in Figure 12.2. Press **Next**.

Report Wizard	
	Which fields do you want on your report?
	You can choose from more than one table or query.

Tables/Queries

Table: tblPropertyRentals ▼

Available Fields:

Selected Fields:

>
>>
<
<<

Date
Property
Description
Income
Expense

Cancel   < Back   Next >   Finish

Figure 12.2: Selecting which fields to add to the report

Do not add any grouping fields yet: just press **Next**.

Do not change the sort order: just press **Next**.

Make sure the **Layout** is set to **Tabular**, the **Orientation** is set to **Portrait** and the **Adjust the field width so all fields fit on a page** box is ticked. Press **Next**.

Select **Formal** and press **Next**.

Name the report **rptPropertySimple** and press **Finish**.

The simple report should look like Figure 12.3. It's just a plain dump of the data from the table.

rptPropertySimple

Date	Property	Description	Income	Expense
31/01/2005	1	Rent paid	800	0
31/01/2005	2	Rent paid	1200	0
28/02/2005	1	Rent paid	800	0
28/02/2005	2	Rent paid	1200	0
31/03/2005	1	Rent paid	800	0
31/03/2005	2	Rent paid	1200	0
21/04/2005	1	Renovations before new ten	0	650
30/04/2005	2	Rent paid	1200	0
31/05/2005	1	Rent paid	900	0
31/05/2005	2	Rent paid	1200	0
20/06/2005	2	Repairs	0	425
30/06/2005	1	Rent paid	900	0
30/06/2005	2	Rent paid	1200	0
05/07/2005	2	New fridge	0	185
31/07/2005	1	Rent paid	900	0
31/07/2005	2	Rent paid	1200	0
31/08/2005	1	Rent paid	900	0
31/08/2005	2	Rent paid	1200	0
30/09/2005	1	Rent paid	900	0
30/09/2005	2	Rent paid	1200	0
31/10/2005	1	Rent paid	900	0
31/10/2005	2	Rent paid	1200	0
30/11/2005	1	Rent paid	900	0
30/11/2005	2	Rent paid	1200	0
31/12/2005	1	Rent paid	900	0
31/12/2005	2	Rent paid	1200	0

15 December 2005

Page 1 of 1

Figure 12.3: Simple report

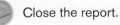 Close the report.

Grouping

If all we wanted to produce was an exact copy of our original table then we may as well have just put it in a spreadsheet. Where Access comes into its own is in the manipulation of data. We can extract just the information we are interested in, and arrange it in more useful ways.

One way of doing this is by arranging the data into groups. Remember that we skipped this option in the wizard when creating **rptPropertySimple**. It might be useful to split the report up so that each property is treated separately. We can do this by making a simple modification to the existing report – we do not have to run the wizard again.

> **Note!**
>
> Grouping in reports works in a similar way to grouping in queries (see Chapter 9).

We will start by creating a copy of the simple report to work on.

 Select **rptPropertySimple** in the **Database** window. From the main menu, select **Edit**, **Copy**. Again from the menu, select **Edit**, **Paste**. A dialogue box appears asking for a new name; type **rptPropertyGrouped** and press **OK**. You should now have two reports: **rptPropertyGrouped** and **rptPropertySimple**.

 Open the new **rptPropertyGrouped** in **Design** view.

Right-click in the grey square in the top-left corner of the report and select **Sorting and Grouping** from the menu that appears, as shown in Figure 12.4. The **Sorting and Grouping** dialogue box appears.

Right-click here

Figure 12.4: Changing the Sorting and Grouping options for a report

Set the **Field/Expression** to **Property** and the **Sort Order** to **Ascending**. Set both **Group Header** and **Group Footer** to **Yes** (notice that new areas appear in the form). Within each property we want the records to be sorted in date order, so add **Date** as a second **Field/Expression** and set its **Sort Order** to **Ascending**, but leave both the **Group Header** and **Group Footer** set to **No**. The dialogue box should look like the one shown in Figure 12.5.

Field/Expression	Sort Order	
Property	Ascending	
Date	Ascending	

Group Properties

Group Header	No	
Group Footer	No	
Group On	Each Value	Select ascending or descending sort order. Ascending means sorting A to Z or 0 to 9
Group Interval	1	
Keep Together	No	

Figure 12.5: Setting a grouping field

Note!

If both **Group Header** and **Group Footer** are set to **No** then the field will just be used for sorting, not for grouping.

Close the **Sorting and Grouping** dialogue box.

Edit the label in the **Report Header** section from **rptPropertySimple** to **rptPropertyGrouped**.

TIP

To change the properties for the whole report, you must either select the report by clicking the grey square in its top left corner, or select **Report** from the drop-down list in the **Properties** dialogue box.

Change the **Caption** in the report's properties from **rptPropertySimple** to **rptPropertyGrouped** to match, as shown in Figure 12.6. (This just affects the report name displayed in the title bar when you view the report.)

Report

Report

| Format | Data | Event | Other | All |

Caption . . . . rptPropertyGrouped
Auto Resize . . . . Yes
Auto Center . . . . No
Page Header . . . . All Pages
Page Footer . . . . All Pages
Grp Keep Together . . . . Per Column
Border Style . . . . Sizable
Control Box . . . . Yes
Min Max Buttons . . . . Both Enabled
Close Button . . . . Yes
Width 15.908cm
Picture . . . . (none)
Picture Type . . . . Embedded
Picture Size Mode . . . . Clip
Picture Alignment . . . . Center
Picture Tiling . . . . No
Picture Pages . . . . All Pages
Grid X 10
Grid Y 10
Layout for Print . . . . Yes
Palette Source . . . . (Default)
Orientation . . . . Left to Right
Moveable . . . . Yes

Figure 12.6: Changing the report's caption

Use the **Label** tool to add labels to the **Property Header** section and the **Property Footer** section, as shown in Figure 12.7. These do not need to be neat because you will be deleting them again soon; it will just be useful to see where they appear in the report.

Label

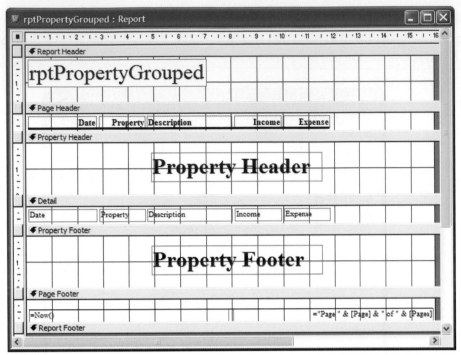

Figure 12.7: Adding labels to the report to highlight the Property Header and Property Footer

View the report using **Print Preview** view. It should look like Figure 12.8.

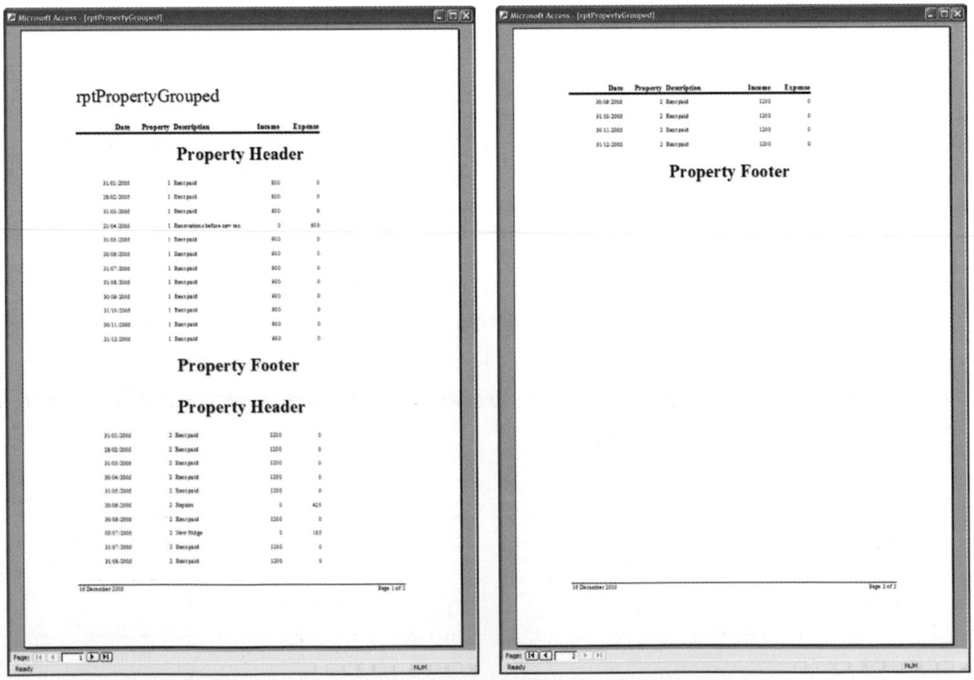

Figure 12.8: The grouped report showing where the headers and footers appear – two pages

Adding totals per group

Let's add a pair of controls to display the total income and expenditure for each property.

 Delete the **Property Footer** label.

 Add a text box control to the **Property Footer** area and delete its label.

> **Syllabus ref: AM5.4.1.3**
> Use formulas, expressions in a report such as sum, count, average, max, min, concatenate.

 Display the properties dialogue box for the new text box. Change the text box's **Name** to **Income Per Property**, its **Control Source** to **=Sum([Income])**, and its **Format** to **Currency**, as shown in Figure 12.9.

Text Box: Income Per Property

Income Per Property

Format	Data	Event	Other	All

Name . . . . Income Per Property
Control Source . . . . =Sum([Income])
Format . . . . Currency
Decimal Places . . . . Auto
Input Mask . . . .
Visible . . . . Yes

Figure 12.9: Adding a calculated field to the report

> **Note!**
> The important change here is where we set **Control Source** to **=Sum[Income]**. The equals sign tells Access that this is a calculation. Because this is in the footer for a group, the sum is restricted to the values in that group; we will create grand totals later by adding a similar control to the report footer.

> **Note!**
> Other functions you could use in a **Control Source** are **Count**, **Avg**, **Max** and **Min**. These work just as they do for queries – see pages 163–166. You can also use **&** to concatenate strings – see the page numbers in the bottom right of Figure 12.7.

 Repeat the previous two steps to create another text box. This time call it **Expense Per Property** and use **[Expense]** instead of **[Income]** in the **Control Source** formula.

 Arrange the two controls beneath the fields they are summing, and add a label **Total per property**, as shown in Figure 12.10.

◆ Detail								
Date		Property	Description		Income	Expense		
◆ Property Footer								
Total per property					=Sum([Incom	=Sum([Expen		
◆ Page Footer								

Figure 12.10: Arranging the fields for the property subtotals

View the report. Each property should look something like Figure 12.11.

Date	Property	Description	Income	Expense
	Property Header			
31/01/2005	1	Rent paid	800	0
28/02/2005	1	Rent paid	800	0
31/03/2005	1	Rent paid	800	0
21/04/2005	1	Renovations before new ten	0	650
31/05/2005	1	Rent paid	900	0
30/06/2005	1	Rent paid	900	0
31/07/2005	1	Rent paid	900	0
31/08/2005	1	Rent paid	900	0
30/09/2005	1	Rent paid	900	0
31/10/2005	1	Rent paid	900	0
30/11/2005	1	Rent paid	900	0
31/12/2005	1	Rent paid	900	0
Total per property			£9,600.00	£650.00

Figure 12.11: Report with subtotals per property (only one property shown here)

Adding grand totals and percentage contributions

Adding grand totals

In **Design** view, make sure that there is a white area in the **Report Footer**. Click and drag the bottom of the **Report Footer** title bar downwards if necessary, as shown in Figure 12.12.

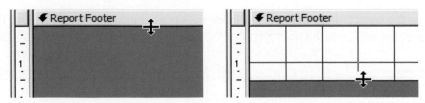

Figure 12.12: Dragging to increase the height of the Report Footer

Click the **Total per property** label and hold down **Shift** while clicking the two **Sum** fields to select all three. From the menu, select **Edit**, **Copy**. Click once in the **Report Footer** area and, from the menu, select **Edit**, **Paste**. Copies of the three controls appear.

Change the text in the new label to **Grand total**.

 Change the **Name** properties for the two new text box controls to **Total Income** and **Total Expense** respectively.

 View the report. The second page should now end with grand totals, as shown in Figure 12.13.

Date	Property	Description	Income	Expense
30/09/2005	2	Rent paid	1200	0
31/10/2005	2	Rent paid	1200	0
30/11/2005	2	Rent paid	1200	0
31/12/2005	2	Rent paid	1200	0
Total per property			£14,400.00	£610.00
Grand total			£24,000.00	£1,260.00

Figure 12.13: Second page of the report, showing grand totals

Some notes about headers and footers

You have just added controls to the **Report Footer** – these will appear only on the last page of the report. Similarly, if you add controls to the **Report Header** then they will appear only on the first page of the report.

Syllabus ref: AM5.4.2.1
Insert a data field to appear within report header, footers on the first page or all pages.

The other sections allow you to add controls to the header or footer of each page, or the header or footer of each group or subgroup. This all works in the same way as you have already seen for forms (Chapter 4).

Adding percentage contributions

We can use these grand totals to calculate what proportion of the total income and expense is contributed by each of the two properties. Let's add a percentage calculation control to show this.

Syllabus ref: AM5.4.1.2
Calculate percentage calculation control in a report.

 Add a new text box control below the first sum in the **Property Footer** area. Delete its label.

Set its **Name** to **Income Contribution**, its **Control Source** to **=[Income Per Property]/[Total Income]** and its **Format** to **Percent**, as shown in Figure 12.14.

> **Note!**
>
> Even though **[Total Income]** is not printed until the last page of the report, it's OK to refer to it beforehand (as we have here). We get the final value of **[Total Income]**, not just the running sum up to the current point in the report.

> **TIP**
>
> This shows why it is a good idea to give meaningful names to the controls you create: it is easier to refer to them in formulas.

Text Box: Income Contribution

Income Contribution	

Format | Data | Event | Other | **All**

Name	Income Contribution
Control Source	=[Income Per Property]/[Total Income]
Format	Percent
Decimal Places	Auto
Input Mask	
Visible	Yes

Figure 12.14: A calculated percentage control

 Create an equivalent control for the expenses.

 View the report.

You should find that Property 1 contributes 40.00% to the income and 51.59% to the expense; Property 2 contributes 60.00% to the income and 48.41% to the expense.

Adding an arithmetic calculation control

Creating the control

Let's add a new control that shows the income minus the expense for each record. (This is an arithmetic control. The method for logical controls is identical.)

> **Syllabus ref: AM5.4.1.1**
>
> Create arithmetic, logical calculation controls in a report.

 Create a new text box to the right of the **Expense** control in the **Detail** section of the report. Delete its label.

Set the **Control Source** for this control to =**[Income]-[Expense]**.

 View the report. The values of this control for the first property should all be one of **800**, **-650** or **900**.

Creating a running total

This new control is not very useful. However, if we convert it to a running total it will show how the cash flow changes throughout the year.

> **Syllabus ref: AM5.4.1.4**
> Create running summaries in a report.

 Edit the properties for the new field: change its **Name** to **Cash Flow** and set its **Running Sum** to **Over Group**, as shown in Figure 12.15.

Text Box: Cash Flow	✕

Cash Flow ⌄

Format	Data	Event	Other	All

Name	Cash Flow
Control Source	=[Income]-[Expense]
Format	
Decimal Places	Auto
Input Mask	
Visible	Yes
Vertical	No
Hide Duplicates	No
Can Grow	No
Can Shrink	No
Running Sum	Over Group

Figure 12.15: Making the field a running sum

> There are three possible values for **Running Sum**:
>
> **No** turns off the running sum;
>
> **Over Group** resets the sum to zero between each group;
>
> **Over All** adds all of the values without resetting the total between groups.

 Change the **Format** for the **Income**, **Expense** and **Income–Expense** fields to **Currency**.

 Add a new label called **Cash Flow** to the **Page Header**, as shown in Figure 12.16. (You can do this by copying and pasting an existing label, so you keep the same style of text.) Resize the underline so that it extends beneath the new label (click the line to select it, and then drag its right-hand resize handle to the right).

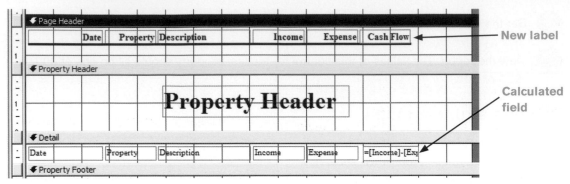

Figure 12.16: New calculated field and its heading label

The report should now look like Figure 12.17.

If you find that the second page is blank, the body of the report is probably wider than the printed page. Switch back to **Design** view and drag the right-hand edge of the report (that is, the border between the white page and its dark grey border) to the left.

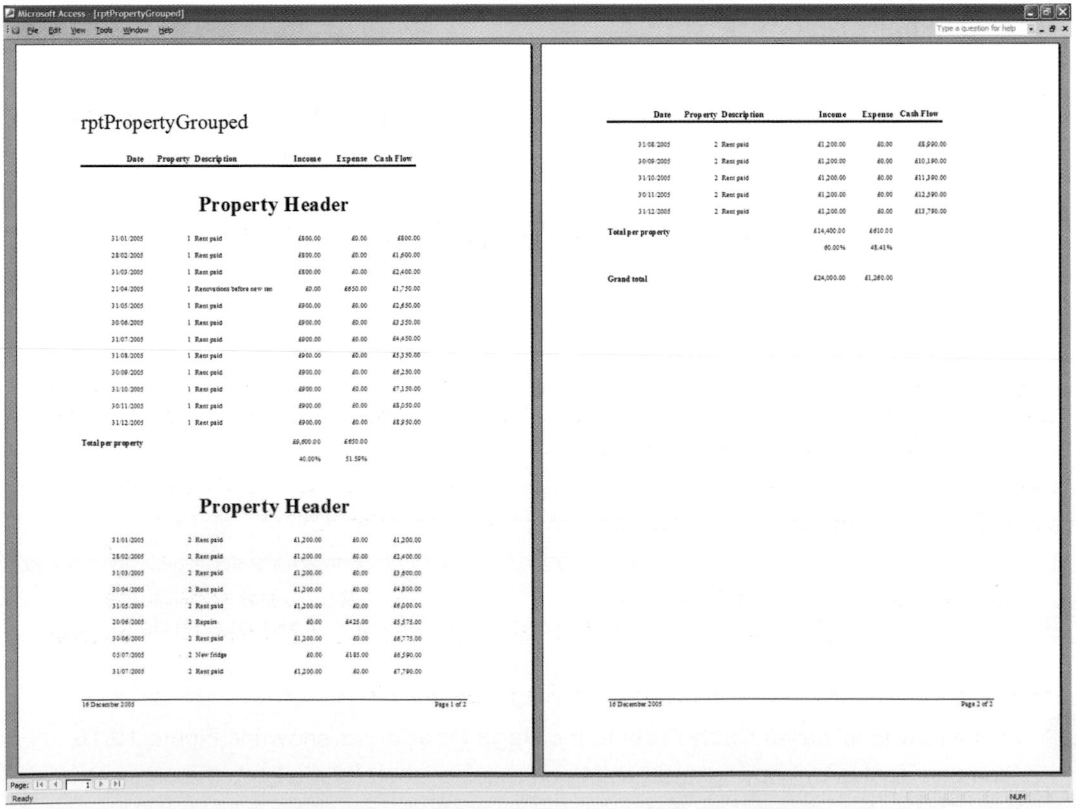

Figure 12.17: Report with a running total for cash flow

Finishing touches

Page breaks

The report would look better if each group (property) started on a new page. We can achieve this by adding a page break to the group footer.

> **Syllabus ref: AM5.4.2.2**
> Force page breaks for groups on reports.

 In **Design** view, select the **Page Break** tool and then click below the existing fields in the **Property Footer**. A page break control appears, looking like a row of dots.

Page Break

 View the report. There should now be three pages: one for each of the properties, and a third page for the grand totals.

Improved headers (using concatenation)

 Change the **Report Header** label from **rptPropertyGrouped** to **Rentals Cash Flow** and centre it on the page.

Delete the label **Property Header**.

Add a new **Text Box** control to the **Property Header** section. Delete the label that appears with it. Set its **Control Source** to =**"Property" & [Property]**.

Use the toolbar to make this control use 16-point, bold, underlined text.

> **Note!**
>
> This is a calculated field. The **&** symbol is used for concatenation. So the field's value will be **Property** (do not forget the space before the closing double quotes) followed by the **[Property]** field, which will have the value **1** or **2**.

We can now get rid of the **Property** column from the body of the report.

 Delete the **Property** label from the **Page Header**, and drag the left edge of the **Description** label to fill in the gap. Make the equivalent change in the **Detail** section.

Arrange the form, if necessary, so that it looks like Figure 12.18.

		Date	Description				Income	Expense	Cash Flow		

Report Header

Rentals Cash Flow

Page Header

| | | Date | Description | | | | Income | Expense | Cash Flow | | |

Property Header

="Property" & [Property]

Detail

| Date | | Description | | | Income | Expense | =[Income]-[Exp |

Property Footer

| Total per property | | | | | =Sum([Incom | =Sum([Expens | |
| | | | | | =[Income Per | =[Expense Pe | |

.....

Page Footer

| =Now() | | | | | | | ="Page" & [Page] & " of " & [Pages] |

Report Footer

| Grand total | | | | | =Sum([Incom | =Sum([Expens | |

Figure 12.18: Final design of the report

 View your report. It should look like Figure 12.19.

 Save and close the report.

Rentals Cash Flow

Property 1

Date	Description	Income	Expense	Cash Flow
31/01/2005	Rent paid	£800.00	£0.00	£800.00
28/02/2005	Rent paid	£800.00	£0.00	£1,600.00
31/03/2005	Rent paid	£800.00	£0.00	£2,400.00
21/04/2005	Renovations before new tenants move in	£0.00	£650.00	£1,750.00
31/05/2005	Rent paid	£900.00	£0.00	£2,650.00
30/06/2005	Rent paid	£900.00	£0.00	£3,550.00
31/07/2005	Rent paid	£900.00	£0.00	£4,450.00
31/08/2005	Rent paid	£900.00	£0.00	£5,350.00
30/09/2005	Rent paid	£900.00	£0.00	£6,250.00
31/10/2005	Rent paid	£900.00	£0.00	£7,150.00
30/11/2005	Rent paid	£900.00	£0.00	£8,050.00
31/12/2005	Rent paid	£900.00	£0.00	£8,950.00
Total per property		**£9,600.00**	**£650.00**	
		40.00%	51.59%	

Property 2

Date	Description	Income	Expense	Cash Flow
31/01/2005	Rent paid	£1,200.00	£0.00	£1,200.00
28/02/2005	Rent paid	£1,200.00	£0.00	£2,400.00
31/03/2005	Rent paid	£1,200.00	£0.00	£3,600.00
30/04/2005	Rent paid	£1,200.00	£0.00	£4,800.00
31/05/2005	Rent paid	£1,200.00	£0.00	£6,000.00
28/06/2005	Repairs	£0.00	£425.00	£5,575.00
30/06/2005	Rent paid	£1,200.00	£0.00	£6,775.00
05/07/2005	New fridge	£0.00	£185.00	£6,590.00
31/07/2005	Rent paid	£1,200.00	£0.00	£7,790.00
31/08/2005	Rent paid	£1,200.00	£0.00	£8,990.00
30/09/2005	Rent paid	£1,200.00	£0.00	£10,190.00
31/10/2005	Rent paid	£1,200.00	£0.00	£11,390.00
30/11/2005	Rent paid	£1,200.00	£0.00	£12,590.00
31/12/2005	Rent paid	£1,200.00	£0.00	£13,790.00
Total per property		**£14,400.00**	**£610.00**	
		60.00%	48.41%	

Grand total

Date	Description	Income	Expense	Cash Flow
	Grand total	£24,000.00	£1,260.00	

Figure 12.19: The final report

Conclusions

This exercise has demonstrated the following points.

 You can change the grouping and sorting options for a report at any time. If a field is set up with no **Group Header** or **Group Footer** then Access merely sorts on that field instead of grouping it.

 The placement of headers and footers in reports is similar to what we saw for forms in Chapter 4. The **Page Header** and **Page Footer** come at the top and bottom of each page, unless the report has a **Report Header**, in which case that comes above the **Page Header** on the first page. The **Report Footer** comes after the last record on the last page. Any headers and footers for grouping levels come immediately before and after their groups.

 You can use formulas – **sum**, **count**, **average**, **max** and **min** – to provide summary information about individual groups or the whole report.

You can use **&** to concatenate values in an expression.

If you refer to a report-level field from a group-level header or footer then you will get the total value for the whole report, not just a running total up to the current point in the generation of the report. This is a good thing – you can easily calculate the **percentage contribution** of values in the current group to a total for the report using division.

 You can perform arithmetic and logical calculations in controls on a report (this works in the same way as for queries).

 The **Running Sum** property for a field can be set to **Over Group** (to keep a running total for each group, resetting it to zero between groups), **Over All** (to keep a running total without resetting it between groups) or **No** (to turn this feature off).

To add a page break between groups, add a **Page Break** control to the group's footer. This is displayed as a row of dots in **Design** view.

Test yourself

Auction database

Let's create a report that compares the total insurance values of each type of goods that have been auctioned. Item types with high values are likely to have contributed most to the auction house's profits, so this is useful information.

1   Create a new report in **Design** view. Use the **Items** table as the **Record Source** for the report. Set the report to be grouped on the **Type** field, and to show a group header for this. We do not need a **Detail** section at all in this report, so reduce its height to zero. In the **Type Header** section, add the **Type** field and another field that calculates the sum of the insurance values, as shown in Figure 12.20(a). When you view the report in **Print Preview** view, it should look like Figure 12.20(b). Save the report as **rptItemValuesByType**.

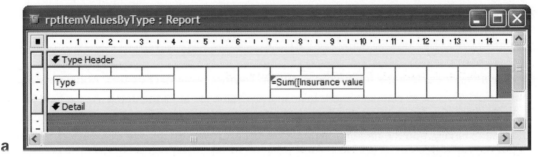

a

BOOKS	£800.00
COLLECTIBLES	£6,500.00
FURNITURE	£116,150.00
GLASS	£1,850.00
JEWELLERY	£55,250.00
MISCELLANY	£11,200.00
POTTERY & PORCELAIN	£34,850.00
SILVER & GOLD	£21,350.00
TOYS	£2,000.00
b WATCHES & CLOCKS	£44,300.00

Figure 12.20: rptItemValuesByType (a) in Design view and (b) in Print Preview view

2   Add a new calculated field between the two existing fields on the report. Use the **&** concatenation operator to display an opening **(** followed by the count of **Item Id**, followed by **items)**. Right-align this control. The first three entries in the report should now look like Figure 12.21.

BOOKS	(11 items)	£800.00
COLLECTIBLES	(66 items)	£6,500.00
FURNITURE	(373 items)	£116,150.00

Figure 12.21: Top of rptItemValuesByType with a calculated field showing the number of items of each type

> **TIP**
>
> The **&** operator is used between values to concatenate them. For example, the formula **="This" & 1+1 & "that"** results in **This 2 that**.

3   Display a header and footer for the report (**View**, **Report Header/Footer**). Add a field to the **Report Footer** to calculate the total insurance value for all of the items. Add a field to the **Type Header** to calculate the percentage contribution of each item type's value to the total value. Finally, add the heading **Item value breakdown by type** to the **Report Header**. Your report should look like Figure 12.22(a) in **Design** view and Figure 12.22(b) in **Print Preview** view.

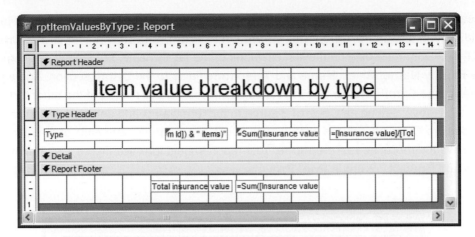

Item value breakdown by type

BOOKS	(11 items)	£800.00	0.27%
COLLECTIBLES	(66 items)	£6,500.00	2.21%
FURNITURE	(373 items)	£116,150.00	39.47%
GLASS	(19 items)	£1,850.00	0.63%
JEWELLERY	(138 items)	£55,250.00	18.78%
MISCELLANY	(89 items)	£11,200.00	3.81%
POTTERY & PORCELAIN	(248 items)	£34,850.00	11.84%
SILVER & GOLD	(161 items)	£21,350.00	7.26%
TOYS	(21 items)	£2,000.00	0.68%
WATCHES & CLOCKS	(91 items)	£44,300.00	15.06%
	Total insurance value	£294,250.00	

Figure 12.22: Final version of rptItemValuesByType (a) in Design view and (b) in Print Preview view

The next exercise involves creating a telephone directory, ordered by surname with a separate page for each letter.

4   Create a report based on the **People** table. Set the report to group on the **Family Name** field, setting **Group Footer** to **Yes**, **Group On** to **Prefix Characters** and **Group Interval** to **1** (so we are grouping on the first character of the family name, not the whole thing). Add the **Family Name**, **Given Name** and **Telephone** fields to the **Detail** section. Add a page break to the **Family Name Footer**. Add a calculated field to the left of the other three in the **Detail** section, setting its **Control Source** to the formula **=1** and setting its **Running Sum** property to **Over All** – this is a clever trick to get Access to number each of the records for us. Save the report as **rptTelephone**. Your report should look like Figure 12.23(a) in **Design** view and Figure 12.23(b) in **Print Preview** view.

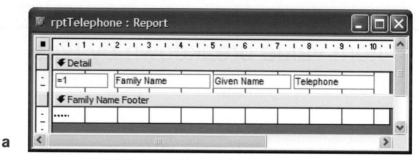

a

Figure 12.23: (a) rptTelephone in Design view

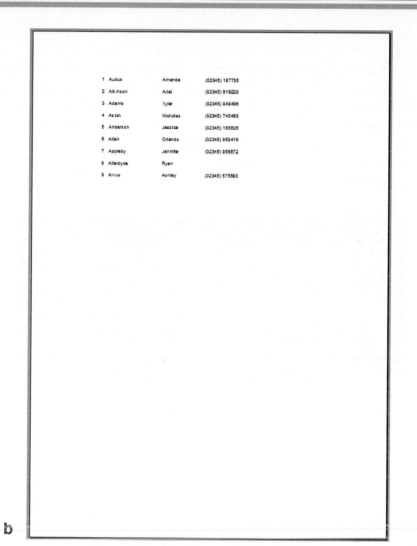

1 Audus	Amanda	(02345) 187735
2 Atkinson	Ariel	(02345) 919220
3 Adams	Tyler	(02345) 848486
4 Aston	Nicholas	(02345) 746493
5 Anderson	Jessica	(02345) 195626
6 Allan	Orlando	(02345) 858419
7 Appleby	Jennifer	(02345) 959672
8 Allardyce	Ryan	
9 Amos	Ashley	(02345) 575580

Figure 12.23: (b) rptTelephone in Print Preview view

Index of syllabus topics

AM5.2.2 Query formulas

AM5.2.3 Refine a query

AM5.3.1 Controls

AM5.3.2 Subforms

AM5.4.1 Calculations

AM5.4.2 Presentation

AM5.5.1 Record & assign macros

AM5.6.1 Data management

Index

Index